Flying into the Future

To
Teeny and Will

Flying into the Future

Air Transport Policy in the European Union

Kenneth Button
Professor of Public Policy
George Mason University, USA

Kingsley Haynes
University Professor of Public Policy
George Mason University, USA

and

Roger Stough
NOVA Professor of Public Policy
George Mason University, USA

Edward Elgar
Cheltenham, UK – Northampton, MA, USA

Published by
Edward Elgar Publishing Limited
8 Lansdown Place
Cheltenham
Glos GL50 2HU
UK

Edward Elgar Publishing, Inc.
6 Market Street
Northampton
Massachusetts 01060
USA

A catalogue record for this book
is available from the British Library

Library of Congress Cataloguing in Publication Data
Button, Kenneth John.
 Flying into the future : air transport policy in the European
Union / Kenneth Button, Kingsley Haynes, Roger Stough.
 Includes bibliographical references.
  1. Aeronautics, Commercial—European Union countries.
 2. Aeronautics, Commercial—Deregulation—European Union countries.
I. Haynes, Kingsley E., 1942– . II. Stough, Roger, 1940– .
III. Title.
HE9842.A4B88 1998
387.7'094—dc21
                   97–43525
                     CIP

ISBN 978 1 85898 799 6

Printed and bound by CPI Group (UK) Ltd, Croydon, CR0 4YY

Contents

Contents

List of Figures

List of Tables

Preface

Air transport is important and is growing rapidly. It is also an area that has, for a variety of reasons, a high profile and possibly attracts even more media attention than its economic importance justifies. There are many issues that are challenging policy makers and academics in the air transport field and they are seldom static in their nature. This adds even more interest to the study of aviation matters.

This book examines one aspect of air transport, namely the organization of air transport in the European Union (EU). It does so in the context of a broad structure, conduct and performance framework by exploring the nature of the industries supplying air transport services and considering the rationale for the institutional structure that currently governs the way air transport services are delivered and its implications.

Analysis is done in the context of both the internal EU market for air transport services and the links between it and the external market. The nature of air networks and the increasing globalisation means that for goals of interoperability and interconnectivity to be realized, the internal EU market for air transport cannot be treated in isolation from the larger international market.

Developments to date have removed many long-standing institutional barriers to efficient provision of air transport services within the EU area. Changes in international air transport, new management strategies adopted by the airlines and the more liberal regulatory environment pose different types of challenges to policy makers.

Particularly, the introduction of new information technologies, reduction of government interference in price and capacity setting and emergence of innovative management techniques have enabled European airlines to circumvent many traditional limitations to interoperability and interconnectivity. Airline alliances, along with other arrangements, have provided an institutional device for circumventing many of the remaining barriers.

Available evidence indicates that liberal markets are generally improving the overall performance of the EU air transport sector, and that many arrangements involving EU airlines are designed largely to facilitate efficient supply.

The issue now is whether the advantages associated with the current structure of a liberalized market, combined with growing integration in the supply matrix, can allow the EU air transport sector to realize its full potential for interoperability and interconnectivity or if remaining market imperfections will act as a serious impediment.

This book stems from a deliverable of the European air transport component of the 'Managing Interoperability by Improvements in Transport System Organisation in Europe' (MINIMISE) project of the European Union. It sets out the current position of European air transport and highlights institutional issues and physical problems impeding the full efficient delivery of appropriate air transport services within the European Union.

Various components of the book have appeared in different guises as reports, conference papers and articles and as such we have enjoyed considerable feedback from a wide range of people. We would like to acknowledge the debt that we owe them. Production of material and editing is time consuming, taking considerable skill and infinite patience, and we would like to thank Mary Baitinger for her help in this regard.

1. Introduction

1.1 BACKGROUND

Air transport is a significant sector in its own right but in providing an important intermediate service helps to stimulate business and more directly facilitates important individual industries such as tourism. It is a fast growing sector but one that has traditionally been extremely heavily regulated. Although if anything social regulations covering such things as safety and environmental effects have been tightened in recent years, the trend has been to significantly liberalize economic controls over pricing, service levels and market entry. The long standing tradition in many countries for their major airlines to be publicly owned is also changing as privatization takes place and commercial carriers are being allowed in traditionally protected markets.

Air transport liberalization has been part of a much wider process. The past two decades have seen remarkable changes in the way economic regulation is viewed. Over time, countries have varied the extent and ways they have intervened in economic markets, particularly in terms of price and entry controls. But the tradition of regulation is well established. In recent years, however, there has been a liberalization of attitude and a withdrawal of states from the interventionist role. In North America, it has been viewed as a period of 'deregulation,' although the UK terminology of 'regulatory reform' is perhaps more appropriate.

While economic regulations have been removed in some cases, there has been tightening of controls of quality factors related to such things as safety. In countries such as the UK and France where there has been privatization of formerly state-owned industries, economic controls over such things as safety have actually been reinforced to replace the direct control of ownership formerly exercised over these large scale undertakings. In some instances, there has also been a tightening of broader industrial policy and labor protection laws as individual sectors have been liberalized,

1

such as the new mergers policy of the EU since 1989. The gradual 'greening' attitudes towards industry has also brought forth new regulations governing the ways the natural environment is treated as well.

While these extend across many spheres of economic activity, changes have been particularly pronounced in the context of transport. The long-standing tradition had been government market intervention to regulate entry and/or price with the intent of protecting customers, third parties and those working in the industry, along with the achievement of social objectives such as service to remote communities and the integration of spatially disparate markets. In many countries, especially continental Europe, transport has traditionally been seen as an input into a wider socio-political-economic process embracing regional, social and industrial policies. As such, it has been manipulated to achieve aims which transcend issues of simple transport supply efficiency.

With a few notable exceptions (namely, deregulation of the UK trucking industry in 1968 and partial deregulation of the railways in 1962), the controls built up from the nineteenth century and developed and rationalized in the inter-war period continued to dominate into the 1970s. The 1930s were a particularly active period for regulators (Button and Gillingwater 1986), and much of the recent change that has occurred effectively rolled back the legislation of that time. An earlier part of this can be explained in terms of society trying to come to terms with new modes of transport (especially the automobile and airplane) which not only offered new technical challenges but also began having a considerable effect on the way people lived. In some ways, the legislation could be viewed as a form of social engineering. However, transport has associated with it a wide range of externalities – it is dangerous, pollutive, and affects many other activities ranging from residential land use to international trade patterns. Issues of overall social efficiency were also at the forefront of the debates of the time.

From the mid-1970s, economic liberalization has spread through transport markets, with supplying industries being freed from price and entry constraints and privatization affecting many areas. The reasons behind the change vary from country to country and sector to sector. The US is often seen as the initiator of most of the reforms with a combination of demonstration and bandwagon effects, together with some clear direct spillovers into international markets, causing other countries to imitate them. The US's claims that it is at the forefront of change in transport policy can be debated – the UK, particularly, may feel it has some precedence – but it has certainly been the US experiences that have received the greatest attention.

During a period from 1976 to the early 1980s, the Airline Deregulation Act (1978), the Staggers Rail Act (1980), the Motor Carrier Act (1980), and the Bus Regulatory Reform Act (1982) essentially liberalized interstate transport in the US, with knock-on effects rippling through to intra-state regulation. Following lags, similar pictures emerge for most other industrialized countries, although the timing and intensity of change has varied enormously. Many reasons exist for this diversity of pace. It is partly explained by the different start points from which liberalization began, but equally, one must consider the nature of the political systems involved; some simply do not have the mechanisms for rapid change, the political philosophy of the different countries, the direct links with other liberalized transport networks, and the degree to which regulations effectively function.

Europe has not in general been at the forefront of this wider liberalization movement but has become a more recent convert[1]. Air transport has been one of the last transport sectors that has been deregulated and even here there remain considerable controls especially over routes external to the European Union. Equally the path towards privatization of airlines and elements of air transport infrastructure has been a slow one and many European carriers remain as state owned undertakings, often enjoying considerable subsidies.

The situation in Europe regarding air transport has, therefore, been fluid but this in itself throws up some important policy issues and challenges. It is with some of these issues that this book is concerned.

1.2   SCOPE

In this book we set out the current position of European air transport and highlight institutional issues and physical problems impeding the full efficient delivery of appropriate air transport services within the European Union[2].

[1]   The early effects of the European Transport Policy in the 1960s also had some liberalising implications for international transport between Member States. For instance, it initiated, albeit limited in number, an EU-wide truck licensing scheme and removed some technical barriers through measures of harmonisation. The impacts were, however, small.

[2]   The book does not cover issues concerning the manufacture of aircraft which is a significant topic in its own right. For example, there is no discussion of the relative levels and forms of governmental support enjoyed by the EU and US aircraft manufacturing companies nor of recent developments in the ways aircraft are sold other than in terms of the implications of this on the airline sector. Matters of airport design are also not considered although they may influence the ability of airlines to make efficient use of some parts of their fleets.

3

The main issues addressed revolve around airline operations. We spend minimal time on other aviation matters such as those concerned with the commercial rivalries between Airbus and Boeing or on the role of European manufacturers in the production of smaller aircraft. Equally, we are interested in the softer policy issues involving economics and institutional matters rather than the more technical questions that are confronting European policy makers. We do not, for instance, look at the respective technical merits of alternative new traffic control systems.

Our geographical domain is the European Union. The title European Union (EU) is new compared to terms previously used such as European Community or European Communities. For simplicity of exposition, EU will be used throughout this book. Currently, it consists of Austria, Belgium, Denmark, France, Finland, Germany, Great Britain, Greece, Ireland, Italy, Luxembourg, the Netherlands, Portugal, Spain, Sweden. Other states, such as Norway and Switzerland, have agreements with the EU on certain aviation and other matters, which tie them to the EU's overall policy.

There are some extremely interesting policy issues within Europe but outside of the EU area. Developments in eastern and central Europe pose a variety of new challenges. These are touched upon in places in this book where of specific relevance but are often of a rather specific nature and are not, therefore, considered in any depth.

Although the main focus of the book is on air services for international markets within the EU, it is totally inappropriate to ignore, for a variety of reasons, the wider international environment where air transport is supplied. Particularly, important features extend beyond the boundaries of the EU. Due to the nature of modern air transport networks, the EU notion of interoperability and interconnectivity must embrace a much wider spatial dimension if it is to adopt scales of production, market strategies and management schemes appropriate to meet the Union's widest economic objectives.

This link between the internal EU market and external markets is not a feature unique to aviation but extends to all EU network industries, including telecommunication and energy distribution. Indeed, it is one that makes policy formulation difficult. The internal and external markets are linked in several important ways:

- Europe itself represents an important transit area for traffic originating outside of the region and destined for locations beyond its borders.
- European airports cater for traffic with origins or destinations internally as well as outside the EU.

- Air traffic control and navigation infrastructure is jointly used by internal EU traffic and traffic with origins or destinations outside of the EU and by traffic overflying EU countries.
- A large number European airlines have extensive operating networks extending beyond EU boundaries and plan and manage their activities to tie these in with their intra-EU services. In terms of long haul traffic, this amounts to less than 15% of international passengers carried but accounts for 50% of their revenue.
- Many airlines have equity involvements with those outside of EU.
- Rapid growth in airline alliances involving EU and non-EU carriers blurs operational boundaries.
- Companies outsourcing EU carriers also serve non-EU airlines and plan commercial activities in this wider framework.
- Many European airlines are in receipt of government subsidies, and there is no distinction whether funds are spent on intra-EU services or external routes.
- Air transport policy is a comparatively new EU concern, and most national policies, which have long been based on much wider international considerations, cannot easily be disregarded.

Links such as these indicate that the air transport policy of the EU has not grown in geographical isolation but has rather entwined with developments elsewhere. Future policies will need to take these linkages into account. Equally, the EU has also been influenced by demonstration effects of events elsewhere; the US deregulatory aviation policies exercised significant influences on EU member countries who, as a result, adopted similar policies. And since they are tailored to meet local and national objectives, EU countries have benefited from hindsight to circumvent some of the problems associated with US reforms.

European developments have not attracted the level of analytical attention as did the US Airline Deregulation Act (e.g. Borenstein, 1992a). This dearth of work, in part, is due to the slower and phased pace in Europe which has made quantitative assessments of policy reforms so difficult. Unlike the US, problems in deploying econometric analysis are compounded because reform is across a range of diverse regulatory systems. At a more practical level it has taken time to develop a good EU data base covering the sector. While lessons may be learned from developments in other aviation markets, there are also many features unique to Europe and specific information is relevant. Finally, there is simply not the tradition of conducting the types of econometric work that one finds in the US; whether this is a good or bad thing we leave open.

1.3   THE BOOK

The focus of the book is to look at ways in which interoperability may be improved in European transport. Interoperability, along with such terms as interconnectivity, is a piece of genuine modern 'Euro-jargon' that transcends national linguistic boundaries. Interoperability reflects the ability of two or more transport systems to operate effectively and efficiently. It aims at making the boundaries between different transport networks effectively invisible. In some instances interoperability involves a technical dimension whereby the various physical pieces of operational equipment and infrastructure can interface effectively. Common rail gauges may be seen as an example. In other cases, and air transport is one example, the major issues are ones of institutional arrangements[3]. There are differing national organizational and juridical structures within Europe that act to impede interoperability.

It is this question of seeking greater interoperability that lies at the heart of the book. The material presented represents an off-shoot of a much larger EU funded project, Managing Interoperability by Improvements in Transport System Organization in Europe (MINIMISE)[4]. This project looks at all the main modes of transport while here the coverage is confined to that of air transport, and within that mainly to air passenger transport.

Initially, this book in Chapter 2 sets down a brief account of EU air transport developments in the context of what is happening globally as well as in the European aviation markets. It also does this in the context of our current understanding of the underlying economics of the air transport operations.

It then proceeds in to look at the important challenges that confront European air transport if it is to continue playing a major role in EU development. It offers an account of the development of European aviation policy and compares it, in Chapter 3, with developments elsewhere and in particular with changes in the US.

It then moves to focus on a number of key issues. In particular the problems now being encountered of congested air transport infrastructure in Europe are reviewed in Chapter 4. The growth and significance of airline alliances involving European airlines are examined in Chapters 5 and 6 in

---

[3]   However, there are many technical issues that still need resolution in air transport, such as a standard European-wide air traffic control system, and the problems of resolving these should not be belittled.
[4]   A project within the European Union's 4th Framework Programme for Research and Technological Development in the Field of Transport (No. ST-96-SC.401)

the context of both their role in circumventing government intervention failures and as a pure efficiency mechanism by which customers enjoy improved service and greater variations in pricing.

Chapter 7 provides a detailed assessment of one special area of interest, namely the longer term stability of the European air transport sector within the current institutional framework. This can be a technical subject, but the more theoretical aspects of the topic are reserved for footnotes and an appendix.

We do not only list constraints, bottlenecks and barriers but rather also explore the problems of providing air transport in the context of the existing imperfect EU world of inadequate information, institutional constraints, inherent market imperfections and imprecise objectives. Discussion is set in the context of the current EU air transport environment that embraces state subsidies, accepted collusive agreements, extensive public provision of infrastructure and a gradual liberalization of internal and external operating regimes.

What this book is not is a textbook on air transport economics or air law. It certainly has an economics bias but that is because many of the issues surrounding the attainment of interoperability in European air transport revolve around economic considerations. There are, however, important legal, political, technical and geographical elements to be considered and these are brought into the discussions. It may, therefore, be seen more as an exercise in political economy.

Finally, the aim of the book is also to be as accessible as possible but at the same time avoid being too trivial or to minimise the difficulties of developing an air transport policy for Europe. To this end technical arguments are not altogether ignored but for presentational reasons they are in general reserved for footnotes and appendices. This, we hope, will make the volume attractive to those who have no training in economics or are not fully up-to-date with the jargon of air transport. We also think it makes the narrative flow more easily.

2. The Development of EU Air Transport Policy

2.1 TRENDS IN AIR TRANSPORT

Globalization and internationalization are two major industrial trends of the late twentieth century (Thurow, 1996). Part of this is reflected in the significant trade growth that has taken place in the 1990s, with real export growth in the industrialized countries that make up the Organisation for Economic Cooperation and Development (OECD) at over 7% per annum. Comparatively, from 1964 to 1992, first world production was up by 9%, exports by 12%, and cross-border lending by 23%. Equally, there has been a significant rise in foreign ownership of assets that are now estimated to total about $1.7 trillion.

Whether these trends are passing fads or genuine long term adjustments to the way production and trade is conducted is premature to judge. Preliminary indications are, however, that they are more than transient.

All this has been taking place when the institutional structure of air transport services provided has seen significant developments. The US's deregulation of its domestic markets for air freight since 1977 and for passengers in 1978, combined with subsequent commitments to an 'Open Skies' approach to international aviation in 1979, has changed the way US policy is conducted but also, through both demonstration effects and direct knock-on effects, the ways in which other air transport markets are now regulated (Button 1990; Organisation for Economic Cooperation and Development, 1993).

The intra-European market is moving rapidly towards a situation found within the United States. Many European countries unilaterally liberalized their domestic markets while the EU, since 1988 through a succession of 'Packages,' has moved to a position that will leave air transport largely free from economic regulation by the middle of 1997(see Section 2.4).

8

These measures, partly stimulated by a number of legal judgments in the European Court, initially opened up regulated fare and capacity bands but then limited fares and entry controls to instances where governments at both ends of a route agreed to them. The creation of a Single European Market from 1993 also means that international air transport within Europe is essentially deregulated, with full cabotage within member states being allowed from 1997.

The majority of national markets in South America have been liberalized with various types of privatization programs. Australia and New Zealand markets have also been deregulated. Additionally, the World Trade Organization (WTO) brought into play (albeit an extremely small role) a new and geographically wider policy making institution to supplement the roles already played by bodies such as the International Civil Aviation Organization (ICAO) and the International Air Transport Association (IATA) (Katz, 1995). Aviation issues are also on the agenda of new regional groupings such as the Asian-Pacific Economic Council (APEC).

This combination of market trends and institutional reforms, combined with rising incomes and increased leisure time, have contributed to the steady growth of demand taking place in aviation markets. Additionally, technology advances have allowed aircraft efficiency to rise and air traffic control systems to handle greater volumes of traffic, thus exerting positive effects on the cost side of the international air transport equation.

As a result, air passenger traffic since 1960 has grown world wide at an average yearly rate of 9% and freight and mail traffic by some 11% and 7% respectively. In 1995, for example, some 1.3 billion passengers were carried by the world's airlines. Civil aviation has become a major service industry contributing to both domestic and international transport systems. It facilitates wider business communications and is a key component in the growth of tourism, now one of the world's major employment sectors.

In addition to passenger transport, aviation is an important form of freight transport, with some estimates suggesting it carries up to 60% of world trade by value and forecast to rise 80% by 2014.

The Association of European Airlines (AEA) members have seen a steady growth in their traffic in geographical Europe since 1992. Overall traffic increased by 8.1% in 1994, the biggest rise for 15 years leaving aside the 9.1% in 1992 following the drop in traffic recorded in 1991. This trend continued in 1995, with growth reaching 6.1% and a new record of 8.3% in terms of passenger kilometers for all the AEA airlines taken together (Table 2.1). This fairly sustained growth in traffic, coupled with a more moderate increase in output, was reflected in an improved load factor for all the national carriers which, like the productivity improvements, brought many of them back into profitability.

9

Table 2.1 *European airlines (AEA members only)*

Short/Medium Haul

		ASKs (billions)	RSKs (billions	FTKs All Services (millions)
1990		129.47	77.34	1,189.9
1991		124.68	72.03	1,047.6
1992		144.09	83.79	1,182.6
1993		158.08	93.05	1,456.7
1994		167.25	101.89	1,652.1
1995		178.50	110.33	1,791.1
1996	Jan	14.71	7.78	148.1
	Feb	13.69	7.49	146.1
	Mar	15.17	9.69	168.3
	Apr	15.71	9.70	156.5
	May	16.25	9.95	150.0
	Jun	16.42	10.64	154.1
	Jul	17.60	11.44	159.7
	Aug	17.87	11.99	150.7
	Sep	16.50	11.20	167.0
	Oct	16.69	10.72	182.5
	Nov	15.48	8.71	181.6
	Dec	15.39	8.61	180.4
1997	Jan	15.78	8.31	154.1
	Feb	14.49	8.20	159.7

Long-Haul

		ASKs (billions)	RPKs (billions)	FTKs All Services (millions)
1990		273.88	192.61	15,688.6
1991		269.44	183.31	15,688.6
1992		297.43	207.06	15,860.0
1993		318.51	223.47	16,789.9
1994		333.53	243.47	17,481.3
1995		319.21	261.90	20,707.0
1996	Jan	29.41	20.48	1,514.4
	Feb	27.09	18.41	1,648.6
	Mar	29.63	23.07	1,926.6
	Apr	30.84	21.93	1,743.2
	May	32.38	22.73	1,756.6
	Jun	32.40	25.09	1,822.9
	Jul	34.59	27.49	1,792.8
	Aug	34.79	28.24	1,720.5
	Sep	33.99	26.98	1,839.6
	Oct	33.88	26.23	1,959.0
	Nov	31.65	22.83	1,907.2
	Dec	32.69	23.14	1,841.3
1997	Jan	32.69	23.74	1,538.4
	Feb	29.27	21.30	1,673.9

After running a deficit for several years, most airlines managed to get back into the black in 1995. Net profits for the 12 main EU airlines are in the region of US$800 million against a net overall loss on the same scale in 1994. However, financial performances have varied with only British Airways, Finnair and KLM achieved universally favorable results over the entire period from 1990 to 1994. Among the medium-sized and regional airlines which have been particularly active since the introduction of the Third Package[1], good results were achieved in 1995 by Regional Airlines and Air Littoral with net profits of Ffr9 million and Ffr8.5 million respectively, by EBA (net profit of Bfr 200 million) and by Tyroletan Airways (net profit of US$3 million). Airlines continued to perform significantly differently in the latter part of the 1990s (Table 2.2)

Table 2.2 *European airline profits in 1996*

Airline	Revenues ($billion)	Pre tax profits ($billion)
British Airways*	13.26	1.02
Lufthansa	13.88	0.46
SAS	5.25	0.26
KLM*	5.96	0.07
Air France*a	8.13	0.04
Iberia	3.77	0.02
Swissair	6.63	-0.36
Alitalia	5.06	-0.78

Notes
* Year end March 1997
a Excluding Air Inter

As a sector, aviation will continue expanding into the foreseeable future, albeit at differential rates, in various geographical sub-markets. A number of international agencies, aircraft manufacturers and airlines regularly produce forecasts of aviation traffic (e.g. Airbus Industrie, 1993; Boeing Commercial Airplane Group, 1996; and International Civil Aviation Organisation, 1994.).While forecasting remains an art rather than a science, it seems likely that passenger traffic will grow at a rate between 5% and 7% into the foreseeable future, much of it in the Asian-Pacific region (up to 9% a year). Forecasts have also foreseen slower growth in the more mature US and European markets.

In line with other sectors, aviation has experienced significant moves towards globalization and internationalization. Indeed, it is the stated objective of the UK carrier, British Airways, that it intends to become a 'global carrier'. In pursuit of wider market coverage and in an effort to

[1]   For details of the various 'Packages' of reforms see Section 2.4

enhance their own internal efficiency, other airlines have followed a similar number of courses. The most recent development, perhaps the most controversial, is the development of various forms of airline alliances.

Later, this book will focus on alliances involving scheduled airline services. These have also been formed involving charter carriers but are less common[2]. There is also one airport alliance (between Schiphol Airport in the Netherlands and Vienna Airport in Austria) which embraces a number of cooperative features and a 1% cross share holding. Scheduled airline services and airport alliances, however, are outside of the scope of this study.

In the past, airlines in Europe have formed alliances to economize on aircraft maintenance. This generally requires fleets of twenty or so large commercial aircraft which few carriers could operate in isolation. In 1968, UTA, SAS, KLM and Swissair formed KSSU – an organization which subsequently underwent a number of metamorphoses as airlines joined and left. Economies of scale and standardization in maintenance were exploited through different carriers specializing in maintaining particular aircraft types. Subsequent groupings, such as Atlas, were of a similar nature. Equally, the cooperation of scheduled airlines to develop computer reservation systems represents another form of an aviation sector alliance. The development of Amadeus in Europe is an example of this (Humphreys, 1994a). The scope and nature of modern strategic airline alliances transcends in importance these early efforts at cooperation.

2.2   THE MARKET FOR AIRLINE SERVICES

Prior to looking at the way air transport markets function, it is useful to set the variety of factors that influence the shape of European air transport into context. Figure 2.1 provides a very simplified flow chart of some of the key linkages. Clearly the underlying nature of the airline market is relevant but so too are the institutional arrangements that shape the parameters of this market. These institutions in the European context do not merely embrace rules and regulations that impact on domestic aviation within a country but also reflect the bilateral arrangements that exist between each pair of countries and the multilateral arrangements, such as those within the EU, that have been established.

There are also external arrangements that, because a lot of air transport within the EU actually originates or is destined for countries external to the Union have implications for air transport within Europe. Also of

[2]   For an account of charter alliances, particularly between UK and German companies, see *Avmark Aviation Economist* (1994).

importance are the non-air transport institutions, such as general competition laws, that influence the structure of the air transport services available.

These institutional structures and the *de fato* ways in which they function have not emerged in a vacuum. They are a product of a variety of factors, not least prevailing political, social and economic theories and of the experiences of previous policies in the region. They can also be affected by developments outside, for instance the experiences of regulatory reforms elsewhere, of the EU that exert an indirect demonstration effect on European thinking.

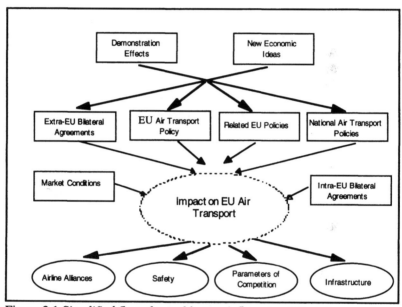

Figure 2.1 *Simplified flow chart of factors influencing EU air transport*

Further, these diversity of forces do not have a single effect on European air transport but rather have varying effects on different attributes of air transport. Some, but not all of these, are reflected in Figure 2.1. The competitive environment is one dimension but is itself complex. Defining the degree of competition in any market is difficult and such measures of price levels, number of suppliers, service levels and size of airlines can all easily be criticized. Safety is another dimension, as is the efficiency with which infrastructure is supplied. The figure also highlights one major factor in the current policy debates in Europe, airline alliances. These may be seen as a component of the competitive structure but have been isolated here to reflect our particular interest.

Finally, the flow chart is a simplification designed mainly to indicate where this and subsequent sections fit into the overall picture. It is not intended to be comprehensive, that would make it too cluttered. Nor does it show important interactions between many of the elements. 'New economic ideas' do not emerge in a vacuum but are a function of experience with previous market structures and institutions. Market conditions can be influenced by the bilateral and multilateral agreements that exist. On the impact side, safety is not independent of infrastructure availability nor the structure of the market.

Turning more directly to the market for air transport, this can be treated much like any other economic activity in terms of the broad ways in which the market functions. There are particular peculiarities of the sector that require careful handling within this framework reflecting, for example, the derived nature of the demand for air services and the technical characteristics of supplying them[3]. The market for airline services deviates, as do all markets in the real world, from the economist's ideal notions of perfect competition. It is the particular nature of these deviations that provide the distinguishing features of air transport.

European airlines differ quite importantly in terms of both their size and the extent to which they engage in services outside of Europe (Table 2.3). The market cannot, therefore, as a whole be seen as conforming to traditional economic notions of perfect competition. This raises questions regarding market entry and the ways in which competition is conducted within the market.

The scale of activities for incumbent operators is often seen in economics to pose problems for potential new market entrants. Economies of scale exist if a doubling of output is achieved with less than a doubling of costs. Such conditions make it difficult for entry except on a large scale. Aviation sector studies, however, reveal little of pure economies of scale. Empirical evidence suggests some benefits for smaller operators, but these are quickly exhausted. They may also exist in specific areas such as marketing and advertising. At least one study of the US domestic aviation industry, however, suggests possible diseconomies at the largest firm sizes (Spraggins, 1989).

Given the complex nature of the air transport industry product, it is not surprising that empirical studies using aggregate measures of airlines'

[3]   Useful textbooks on the economics of air transport include, Doganis (1994) and Hanlon (1996). Oum (1995) offers a collection of more advanced papers.

output can give inconclusive results. If measured as revenue passenger miles, the scale of operations of a carrier can be extended by increasing *ceteris paribus*, the flight frequencies or the number of passengers per flight. Frequency changes could theoretically lead to economies of network size, where density effects might occur in connection with the amount of use made of the networks involved.

Table 2.3 *Airlines' passenger traffic, 1994*

Airlines	Seat-kilometers (x106)	Passenger load factor (%)	Seat-kilometers: % Europe
Top 3			
British Airways	121215.0	71.1	16.9
Lufthansa	83224.3	67.9	22.3
Air France	68570.2	73.1	15.0
Sub-top			
KLM	56383.3	72.4	13.4
Alitalia	39148.8	68.9	26.6
Iberia	32856.8	68.6	26.0
Swissair	29031.6	63.4	25.7
SAS	28153.6	65.6	43.9
Middle-group			
Turkish Airlines	14314.6	59.7	49.2
Olympic Airways	13087.6	64.4	39.5
Sabena	12480.7	60.1	41.3
TAP-Air Portugal	11047.2	68.7	40.0
Finnair	10326.8	62.8	48.5
Aer Lingus	6010.9	71.2	42.1
Austrian Airlines	6307.7	60.8	56.7
Small			
Cyprus Airways	3943.2	71.3	93.0
Balkan	3899.4	52.4	41.0
Icelandai	3258.8	70.2	44.3
British Midland	3619.9	61.2	55.8
CSA	3152.1	62.7	40.6
Malev	2907.5	56.9	76.9
Air Malta	2792.8	65.2	88.4
Luxair	660.5	54.7	100
Adria Airways	656.7	50.2	100

In more detail, regarding economies, evidence suggests that airlines' unit costs do not fall greatly as they expand (e.g. Caves *et al,* 1984).

Strictly the evidence indicates that within any city pair markets there are rapidly declining costs of service but that there are approximately constant returns to scale for airline systems that have reached the size of the US trunk carriers. Savings come from attracting more traffic rather than expanding the network to cover additional origin/destinations; any additional routes increase the operator's quasi-fixed costs which may negate the benefits derived from more traffic. Further, good regional connections may be a more effective marketing tool than large, less coherent networks.

The US domestic market experience overall since market liberalization (see Section 3.1), particularly as the result of widespread merger activity, has increased concentration within the industry. As we see below, in recent years, there have also been significant mergers and other forms of joint activities by European airlines, especially within the EU. As liberalization has gradually spread across the international market, global passenger traffic concentrated on the 10 largest carriers slightly rose in the decade up to 1993, from 44% to 46%, with similar trends in cargo.

However, evidence on route pairs suggests, on average, less concentration at the city-pair level. Prior to 1993, European domestic routes operated in a liberalized environment with international routes and enjoying a liberal bilateral agreement exhibited more competition than those where entry was much more restricted.

While substantial traditional economies of scale may be absent in the aviation industry, others related to the nature and size of operations exist which explain the growing market concentration and barriers to new market entry and exit. These might be thought of as quasi-scale effects.

Standard economic analysis focuses on firms producing a single output. This does not adequately reflect the complexity of relationships in the international aviation industry. It produces a range of outputs by operating more than one service on any given city-pair route and providing a number of interconnected ones. Economies of scope occur when it is less costly for one airline to provide a range across a fixed network than for a number of airlines to provide them separately. They have traditionally been associated with other forms of activity, especially those where potential exists for consolidation and transshipment. In terms of market entry, economies of scope imply that entry needs to be across a range of markets if costs of the entrant are to match the incumbents. Conversely, successful entry of low-cost point-to-point airlines in the 1990s US domestic market demonstrates that costs can in some cases be lower for such services than for larger networks.

US regulatory reforms have airlines seeking this diversity of service, primarily via hub-and-spoke operations. In the international market, flag carriers tend to focus their operations on national hub airports. The empirical evidence is not conclusive that this generates significant economies of scope. One of the main difficulties has been isolating potential effect from other aspects of airlines' cost functions. Further, a major rationale comes as much from marketing advances (i.e. on the demand side) as cost savings. Providing a diverse range of services leads to market visibility and makes frequent flyer programs more attractive, thus enhancing customer loyalty. These attributes are features of network value or 'value of presence and utility to customer'.

A related issue is that smaller operators and new market entrants can enjoy some marketing benefits of diversity by forming alliances. Arrangements can include code-sharing agreements, reciprocal frequent flyer programs, and sharing lounge facilities (British Midland, the UK's second largest carrier, has vigorously pursued this approach). While these may remove an airline's full control over operations, the advantage in code-sharing is that customers travel through hubs on a common airline code and, to all intents and purposes, are on-lining.

Reaping economies from traffic density is often as important as exploiting economies of scope, although their effects are entwined[4]. As more passengers travel, it becomes possible to use larger aircraft that are cheaper to operate per seat kilometer and offer more frequent services. This lowers the cost per available seat kilometer. As we have said, economies of density occur when unit costs fall as the size of the market increases. Hub operation adoption, by increasing city-pairs served, allows a carrier to utilize better its unsold seats inventory. Early empirical evidence from the US domestic market points to significant economies of density, with a 1% rise in passengers an airline carries over a given network, increasing total costs by only 0.8% (Caves *et al.*, 1984). Recent studies point to a possibility of greater economies. Competitive market entry on any route in these conditions again requires entry on a large scale. Recent low-cost carriers on

---

[4]   Strictly, economies of scope relate to falling costs of providing services as the range of services offered by a carrier increases, while economies of traffic density refer to falling costs as the amount carried increases between any given set of points served (Bruecker and Spiller, 1994).

The technical distinction between economies of scale and scope can be seen by reference to the following equation where C denotes cost and Q is output. Economies of scope are assessed as:

$S=[C(Q^1) + C(Q^2)) - C(Q^1 + Q^2)\} / \{C(Q^1 + Q^2)\}$

$C(Q^1)$ is the cost of producing Q^1 units of output one alone, $C(Q^2)$ is the cost of producing Q^2 of output two alone, and $C(Q^1 + Q^2)$ is the cost of producing Q^1 plus Q^2. Economies of scope exist if S>0. There are economies of scale if C/Q falls as Q expands.

US and European routes, however, again suggest that some markets are amenable to a smaller-scale entry.

Economies in operating a standard fleet of aircraft also seem to exist. Particularly, communality of spare parts, maintenance procedures and flight crews can reduce unit operating costs. This is exemplified in the US domestic market by the savings Southwest Airlines has achieved, partly through its total reliance on Boeing 737 aircraft and ValuJet's reliance on DC9s for the same reason. These economies are being exploited in short-haul markets, with few impediments to market entry. In some instances, airlines make use of the large second-hand market to equip themselves from the outset with a standard fleet of aircraft.

Even in the absence of specific economic regulation, international aviation does not, therefore, conform to ideas of actual perfect competition or contestability. However, while empirical evidence exists that imperfections due to scope, density and standardization effects are possible, recent US and European experiences suggest that new market entry is occurring. The issue is one of the overall importance of ensuring efficient market entry and exit and, if policy actions are required, the nature of the appropriate official response to minimize any adverse impacts. The policy challenge is to design regulatory instruments which prevent artificial competition suppression while ensuring that where genuine economic benefits exist of restricted competition, they are fully realized.

One recent outcome of aviation liberalization is the ability of many incumbents to remain in the market and strengthen their position. There may, therefore, exist economies of experience. Part of this effect can be due to residual endowments of market power after reforms (those, for example, associated with the grandfathering of landing slots) and partly to initial diversity and scope of an incumbent's operations. Even accepting these advantages, an additional effect associated with their very existence emerges in the market and the experiences gained from it.

Experience provides incumbents with buffers against new market entrants in a number of ways:

- Goodwill. When confronted with a number of carriers, potential users of aviation have varying levels of information and quality of services. Risk aversion encourages a 'better the devil I know' mentality that favors incumbent suppliers. The need to circumvent this with advertising and promotions pushes up costs for new entrants.
- Knowledge. Incumbent supplies have more information on the market being served and can tailor service to specific customer needs. New entrants must sink resources into acquiring such information.

18

- Organization. New entrants must assimilate needs of the new service over their other routes, and this entails learning costs throughout the remainder of their organization.

While these effects can be intellectually isolated, the important question concerns quantitative importance. Empirical evidence is scant and exact causal links difficult to define. After federal deregulation, The US domestic experience established that existing intra-state airlines had a much larger impact on the interstate market than did newly established carriers. The evidence from Europe is only slowly emerging.

Aviation markets have attracted considerable attention on both sides of the Atlantic, with two major official studies released from Brussels and Washington in the mid-1990s[5]. Both came to the same general conclusion that competition was important to the health of air transport. Equally, however, both to varying degress argued that public policy medicines or incentives should be given to particular constituent airlines to prevent excessive ailing in such a market. What is less clear is an exact definition of what competition means in air transport markets.

As we have seen, like most suppliers of transport, communication and other network services, airlines operate under a variety of conditions influencing cost structure and the patterns of demand that they respond to. While a wide range of academic writing exists on the sector, very little agreement has been reached on what the inherent underlying market structure implied by this cost configuration looks like (Doganis, 1991).

At one extreme in the late 1970s, confidence was expressed that aviation markets are naturally contestable, and even in the absence of actual competition, continued threats of potential market entry would act as a stimulus to limit any excessive harmful monopolies exploiting the activity of incumbent carriers.

Others with less confidence in potential competition argued that, while perfectly competitive aviation markets are unlikely, there is sufficient competition to constrain exploiting behavior without the possible theoretical distortions often accompanying imperfect government interventions. Aviation markets were seen to be workably competitive[6].

---

[5]   These were Comité des Sages for Air Transport (1994) and the US National Commission to Ensure a Strong Competitive Airline Industry (1993).

[6]   Alternatively, the notion of imperfect oligopolies was used to characterize the natural outcome of a free aviation market with limited competition between larger carriers partly being augmented by smaller actors (Keeler, 1990). If this is true, then some form of government control over fares would be needed.

The development of hub-and-spoke operations, where carriers feed services into a small number of major airports and distribute them to their destinations, has, in part, been brought about by these cost features[7].

In their hub-and-spoke operations, US major carriers generally use one or more large airports, with some secondary hubs designed to meet the demands of the domestic market. Flights are arranged in banks which allow passengers continuing on to be consolidated on outbound flights to further destinations. In the context of international flights, there are usually major hubs in each of the countries involved.

Figure 2.2 offers a very simple example of hub-and-spoke operations in international markets. Services feed traffic into a hub in country A, where traffic destined for country B is consolidated and moved, usually by a larger aircraft. On arrival, passengers not destined for locations immediately around the gateway airport are combined with domestic traffic or traffic to other foreign destinations on other flights to their final destinations.

Coupled with these operational benefits are economies on the demand side. Hub-and-spoke operations provide carriers with the appearance of greater market presence. These stem from the ability to attract more passengers beyond the wider range of services offered. Particularly, flights throughout the day, combined with an extensive geographical network, allow passengers temporal and spatial flexibility when planning. The hub-and-spoke system, by offering a wide range of origins and destinations, therefore, helps carriers exploit other economies of market presence. Combining substantial domestic traffic flows with international traffic through hubs further enhances this advantage.

At the international level, evidence from 1989/1990 data shows that European airlines serving Europe and trans-Atlantic markets through large

---

[7]   There are a number of ways in which airline hub-and-spoke structures have been delineated.
- linear networks simply link separate airports and there is no dominant focus;
- simple hubs involve various 'spoke' services operating independently of each other;
- complex hubs involve flights connecting with arrivals and departures scheduled within a short period of time;
- directional hubs form an hour glass pattern with, for example, flights from the east coordinating with those to the west but with limited coordination with either south or north traffic;
- multiple hubs exist when the operations of an airline through several hubs are coordinated, often this may involve combining directional hub activities especially when there are long-haul operations involved.

hubs are more attractive to passengers than North American carriers. But this advantage is removed if the comparison is made only with the US airlines (such as American, Delta and United) who offer extensive domestic networks as well as international services (Dresner and Windle, 1995).

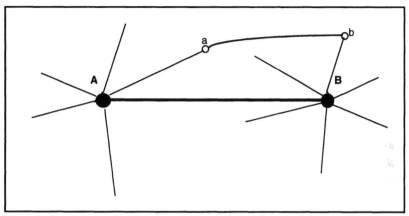

Figure 2.2 *Pattern of hub-and-spoke operations*

While economic forces in many international situations are a factor, the hub-and-spoke structure has often been less a consequence of market forces and more the result of institutional arrangements. In Europe, state-owned carriers have enjoyed extensive monopoly rights, both for domestic and international carriage, and used this to create protected hub-based operations. Relaxation of regulations within the EU area has seen new entry into domestic and short-haul markets, with traditional flag carriers' monopolies being eroded.

The nature of hub-and-spoke operations, evolving in recent years as conditions of market competition, have changed and improved management techniques introduced. Particularly, hub-and-spoke operations now generally involve the concentration of traffic at hub airports in a series of banks, thus refining the optimizing of these structures.

What technically constitutes a hub-and-spoke structure is opaque, but a general rule has been thought to entail carriers feeding three or more banks of traffic daily through an airport from some 40 or more cities. Realistically, however, this may not prove a viable economic structure in the future, as crucial cut-off points for the number of banks and the linked cities may be different.

Besides potential periodic congestion, banking was traditionally seen as posing few economic problems. But it can lead to considerable periods of idle time when the number of banks per day is relatively small. Ground staff

21

and other resources are left with little to do, and aircraft are used much less effectively. Now it is recognized that while airlines may enjoy economies of network presence from having large-scale hub-and-spoke operations, -diseconomies need to be considered in some cases.

Indeed, some air carriers are extremely successful in engaging in non-hub-and-spoke operations. They have either focused on taking radial traffic from some hubs to nodal points or have offered direct services between smaller cities. (In terms of Figure 2.2, carriers may offer direct flights between a and b.) Several new EU start-up carriers, such as the former EBA, can be categorized in this way.

More recently, some major US carriers such as Northwest and Continental have truncated or withdrawn services at smaller, secondary hubs. Sophisticated accounting procedures reveal that marginal revenues generated by higher traffic volumes attained from these elements of their operations are more than off-set by the fixed costs of the structure (Treitel and Smick, 1996). The trend is not so pronounced in Europe, although outside of the EU, Swissair's reduction of long-haul flights from Geneva may fall into this type of hub restructuring.

Long-haul international traffic can pose another challenge due to additional constraints such as differing time zones. Night curfews at airports and travelers' desire to arrive within certain times, limits flexibility in operations. And the need for specific aircraft for long haul can also affect a carrier's fleet composition. These factors may make it difficult for international carriers to provide hub type arrangements at both ends of a flight, although the size of aircraft would ideally mean that linked feeder services would be desirable. This is one of the reasons why increased cooperation exists between carriers of different countries; in effect, they seek to generate additional synergy effects from combining their respective hub activities.

It is not only with regard to monitoring their costs that airlines have become more sophisticated. On the demand side, air travel is generally considered as derived, not wanted for its own sake but rather for the benefits at the end of a trip. While all forms of air travel are increasing, leisure travel is growing more in importance – globally, its ratio to business travel is now 80:20. This reflects the importance of leisure activities at a time of rising incomes and the increased non-working time people now enjoy.

Yet business travel is much less price elastic than the demand for leisure travel, thus offering the opportunity for airlines to change higher market fares. Careful yield management[8], whereby airlines adjust fares and

---

[8]   Airline services are non-durable in the sense that if a seat is not sold when an aircraft takes off, that service is lost forever. Those demanding air

impose constraints on tickets to reflect various fare elasticities of potential travelers, enables carriers to exploit these differences in elasticities[9].

Indeed, systems of yield management have become so sophisticated that British Airways now obtains about 70% of its revenues from 30% of its passengers in this manner. Business travelers are less price sensitive but exhibit more demands on quality of service (e.g. time and frequency of flights, lounge facilities and frequent flyer bonuses). By offering flexible tickets, comfortable on- and off-plane amenities and scheduling convenient

transport services are not a uniform group but represent a wide range of individuals - business travelers of differing seniority, holiday-makers etc. - with various priorities. This combination of non-durability of service and heterogeneous demand has led many airlines to adopt yield management techniques to maximise their revenue flow.

One can see the economic rationale by recourse to a simple diagram. Yield management is essentially a dynamic form of price discrimination whereby rather than an identical fare being charged to each passenger (such as c below) users are charged different fares (e.g. a,b,c) reflecting their elasticities of demand. The availability of modern computer systems allows airlines to track how sales are going on each service and to adjust fares and the conditions attached to them so that maximimum revenue is obtained.

As with any form of price discrimination this allows the airline to convert consumers' surplus (the difference between the price the user pays and that he is willing to pay) into producers' surplus. In the case of yield management, the airlines adjust their prices of seats over time as sales proceed; slow sales precipitating a fall in price in the next period. See, Kraft *et al* (1986); Oum *et al* (1986)

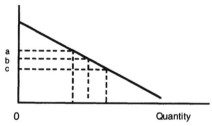

[9] The natural reaction of any incumbent actor in a market that has previously enjoyed some measure of shelter from competition is to attempt to limit the erosion of the market power that it has accumulated. Gillen *et al* (1988) offers some insights in terms of this effect with respect to the Canadian air transport market. See, Organisation for Economic Cooperation and Development (1997) for a more general discussion in terms of international markets.

to business needs at a premium price, carriers can exploit this willingness to pay.

The fact that business trips are paid for by companies means that the choice of airline is often not in the hands of the flyer, thus technically isolating the principal from the agent in the travel choice equation. This is one reason why airlines use incentives such as frequent flyer programs and business lounges; they are benefits directly enjoyed by the traveler.

Given these features, airlines pursue a number of different strategies to achieve their objectives. These objectives themselves may vary. In the case of private, commercial airlines profitability is normally the driving force, although over what periods profits are to be assessed is not always agreed upon. Nationalized airlines often operate under somewhat different criteria and with different concerns regarding uncertainties in their financial accounts. Closer interactions with government can lead to management having less precise ideas of what exactly they should seek to achieve. They may technically be required to make a target rate of return or to act commercially but in many instances, particularly within Europe, the large-scale subsidies are given by governments to their flag carrying airlines. Here, clear objectives are not set and economic efficiency is often sacrificed, sometimes at the behest of governments seeking to meet a wider political agenda.

2.3   CHANGING VIEWS ON ECONOMIC REGULATION

Air transport has traditionally been the subject of a wide range of regulations and controls. Changes in the way economists and policy makers think about regulation have been important underlying forces influencing recent developments in EU regulatory policies[10]. Here we offer a brief outline of the changes in thought that have occurred.

It is difficult to explain all past policy changes entirely in terms of the widespread acceptance of these new ideas; reforms of UK road haulage regulations in the 1968 Transport Act were well in advance of the new ideas, and those responsible for the deregulation of US aviation seem not to fully subscribe to all of them (e.g. Kahn, 1988). Nevertheless, they were potent forces in more recent debates about European aviation. Two particular developments in economic theory are of special importance:

[10]   To paraphrase the British economist, John Maynard Keynes, all practical men are influenced by the ideas of some long deceased economic scribbler, although in this case many of the actors are still with us.

By the mid-1970s, a growing body of opinion, led by the Chicago School of economists, suggested that economic regulation might not always be initiated with the public interest in mind. Even if this was the original intent, it might subsequently cease to serve that particular interest. One reason for this could be that legislation and/or regulations might be captured by those whom it was intended should be controlled, and regulators might well have a vested interest in expanding the system to meet their own aspirations for power (Stigler, 1971).

A major difficulty with any form of regulation is to ensure the regime is appropriately updated as conditions change. Moreover, those with specialized knowledge needed to carry this through are normally those involved in the industry and hence having the power of manipulation. Under these circumstances, the Chicago School argues that the onus of proof should be on the shoulders of those advocating regulation and where there is doubt, a liberal policy should be preferred. There was considerable debate in the US about the applicability of such arguments with regard to transport and particularly aviation industries (Keeler, 1984), and this thought permeated within Europe.

The second important development in economic thinking concerns the power of potential competition. Traditionally, market intervention in aviation has been justified as important to contain the power of monopoly suppliers of services, especially on thin routes where efficiency may mean only one airline could viably operate. Provided there is free entry to and exit from a market (i.e. there are no 'sunk costs'), contestability theory argues that the threat of potential competition will deter any efforts by a monopoly or quasi-monopoly operator to exploit air travelers (Baumol *et al.*, 1982). If no sunk costs exist associated with providing a particular service, then the simple threat of hit-and-run entry would deter incumbent operators from charging sub-optimally high fares.

While perfectly contestable markets are unlikely to be achieved (any more than perfectly regulated markets ever exist), a high level of contestability is possible in the aviation industry. Aircraft, for example, are easily switched between routes at a negligible cost. The logic of the arguments together is that government regulations may well lead to intervention failures that have adverse implications in excess of the market distortions they are meant to correct. More particularly, the contestability argument provides a framework within which perfect competition becomes a special case. There is no need for the myriad of competitors that perfect competition theory implies but rather actors can be kept on their toes through the threat of competition. Advocates of liberalization, therefore, argue that removal of entry, exit and pricing regulations would, in these circumstances, be preferable to existing regulatory regimes. In these terms,

Keeler (1990) has implied that aviation markets can be made 'workably contestable' in that liberalization generates a more efficient, if not perfect, system than one of economic regulation.

We return to this later when considering the factors that have shaped EU thinking on aviation policy reform.

2.4   AIR TRANSPORT POLICY DEVELOPMENT IN THE EUROPEAN UNION

While there has been a Common Transport Policy since the signing of the Rome Treaty in 1957, aviation was initially excluded. Countries regulated their own domestic aviation and a bilateral system of agreements, evolved from the Chicago Convention of 1944, governed international air transport within the Union, as well as outside of it. Policies were essentially concerned with the regulation of scheduled fares, service provision and market entry.

Coupled with this was the growth of a very large European charter market that met north-south tourist traffic demands. This market was less rigorously regulated and served by low cost operators. The long term contracts carriers, with tour operators, provide a buffer against market fluctuations that could be interpreted as a coalition mechanism in the context of core theory (see Chapter 7).

The EU has also never had a single regulatory body with responsibility for international air transport like the former Civil Aeronautics Board (CAB) that regulated US interstate aviation. The bilateral air service agreements that emerged after the 1944 Chicago meeting were piecemeal arrangements, although common motivations often led to standard features[11]. They were generally restrictive and often allowed only one airline from each country to operate a route.

While this type of restriction may be similar to the CAB's entry policy to US interstate routes prior to 1978[12], the European situation was more stringent; over 90% of bilateral agreements involved controlled capacity with obligatory 50:50 revenue pooling. Further, some 900 of the

---

[11]   Articles 1, 6 and 17-20 of the Chicago Convention were particularly important in recognizing each contracting state's complete and exclusive sovereignty over the airspace above its territory, the requirement that aircraft should have a nationality by being registered in one particular state, and the consequent need for aircraft registered in any state to obtain the permission of a state in order to operate air services to or from its territory.

[12]   For more details see Chapter 3.

agreements excluded fifth freedom rights. The two countries involved agreed on the airfare, and competitive pricing was excluded. Finally, many of the airlines were 'flag' carriers that were largely state owned and often in receipt of substantial state subsidies.

Within the EU, overlapping philosophies and approaches to economic regulation extended into the supply of aviation services and make the creation of a unified policy difficult. The patchwork of controls over such things as market entry, fares, and conditions of operation that existed in 1957 have grown with time. To a large extent, they were initially a reflection of these differences. Countries such as France, Spain and Greece where domestic aviation is relatively important have a tradition of heavily regulating entry and fares, and this has extended to their views of international aviation policy.

This degree of regulation has frequently been justified by governments in terms of serving the public interest by ensuring market stability, maintaining safety standards, protecting the public from monopoly exploitation and providing a comprehensive network of services. From this perspective, the view of air transport is as a public service where regulation is seen as necessary with regular services being offered at the lowest possible fares, that are consistent with a reasonable rate of return being earned by carriers.

These controls also serve, perhaps less explicitly, as important instruments for the protection of other aspects of the national interests by maintaining flag carriers who meet wider economic and military criteria. From a foreign policy perspective, 'showing the flag', was a feature of nineteenth century maritime policy but the idea has continued into the aviation age. Exporting aviation services can also represent an important element of 'invisible' earnings from foreign trade. In addition, there is the question of status and market presence. In many countries (e.g. Greece), aviation is provided through statute by national, state-owned airlines. Such direct controls not only influence provided air transport services but can also be deployed to regulate the purchase of aviation equipment which can also form a major item in foreign trade accounts.

Such a regime of *ad hoc*, state-based regulations and controls is unlikely to generate the most efficient air transport system for Europe. While some countries may benefit because of their bargaining position or through historical accident, overall it will tend to protect inefficient operations and distort the overall pattern of services being provided. It effectively acts as a restraint on trade and associates with it the same undesirable economic implications as other restraints such as tariffs. The problem is that countries with well-entrenched systems of market controls, even if appreciative of the probable adverse implications of this for the overall welfare of the Union, have effectively cushioned their airlines from competition and, in consequence, would find it difficult suddenly competing in a more market-orientated environment.

Change has come slowly and taken four broad thrusts:

2.4.1 Domestic reforms

There have been reforms of domestic aviation policy within a number of EU members. Some, as in the UK, were *de facto* changes and did not entirely free up the market. Rather, they saw the national regulatory agency being more liberal in the allocation of licenses and acceptance of fare flexibility (UK Civil Aviation Authority, 1988). Other countries such as France, Spain, Italy, and Germany have been less inclined towards unilateral domestic liberalization.

Reforms have gradually been accompanied by greater private sector involvement in the provision of aviation services (Meersman and van de Voorde, 1996). In some instances (most notably British Airways), there was complete privatization of former state companies at an early stage. More common (in Germany and the Netherlands) has been a gradual selling off of stock. Implications of these different approaches to privatization (albeit in terms of looking at British Airways and Air Canada) suggest that complete private sector ownership has distinctly positive implications for aviation markets (Eckel *et al*, 1997)[13].

Airports and other fixed infrastructure, outside of the UK where the main airports have been privatised as the British Airports Authority in 1987, has tended to remain in the public sector.

2.4.2 Reforming bilateral air service agreements

Since the mid-1980s, there has been a move to liberalize bilateral agreements between some members. In 1984 the UK and the Netherlands concluded a new agreement that very significantly relaxed the rules concerning traffic between the two countries. The main features of the agreement were as follows. Access to routes was opened up: any airline (based in either country) could fly between the two signatories. Tariff freedom was established: there was no compulsory consultation with other airlines and fares were to be set by the country from which the flight originated. Capacity offered was left to the airlines to determine. In 1985 these two countries went further when a double disapproval system was

[13]   Prodromidis and Frangos (1995) offer further empirical evidence of the greater efficiency of private airlines.

introduced. Previously fares had been subject to approval by the country of origin. From 1985 an airline was free to modify its fares unless both countries disapproved.

Subsequently the Anglo-German (1984), Anglo-Belgian (1985), Anglo-Luxembourg (1985), Anglo-Italian (1985) and Anglo-Irish (1988) agreements were all subjected to varying degrees of liberalization. Whilst these developments were a step forward, what was still lacking was a Union-wide act of deregulation. This was something that could only be accomplished by the Council of Ministers.

The changes did, however, initiate liberalization into fragments in the European international market and offered important insights into its implications. It encouraged new entrants and brought response from incumbents. Empirical evidence from Irish-UK routes, for example, point to lower fare levels and benefits estimated in 1989 to £24.9 million for the 994,000 passengers already using the route at the time of regulatory change and £16.2 million for 1.3 million additional passengers generated post liberalization (Barrett, 1990). The immedate impact of the Anglo-Dutch liberalisation was much more muted although this can in part be explained in terms of its timing in the trade cycle and the fact that the existing bilateral was not excessively restrictive.

2.4.3 'Open Skies' agreements

Not all liberalizing measures have been exclusively within the Union, such as the Anglo-Swiss bilateral free access capacity provisions with limited tariff constraints. Of particular importance are agreements involving the US whose 'Open Skies' policy, since 1979, has attempted to develop liberal bilateral air service agreements with individual EU states. The bilateral agreements between the US and individual EU countries had traditionally varied by country (Table 2.4) but in general were relatively restrictive on capacity and entry points as well as 5th freedom rights.

There has been a gradual change in the 1990s but, to date, the only long standing liberal agreement is with the Netherlands.

In 1994, however, the US initiated liberal bilateral agreements with a number of European countries, although none has been a major international airline. In 1996, an interim arrangement was reached with Germany, amounting to an Open Skies agreement. The impact of both types of development and stance the US has taken is to help bring European aviation closer to the global marketplace[14].

---

[14]   The liberalization of the North Atlantic has not entirely been painless in the short term. Between 1984 and 1990 the six countries with the most liberal

Table 2.4 *Selected US/EU bilateral air service agreements pre-'Open Skies'*

	Germany	France	Spain
European 3rd/4th freedom	25 US points	9 US points served	11 points in USA
European 5th freedom	Unrestricted	Very limited	Substantial
US 3rd/4th freedom	Unrestricted	From 15 US points	6 US points to Madrid and Barcelona
US 5th freedom	Unrestricted	Frozen: limited	Substantial
Designation	Unrestricted	Frozen	Single
Capacity	Restrictions on US capacity	Restricted	Unrestricted
Fare approval	Country of origin	Double approval	Double approval
Code-sharing rights	Specified number per year	None	To 15 points in the USA

A longer standing issue, in the context of an EU air transport policy, is whether it is still appropriate for individual Member States to engage in such bilateral arrangements or if a common EU negotiating position should be taken (Association of European Airlines, 1995). In 1996, EU states gave over some soft-negotiating rights to the Commission but major players in the trans-Atlantic market, and especially the UK, have resisted relinquishing their individual negotiating rights.

2.4.4 EU air transport policy

The development of the EU's air transport policy should be put into context[15]. The foundations of post-war international regulation of scheduled air passenger services were, as stated earlier, laid shortly after the Chicago Convention of 1944. Interstate services in Europe were no exception. The Convention gave rise to a United Nations agency – the International Civil

bilateral air service agreements with the US (Belgium, Denmark, France, Germany, Spain and the Netherlands) lost market share while those with more restrictive agreements (Greece, Denmark, Italy, Portugal and the UK) gained market share. Over the same period, overall the US carriers took a larger proportion of the fast growing non-US citizens traffic on the Atlantic.

[15] For more details see Button and Swann (1989; 1992); Vincent and Stasinopoulos (1990); Stasinopoulos (1992; 1993); Doganis (1994); Borenstein (1992b); McGowan and Seabright (1989); Pelksman (1986) and Good *et al* (1993); Stevens (1997).

Aviation Organization (ICAO). In practice its role was largely concerned with technical standards, the collection of statistical data, etc., rather than detailed economic regulation.

The discussions within the Convention were dominated by the fact that governments claimed absolute sovereignty over the airspace over their national territories. The hope that lay behind the discussions was that those who signed the Convention would grant to all other signatories freedom of access to this airspace and to airports beneath them. To this end certain freedoms of the skies were identified[16].

In practice the Convention did not make a great deal of progress since the commercially important third, fourth and fifth freedoms were not, with some minor exceptions, settled on the hoped-for multilateral basis. Instead states preferred to enter into bilateral deals. This gave rise to a network of bilateral air services agreements – e.g., the UK and US concluded the first Bermuda Agreement in 1946. Under these bilateral agreements the two countries agreed upon the gateway airports through which each could enter the other's territory, restricted the entry of airlines to routes and shared out the traffic. This also meant that fifth freedom operators could only fly on the routes involved if the regulatory authorities at both ends agreed.

These bilateral agreements were primarily concerned with access to gateways and routes. The matter of airfares was in the first instance

---

[16]   The 'Freedoms of the Skies' are:

- 1st freedom. The right of an airline of one country to fly over the territory of another country without landing.
- 2nd freedom. The right of an airline of one country to land in another country for non-traffic reasons, such as maintenance or refueling, while en route to another country.
- 3rd freedom. The right of an airline of one country to carry traffic from its country of registry to another country.
- 4th freedom. The right of an airline of one country to carry traffic from another country to its own country of registry.
- 5th freedom. The right of an airline of one country to carry traffic between two countries outside of its own country of registry as long as the flight originates or terminates in its own country of registry.
- 6th freedom. The right of an airline of one country to carry traffic between two foreign countries via its own country of registry. This is a combination of third and fourth freedoms.
- 7th freedom. The right of an airline to operate stand-alone services entirely outside the territory of its home state, to carry traffic between two foreign states.
- 8th freedom. The right of an airline to carry traffic between two points within the territory of a foreign state (cabotage).

determined within the ambit of another body. This was the International Air Transport Association (IATA), which came into existence in 1945. It operated a series of conferences where airlines discussed and coordinated fares, the resulting fare agreements being subsequently ratified by governments. Thus the scheduled fares between London and Paris were subject to the final approval of the British and French regulatory authorities. At a later stage the activities of IATA were subjected to attack by the US government and were undermined by competition from non-member airlines from the Far East.

At a still later stage membership of IATA did not require airlines to be bound by conference fare decisions and in some sectors (e.g., the North Atlantic routes) fixed rates were replaced by zones of reasonableness.

The European bilateral system was, however, relatively tightly regulated although, as we shall see later, toward the end piecemeal deregulation began to break through. Bilateral agreements involving EU members were inevitably not uniform but there were typical features:

- Access to the market was not free but was indeed severely restricted. Often only one airline from each country was allowed to fly on a particular route. This was referred to as single designation. As late as 1987, out of 988 routes within the Union air services network only 48 had multiple designation, i.e., more than one airline from either side.
- Fifth freedom competition was the exception – of the above 988 routes only 88 allowed fifth freedom rights. The capacity offered by each bilateral partner was also restricted. Generally each country enjoyed 50% of the traffic between the two countries.
- The division of the market was often accompanied by pools in which the airlines shared the revenue in proportion to the capacity employed. Thus even if one airline obtained 54% of the revenue and the other enjoyed only 46% they would nevertheless split the proceeds equally.
- Fares were finally approved by the regulatory bodies of the bilateral partners and there was no competition on price, as opposed to service, on particular routes.
- The airlines designated by each country had to be substantially owned and controlled by the country designating it, or by its nationals.
- In some cases airlines, many of which as we will see were wholly or partially government owned, enjoyed what were in effect competition distorting state aids.

The Rome Treaty, signed in 1957, came into operation on January 1, 1958. It originally comprised six member states – West Germany, France, Italy, the Netherlands, Belgium and Luxembourg. Subsequently it was enlarged – in 1973 the UK, the Irish Republic and Denmark became full members. In 1981 Greece was admitted and in 1986 the Community was further enlarged to include Spain and Portugal. Sweden, Austria and Finland are now members. The Rome Treaty provided for the creation of the European Economic Community that is centrally concerned with the integration of the various national economies.

The Treaty required that there should be free competition across frontiers and this called for the removal of all protective tariff, quota and non-tariff barriers to the free circulation of goods. The Treaty also envisaged free competition across frontiers for services – each state would enjoy the unrestricted freedom to sell its services to all the other member states. Around the island of free trade there was to be a protective ring fence of the common external tariff. Finally, the Community envisaged free movement of factors. Labor, capital and enterprise should be free to move and set up in production in all the other member states. All of this technically constituted a common market.

Three features of this common market arrangement had the potential to undermine the system of economic regulation we described earlier. First, Article 3 of the Rome Treaty lays down the objectives of the European Economic Community. Article 3(f) declares that one of the key aims is the creation of conditions of undistorted competition. Indeed, the integration of the national economies was to be a process based on competitive trade (in goods and services) interpenetration. Quite clearly the system of airline regulation as described above was anti-competitive and fundamentally at variance with the competitive ethos of the Rome Treaty.

Secondly, the requirement to abolish non-tariff barriers applied not merely to goods but also to services. Antitrust-type restrictions constitute such a barrier and Article 85 of the Rome Treaty provides the European Communities Commission with the power to ban cartel arrangements[17], Article 86 provides a prohibitory power in respect of abuses by firms in market dominating positions[18] whilst Article 90 applies these provisions in

---

[17]   Strictly, it declares as incompatible with the common market '...all agreements between undertakings, decisions by associations of undertakings and concerted practices which may affect trade between Member States and which have as their objective or effect the preservation, restriction or distortion of competition within the common market...'

[18]   Strictly, 'Any abuse by one or more undertakings of a dominant position within the common market or in a substantial part of it shall be prohibited as incompatible with the common market in so far as it may affect trade between Member States'. These and other general EU policies of special relevance to air transport are considered in more detail in Section 2.5.

modified form to public enterprises. Thus the price-fixing and revenue-pooling arrangements of the airline regulatory system appeared to be extremely vulnerable to attack.

Thirdly, a key feature of the regulatory system contained in the bilateral agreements was the restrictions on access to routes. They were at variance with the idea of freedom to supply services. The latter suggested that, for example, Lufthansa ought to be free to compete on the London/Paris routes whereas under the UK/France bilateral it could be debarred, the traffic being reserved for Air France and British Airways. If the problem was that only British – or French – owned or controlled airlines could fly on those particular routes then that matter appeared to be capable of resolution by Lufthansa taking advantage of the Treaty's free movement of enterprise provision (the Right of Establishment). Article 52 of the Treaty envisages that such an established company should enjoy similar rights to nationals.

Whilst the Rome Treaty theoretically appeared to threaten the system, it has to be admitted that not only in the air transport sector but right across the board the Community made only limited progress in removing the restrictions on the free movement of goods, services and factors. Indeed it was this shortcoming that explains the signature in 1986 by the then 12 Member States of the Single European Act. This recognized the Union's failure to complete the Single European Market and set the end of 1992 as the target date for its completion. This was bound to have implications for international airline regulation within the Union.

An explanation of how and why deregulation finally emerged requires identification of the players and forces at work.

The European Communities Commission is basically charged with the task of ensuring that the aims of the Union (as laid down in Article 3 of the Rome Treaty) are achieved. To this end it makes policy proposals for Union law and plays an executive role (e.g. it hands down antitrust prohibitions). But the power to make Union law lies not with the Commission but with the European Communities Council of Ministers.

The key legislative players in this area of policy are the Member State governments. They appear in two guises. First, they were the parties to the regulatory arrangements which did not proceed from actions under the Rome Treaty but predate it by more than a decade. Secondly, their ministers of transport make up the Council of Ministers (on transport matters) and as the Union's lawmakers have been in a position to undo the regulatory knot that they have tied on an intergovernmental bilateral basis. The European Court of Justice has the power to uphold or overturn the actions of these other EU institutions and to render preliminary judgments on issues of European significance arising in national courts.

Whilst the court is essentially reactive, its influence can be decisive. The airlines are a diverse group including the national scheduled flag carriers but also regional and charter carriers. Next there is a collection of bodies including user groups, individual investigators, etc. They have had the capacity to expose the regulatory system to criticism and to mobilize public opinion. Finally there were autonomous forces. This is a catchall category since it brings to bear not only the impact of changing attitudes to regulation but also the international demonstration effect arising from acts of deregulation elsewhere.

At the outset, the balance of forces favored the existing regulatory system. It is true that the Commission was charged with the implementation of a treaty that quite clearly embraces a pro-competition philosophy. However, the competitive rigor of the Commission's policy stance was bound to be conditioned by the prevailing orthodoxy, and in the early days of the Commission's existence regulation was regarded as being in the public interest whilst competition was seen as inimical to safety, stability, etc.

Moreover the Commission was faced with some uncertainty over the position of air transport under the Treaty. Article 3(i) provided for a separate regime for transport – i.e. a Common Transport Policy (CTP) which might possibly, because of the alleged peculiarities of transport, be somewhat different from the rest of the Treaty. However whilst the Rome Treaty is rather sparing when it comes to spelling out the detailed nature of the CTP, the provisions that are revealed are liberalizing. Moreover when the Commission came to put policy flesh on the Treaty it chose to adopt a competitive stance. Having said that, it has to be recognized that the CTP only applied to road, rail and inland waterway – air and maritime transport were not included in the policy[19].

Other players and forces were also favorable to the existing regulatory system or were relatively quiescent.

Member State governments had created the regulatory system and the prevailing orthodoxy plus inertia did not dispose them to undo it. Scheduled flag carriers enjoyed the protection of the system and, given that those flag carriers were often publicly owned, were hardly likely to deviate from the position taken by their governments. Free and intensified competition carried with it the possibility of losses that would fall upon national exchequers and therefore member state governments were disposed to

---

[19]   Technically, the Council of Ministers was left with the power to decide what provisions should be made for air and sea transport; '...[t]he Council may, acting unanimously, decide whether, and to what extent and by what procedure appropriate provisions may be laid down for sea and air transport'.

preserve the protected *status quo*. The non-scheduled airlines were carving out a role for themselves but as yet they had not gained enough confidence to mount a direct assault on the preserve of the scheduled carriers. It was only as air travel grew that users became an increasingly significant pressure group – in due course they and others were encouraged by change in the prevailing orthodoxy. Autonomous forces had not yet delivered that change.

In 1974, however, the first significant change occurred thanks to the reactive influence of the Court of Justice. In the *French Merchant Seamen* case (European Court of Justice, 1974), the court declared that the general rules of the Treaty, and therefore by implication those relating to competition, applied to sectors such as air transport. This appeared to open up air transport regulation to attack under the Treaty. However this was not so for various reasons.

Articles 85 and 86 allow the Commission to prohibit activities such as collusive price fixing and abuses of dominant positions. But even if they were applicable to air transport there was still the problem that the Commission lacked powers to implement these rules directly itself. Article 87 enables the Council of Ministers to confer implementing powers on the Commission. This the Council did not do in the case of air transport, and the Commission had to rely on the inadequate implementing provisions of Articles 88 and 89. These require the Commission to investigate infringements in collaboration with the Member States, a situation which might be described as a case of the gamekeeper requiring the poachers to cooperate in organizing the latter's prosecution. The Commission also lacked the power to directly impose penalties.

There was a further complication. In 1981 Lord Bethell attempted to take the Commission to task for not applying competition rules to fare-fixing restrictions. But the Commission replied that it was not guilty on the ground that fare-fixing was an autonomous act of government whilst the competition rules (Articles 85 and 86) applied to enterprises (Kuijper, 1983). This did not entirely settle the matter since the Rome Treaty does require member states to act in conformity with the Treaty and to abstain from measures that impede attainment of its objectives. Unfortunately these are somewhat unspecific injunctions and do not provide a firm basis for action.

A further difficulty arose in connection with designation. Licensing was often tight with only one airline operating from either bilateral partner and added to this was the nationality rule. This appeared to conflict with the freedom to supply services. However, Article 90 indicates that the Member States could take refuge behind its provisions. It applies to public enterprises and enterprises to which member states grant special privileges. It goes on to declare that the competition rules apply to both categories of enterprise. It then qualifies this by saying that in respect of the second category the rules of the Treaty should not be applied if their application would obstruct those enterprises in the tasks assigned to them. It was therefore possible for Member States to declare that their national flag carriers were enterprises granted special privileges and that the strict licensing principle was essential.

Putting it another way, the unrestricted freedom of entry implied by the freedom to supply services was therefore undesirable. The Commission was also aware that in the *Saachi* case the Court of Justice had supported such a view (European Court of Justice, 1994). Even if a non-bilateral airline took advantage of the right of establishment principle and established itself, the state in which it was now established could still refuse it a license. The State could argue that all it had to do to avoid breaching the right of establishment principle was to treat such an established airline in the same way as it treated its own nationals. This it could do by pointing out that in its licensing it refused licenses to its own nationals as well as established airlines. There was, therefore, no discrimination on the ground of nationality.

All these inhibitions arose because of policies pursued by Member States and what they had done on an intergovernmental basis they could undo on a Community basis as members of the Council of Ministers.

At this point we turn to autonomous forces that played a key role. Prior to the 1970s economic regulation was with few exceptions viewed as being in the public interest. The origins of regulation could indeed be stated in terms of syllogism:

- Market failure provided a rationale for a system of regulation in the public interest.
- Governments did in fact regulate.
- Therefore such regulation had its origins in a desire to protect the public interest.

As we saw in Section 2.3, in the 1970s, and indeed before, there was a process that can be described as the undermining of the public interest theory. Revisionist historians and political scientists were influential in the 1950s and 1960s but the most notable contribution came from Stigler (1971). Prior to Stigler, it was possible to envisage regulation as the product of a benign and disinterested state that interfered in the workings of the market solely to protect the general good. After Stigler the state is seen less as a benign actor and more as a market place where producer groups and politicians traded private advantages – i.e. regulation for political support.

The intellectual defense of economic regulation ultimately boiled down to the proposition that in the long run, competition is either not feasible or not desirable - i.e. natural monopoly conditions existed or excessive competition would ensue. It is possible to point to a series of contributions that across the board weakened the general case for regulation by making a case for competition and for the free play of market forces. The Chicago contribution was extremely important. Apart from Friedman's (1962) views on the connection between economic and political freedom and his attack on specific forms of government interference, Demsetz (1968) reawakened the idea that natural monopoly does not preclude competition. Competition for the field can be substituted for competition in the field.

Finally, there was the development of contestable market theory (Baumol *et al*, 1982). It is highly relevant to those situations where the number of enterprises in the market is limited. Fewness, following a conventional view, may suggest that some regulatory controls on prices are called for. The theory of contestable markets suggests that it is possible to have a competitive outcome even if there is only one firm in the industry, provided that the firm is constrained in its pricing behavior by the existence of potential as much as actual competition. The latter influences depend upon the existence of free entry that in turn depends on the existence of free exit. It is not economies of scale that constrain entry but sunk costs. There will be freedom of exit if no sunk costs are laid upon entrants. If this is so then an airline can contemplate entering a specific passenger route with equanimity since if the worst comes to pass it can also leave in a relatively cost free fashion – e.g. it can switch its aircraft to another route or sell them. In other words, the theory envisages that competitors can hit and run if necessary. As a result of all this, any attempt by an incumbent airline to raise prices above competitive levels, or to allow costs to drift up, will provoke entry.

To that extent regulation of prices will not be necessary, potential and actual competition will perform the necessary policing role. The theory suggests that airline operation is a likely industry in which to find highly contestable markets, provide arrangements exist to take care of the sunk cost problems. The theory also suggests that those features of regulation that impede exit, such as refusals to abandon unprofitable routes, will impede entry and are therefore likely to be counterproductive. Some sluggishness in the pricing response of incumbents to entry will also facilitate contestability, although such a condition is not absolutely essential. The theory emphasizes that the number of firms in the market does not determine the extent of its competitiveness.

Whilst the change in the climate of thinking was influential still more significant were actual decisions to deregulate and their effects. In practice, it was the decision of the US Congress in 1978 to totally scrap economic regulation and sunset the CAB that attracted European attention.

The changing climate of opinion and the US example had a noticeable effect on several of the key players.

The European Communities Commission was in 1979 encouraged to take a bolder line in terms of the kind of regulatory reform that it felt it could credibly propose. Thus it issued what became known as *Civil Aviation Memorandum No. 1*. Its rather modest proposals were as follows:

- Increased possibilities of market entry and innovation were desirable but full freedom of access was a long-term prospect.
- There was a need for the introduction of various forms of cheap fare.
- There was also a need to develop new cross-frontier services connecting regional centers within the Community – this was acted on later.
- An implementing regulation applying Articles 85 and 86 directly to air services was essential – a proposal on these lines was made in 1981.
- Increased competition emphasized the need for a policy on state aids to airlines.
- Whilst the right of establishment applied directly to airlines, Council action was necessary since practical and political obstacles would otherwise still exist.

By 1984 the Commission had become much bolder and in *Civil Aviation Memorandum No. 2* moved the discussion on from the 1979 statements of desirability to more specific liberalization proposals. The new elements when compared with the 1979 idea were:

- Scope for greater airfare freedom had been under discussion since the 1981 airfare report. Fares should be subject to a zone of flexibility system. A reference fare level and a zone of reasonableness around it would be arrived at on the basis of official double approval – i.e., both sides would have to agree. Having thus determined the scope for flexibility, airfares within the zone of flexibility would be subject to country of origin approval or double disapproval.
- In the case of designation a relatively weak proposal was made. The dominance of national flag fliers within the bilateral system was to remain relatively undisturbed except for a minor change to the effect that other airlines would be allowed to enter and take up any unused route operating rights.

- In the case of the 50/50 division of traffic between the national flag fliers of each state a bolder proposal was made whereby state A could not oppose a build up of traffic by state B until state A's share had fallen to 25%.
- Interairline agreements should be subjected to control. Capacity agreements would be permissible provided airlines were free to withdraw whilst revenue sharing pools might be exempted provided their revenue redistributing effect was minimal.

The changing climate of opinion also had an influence on user groups and various bodies who investigated the European system of regulation. The growth of air travel generated a growing interest group that could be mobilized in favor of change. Various bodies championed the cause.

The European Civil Aviation Conference (1981) showed the restricted nature of competition in European aviation. It indicated that only on 2% of city-to-city routes was there more than one airline operating per state. On 93% of routes there were apparently limitations on the number of flights that airlines could put on. Revenue pooling arrangements covered between 75% and 85% of total ton-kilometers flown. Inevitably comparisons were made between air fares in Europe and those in the US. According to the House of Lords, certain selected fares were double the US fares for similar distances, although the differences for return fares were much less marked. Other studies emerged supporting the view that European air fares were significantly higher.

The Commission of the European Communities (1981) also carried out its own investigation. Just as scholars in the US had been able to compare the free competition fares of California with the CAB regulated rates, so it was possible in Europe to compare bilateral regulated rates with those offered by the competitive charter sector. Barrett (1987) reviewing the Commission's conclusions based on cascade studies draws attention to the Commission's observation that,

> ...it would appear that only a relatively small proportion of the difference between scheduled and charter costs cannot be attributed to inherent differences between the two modes of operation.

The final precipitating factors were two in number. First, in 1979, the European Parliament was for the first time directly elected by the people rather than being representatives of national parliaments. This greatly enhanced its authority and as a reflection of that fact it put forward a far-reaching draft Treaty of European Union. This and other initiatives led to an Intergovernmental Conference. Whilst the Member States did not agree to go along with Parliament's visionary scheme they did recognize the need to revive the idea of closer economic union. This led to the 1986 Single European Act, referred to earlier, a key feature of which was the economic commitment to complete the internal market by the end of 1992. Part of that program involved the need to address the continuing restrictions in air transport.

The final push however came from a player who had hitherto been relatively quiescent – the European Court of Justice. It finally helped to precipitate the deregulatory measures of 1987. This initiative centered around the *Nouvelles Frontieres* case (European Court of Justice, 1986) which concerned the airfare cutting activities of, amongst others, a French travel agent. Tickets had been sold below the price approved by the French Minister for Civil Aviation – a violation of the Civil Aviation Code (*Code de l'Aviation Civile*). The resulting legal proceedings in France in turn generated an appeal for a preliminary ruling from the Court of Justice as to the conformity of the Civil Aviation Code with the law of the European Community.

The result of the Court's judgment was to encourage the Commission in the view that its powers to attack fare fixing activities were greater than the lack of an implementing regulation (in respect of Articles 85 and 86) might suggest. Basically, the Court said that if the Commission, or an appropriate national authority, was to pronounce adversely on an airline restriction, then a national court would have to take account of that fact. A party with standing might therefore bring an action against such a restriction in a national court and the restrictive arrangement in total might fall. The same thing could happen if the national court turned to the Court of Justice for guidance.

The impact of all this on the Council of Ministers was dramatic. There were differences between Members on the desirability of competition. Some were reluctant and others were prepared to make progress but not necessarily to throw the market into a state of free competition. Yet this might happen if the courts were to be besieged by appropriate cases. The Council was in danger of losing control of the situation. At this point the Commission, itself anxious to force the Council to deregulate, decided to increase pressure. It decided to instigate proceedings against certain airlines. The Council therefore decided that the best way to regain control was to agree to introduce deregulation but of a kind, and at a pace, of its own choosing. Hence the 1987 deregulation package – the 'First Package'. The Commission having achieved its key objective obligingly then decided to withdraw the proceedings.

The basic philosophy of the 1987 package was that deregulation would take place in stages – evolution rather than revolution being the watchword and workable competition being the objective. The details of what became known as the 'Packages' are set out in Table 2.5.

A regulation was adopted that enabled the Commission to apply the antitrust Articles 85 and 86 directly to airline operations. Only interstate operations were covered; the intrastate services and services to third countries were not at this stage affected by this measure. Certain technical agreements were also left untouched.

Whilst the above regulation enabled the Commission to attack directly agreements restricting competition (and abuses by firms in a market dominating position), another regulation was introduced that allowed airlines to continue to collude in respect of certain matters[20]. This enabling regulation in fact allowed the Commission to exempt *en bloc* three categories of agreements:

- agreements concerning joint planning and coordination of capacity, revenue sharing, consultations on tariffs and aircraft parking slot allocation;
- agreements relating to computer reservation systems;
- agreements about ground handling services.

But this block exemption power was of limited duration – it had to be revised by June 30, 1990 and Commission regulations made under it expired by January 31, 1991. Argyris (1989) points out that any proposal to prolong block exemption would on past evidence have been closely linked to the extent of further deregulation. If the Council of Ministers failed to agree to more liberalizing measures then the block exemption power would automatically lapse.

The block exemption issue vividly illustrates the political horse trading that took place in 1987. It is best viewed as a stratagem on the part of the Commission designed to persuade the Council to adopt a program of progressive liberalization. In other words, the immediate shock arising from more competition would be cushioned. The airlines would be able to collude for a period even though the Council regulation was designed to enable the Commission to apply Article 85 (and 86) directly. Airlines could, as a result of these exemption provisions, discuss fares.

[20]   Article 85, which attacks agreements, is not based on the *per se* principle. Rather it prohibits but holds out the possibility of exemption when certain defined benefits can be brought forward in defense.

Table 2.5 The EU 'Packages' of air transport policy reform

	1st Package From 1st January 88 International scheduled passenger transport	2nd Package From 1st November 1990 International scheduled passenger transport	3rd Package From 1st January 93 International scheduled passenger transport
Relevant Legislation	Regulation 3975/87 on the application of the competition rules to air transport. Regulation 3976/87 on the application of the Treaty to certain categories of agreements and concerted practices. Council Directive 87/601/EEC on air fares. Council Decision 87/602/EEC on capacity sharing and market access.	Council Regulation 2343/90 on market access. Council Regulation 2342/90 on air fares. Council Regulation 2344/90 on the application of the Treaty to certain categories of agreements and concerted practices.	Council Regulation 2407/92 on licensing of air carriers Council Regulation 2408/92 on market access Council Regulation 2409/92 on fares and rates
Fares	Fare Type ref. Fare by States Discount 66-90 Automatically Deep discount 45-65 Automatically All other Double approval	% of Fares approved Fare Type ref. Fare by States Fully flexible 106 Unless double disapproval Normal economy 95-105 Automatically Discount 80-94 Automatically Deep discount 30-79 If double approval All others	Provisions made for the States and/or the Commission to intervene against. • Excessive basic fares (in relation to long term fully allocated costs) • Sustained downward development of fares

Designation	• Multiple designation by a State allowed if:
	  250,000 pass (1st year after integration)
	  200,000 pass or 1,200 rt flight (2nd year)
	  180,000 pass or 1,000 rt flights (3rd year)
		• Multiple designation by a State allowed if:
		  140,000 pass on 800 rt flight (from January 91)
		  100,000 pass or 600 rt flight (from January 92)
			No longer applicable

Capacity	• Capacity shares between states
	  45/55% (from January 88)
	  40/60% (from October 89)
		• Capacity shares of a State of up to 60%
		• Capacity can be increased by 7.5% points per year
			Unrestricted

Route Access	• 3rd/4th freedom region to hub routes permitted. • 5th freedom traffic allowed up to 30% of capacity • Additional 5th rights for Irish and Portuguese • Combination of points allowed • Some exemptions	• 3rd/4th freedom traffic between all airports • 5th freedom allowed up to 50% of capacity • Public service obligations and certain protection for new regional routes • A 3rd/4th freedom service can be matched by an airline from the other State • Scope for traffic distribution rules and restrictions related to congestion and environmental protection	• Full access to international and domestic routes within the EU (exemptions for Greek island and Azores) • Cabotage unrestricted from April 1997. Restricted cabotage allowed for up to 50% of capacity until then. • Reformed public service obligations and some protection for new thin regional routes • More scope for traffic distribution rules and restrictions related to congestion and environmental protection
Competition Rules	Ground exemption regarding • Some capacity coordination • Tariff consultation • Slot allocation • Common computer reservation systems • Ground handling of aircraft, freight, passenger and inflight catering • Some sharing of pool revenues	Ground exemption regarding • Some capacity coordination • Tariff consultation • Slot allocation • Common computer reservation systems • Ground handling of aircraft, freight, passenger and inflight catering	Ground exemption regarding • Some capacity coordination • Tariff consultation • Slot allocation • Common computer reservation systems • Joint operation of new thin routes
Licensing of Air Carriers	Not provided for in 1st and 2nd Packages		Uniform conditions across EU: notion of Union ownership and control; and small carriers subject to looser regulatory requirements

Yet in the past the Commission seldom saw any virtue in price-fixing arrangements that had a significant impact on competition. Apparently the Council would have preferred the Commission to be bound by the wording contained in enabling regulation but the Commission avoided that.

The Commission maintained that it and not the Council was endowed with the power to approve the block exemption provisions. This gave it an opportunity to tighten up the details.

The Council also adopted a directive designed to provide airlines with greater pricing freedom (Regulation No. 3976/87). Whilst airlines could collude (though this is likely to be temporary) the hope was that they would increasingly act individually. The degree to which competition emerged was recognized as depending on the degree to which airlines exhibited a competitive spirit in their approach to airfare applications made to national civil aviation authorities. Article 3 of the directive declared that member states shall approve fare applications provided they were reasonably related to the long-term fully allocated costs of the applicant air carrier, while taking account of other relevant factors. In this connection they had to consider the needs of consumers, the need for a satisfactory return on capital, the market situation, including the fares of other air carriers operating the route and the need to prevent dumping. State authorities were not allowed to keep price competition at bay by refusing to approve a fare application simply because it was lower than that offered by another carrier.

Airfare applications were approved by the authorities of the states. Also the new arrangements did not constitute free competition – an element of regulation still remained in place. Whilst conditions were laid down that reduced the national authorities' room for maneuver in rejecting airfares, they could still do so. However, if there was disagreement on a fare the disagreeing party lost the right of veto. This arose because in such disagreement situations a right of arbitration was provided for. Under arbitration the disagreeing party could find its case being overturned.

The key fares in the approval procedures were economy fares. These reference rates provided a benchmark. The directive provided scope for discounts. Provided certain travel conditions were met, fares could be reduced below the benchmark by varying amounts. This discounting and deep discounting was an automatic right. There was an additional degree of flexibility for fares which, when the directive was introduced, already fell below the bottom of the deep discount zone. Fifth freedom operators could match these discounted fares.

The Council's 1987 package also made a start on liberalizing access to the market. To this end it adopted a decision in December 1987 (Regulation No. 3975/87). This provided for a deviation from the traditional air services agreement 50/50 split. The capacity shares related to total traffic between the

44

two countries. Member states were required to allow competition to change the shares up to 55/45 in the period to September 30, 1989 and thereafter to allow it to change to 60/40. Normally they could only take action if capacity shares threaten to move beyond such limits. Fifth freedom traffic was not included in these ratios but came on top. There was also a provision in which serious financial damage to an air carrier could constitute grounds for the Commission to modify the shift to the 60/40 limit.

The decision also required member states to accept multiple designation on a country pair basis by another member state. A member state was not obliged to accept the designation of more than one air carrier on a route by the other state (i.e. city pair basis) unless certain conditions were satisfied. These conditions become progressively less restrictive over time.

The decision also made a limited attempt to open up the market to fifth freedom competition (Directive No. 87/60). Certain fifth freedom rights became automatic but these were hedged around with safeguards and indicate the reluctance of the Council of Ministers to go too far too fast. The fifth freedom flights in question had to be extensions of a service from the state of registration or a preliminary of a service to the state of registration. An example of the latter would be that Aer Lingus might already have a right to fly between Birmingham and Dublin. It could now enter the Brussels to Birmingham route normally reserved for UK (and Belgian) bilateral operators, i.e. it could drop off in Birmingham passengers picked up in Brussels on a flight en route to Dublin. But there were more restrictions. One of the airports had to be a category-two airport – this prevented competition on the key routes between main airports. The above example by involving Birmingham (category two) and Brussels (category one) met the condition. There was also a ceiling on the proportion of passengers who could be in the fifth freedom category – on an annual basis not more than 30% of the people carried could be in the Brussels to Birmingham category.[21]

In December 1989 the Council of Transport Ministers returned to the issue of air transport deregulation. An agreement – the 'Second Package' – involving more deregulation was entered into.

- In respect of the freedom of airlines to make competitive fares, from the beginning of 1993 a system of double disapproval was accepted (Regulation No. 2343/90). Only if both civil aviation authorities refuse to sanction a fare application could an airline be precluded from offering

---

[21]   Both the fare directive and the access decision represented minimum degrees of liberalization that had to be accepted by all member states. More flexible arrangements were permitted.

it to its passengers. The regulation essentially provided for a revised system of discount fares based on a reference fare within which all fares meeting the specified criteria were approved automatically[22].

- From the same date the old system of setting limits to the division of traffic between the bilateral partners was to totally disappear in a phased manner (Regulation 2343/90).

- Member States have endorsed the vital principle, advanced by the Commission, that governments should not discriminate against airlines provided they meet safety and technical standards and run economically[23].

- The Council of Ministers agreed to address the problem of ownership rules. As indicated earlier, an airline has typically had to be substantially owned by a European state before it could fly from that country. The Council abolished this rule over a 2-year period. The implication was that fifth freedom rights became fully automatic whereas in the 1987 package they were granted on restricted terms. Another way of putting it is that airlines could enjoy fifth freedom rights provided they are registered in the Community.

- Air cargo services were liberalized so that a carrier operating from its home state to another member country can take cargo into a third member state or fly from one member state to another and then to its home state. Cabotage, or operations between two free standing states, was not liberalized.

The final reform – the 'Third Package' – came in 1992 to take effect from the following year. This initiated a phased move that, by 1997, resulted in a regulatory framework for the EU similar to US domestic aviation. Important questions, however, exist regarding the EU's role with respect to international aviation outside of the Union (Close, 1990).

- The measures removed significant barriers to entry by setting common rules governing safety and financial requirements for new airlines

---

[22]   The zones based on the reference fare (i.e. the standard air fare for each route at 100%) were 95% to 105% (normal economy), 80% to 94% (discount) and 30% to 79% (deep discount).

[23]   This was reported to be a response to a case made by UTA, the French overseas airline, which lobbied the Commission because the French civil aviation authorities refused to allow UTA to compete on European routes served by Air France.

(Regulation 2407/92)[24]. Since January 1993, EU airlines have been able to fly between member states without restriction and within member states (other than their own), subject to some controls on fares and capacity (Regulation No. 2408/92). In practice, though, some difficulties exist in implementation e.g. the European Court of Justice having to rule on non-French access to Orly-Paris Airport.

- National restrictions on ticket prices were removed (Regulation No. 2409/92) with only safeguards if air fares fell too low or rose too high[25].
- Consecutive cabotage was introduced allowing a carrier to add a 'domestic leg' on a flight starting out of its home base to a destination in another member state if the number of passengers on the second leg did not exceed 50% of the total in the main flight. Starting in 1997, full cabotage has been permitted, and fares are generally unregulated (Commission of the European Communities, 1994).
- Foreign ownership among Union air carriers is permitted, and they have, for EU internal purposes, become European airlines. This change does not apply to extra-Union agreements where national bilateral arrangements still dominate the market. One result has been a considerable increase in cross-share holdings and the rapidly expanding number of alliances among airlines within the Union (Table 2.6). Details of the main cross-ownership and airline alliances between EU and non-EU airlines are set out in the UK Civil Aviation Authority (1994).

Early analysis of reforms by the UK Civil Aviation Authority (1995) indicated that the reforms of the 1990s produced, in terms of multiple airlines serving various market areas, greater competition on both EU domestic routes and on international routes within the Union (Table 2.7). The changes varied but countries such as Greece and Portugal increased the number of competitive international services considerably. Many routes, however, either because multiple services are simply not technically sustainable or institutional impediments still limited market entry, remained monopolies in 1994.

---

[24] There were reforms to charter as well as scheduled services. Charter operators are allowed to set up in any European market and can sell tickets to private individuals on a seat-only basis at both ends of a service.
[25] See Chapter 7 for an examination of the logic of this restriction on fare setting.

Table 2.6. *European alliances and mergers involving major EU airlines*

Airline	Linkage
Air France	Ownership stakes in Austrian Airlines (1.5%), Air Charter (80%)
	Agreements with Lufthansa, Austrian Airlines, Sabena, Alitalia, Atlas[1]
Alitalia	Agreements with Finnair, British Midland, Air France, Atlas[1]
British Airways	Ownership stakes in Deutsche BA (49%), TAT (100.0%), Air Liberté (67.0%)
	Agreements with Aer Lingus, Deutsche BA, GB Airways, Maersk Air, TAT
Iberia	Agreements with Austrian Airlines, British Midland, Finnair, Lufthansa, TAP, Atlas[1]
KLM	Ownership stakes in Air UK (100.0%), Martinair (50.0%), Transavia (80.0%)
Lufthansa	Ownership stakes in Cargolux (24.5%), Condor (100.0%), Luxair (13.0%), Lauda Air (39.7%).
	Agreements with Air France, Austrian Airlines, Finnair, Cargolux, Lauda Air, Luxair, Iberia, Atlas[1]
Sabena	Ownership stakes Sobelair (72.3%)
	Agreements with Air France, Aer Lingus, Virgin Express, Maesk Air, Atlas[1]
SAS[2]	Ownership stakes in British Midland (40.0%), Spanair (49.0%)
	Agreements with British Midland, Austrian Airlines

[1] Atlas is a maintenance consortium involving Alitalia, Iberia, Lufthansa and Sabena
[2] 28.6% of SAS is Danish. The remaining ownership is in Norway and Sweden

Source: Derived from *Airline Business*, June 1995, December 1995 and June 1997, which contain further details of the exact nature of agreements.

More recently, the EU Commission in examining the immediate impact of the Air Transport Third Package finds evidence of significant changes in the industry (Commission of the European Communities, 1996). The Commission points to important consumer benefits being generated by the liberalisation that has taken place. It argues that in terms of service choice, the number of routes flown within the EU geographical area rose from 490 to 520 between 1993 and 1995. Further, 30% of Union routes are now served by two operators and 6% by three operators or more and 80 new airlines have been created while only 60 have disappeared.

In terms of the price of using the network, air fares have fallen on routes where there are at least three operators and overall, when allowance is made for charter operations, 90–95% of passengers on intra-Union routes are traveling with reduced fares. A caveat here being that there have been quite significant variations in the patterns of fares charged across routes.

There has been little change in fares on routes that remain monopolies or duopolies. The number of fifth freedom routes doubled to 30 between 1993 and 1996 although this type of operation remains a relatively small feature of the market and seventh freedoms have been little used. Indeed, much of the new competition has been on domestic routes where routes operated by two or more carriers rose from 65 in January 1963 to 114 in January 1996 with the largest expansions in France, Spain and Germany. The charter market has also continued to grow and in some countries accounts for more than 80% of traffic.

Table 2.7. *Changes in competition on selected EU scheduled routes.*

| | Proportion of round trip flights on routes with two or more competitors | | | |
| | Domestic Routes | | International Routes | |
	December 92	December 94	December 92	December 94
Austria	0%	0%	12%	12%
Denmark	3%	4%	8%	11%
Finland	9%	9%	7%	0%
France	10%	9%	26%	35%
Germany	36%	40%	10%	15%
Greece	0%	0%	0%	16%
Ireland	0%	0%	36%	46%
Italy	28%	26%	7%	15%
Netherlands	0%	0%	20%	18%
Norway	27%	38%	0%	9%
Portugal	47%	35%	14%	37%
Spain	0%	60%	14%	20%
Sweden	47%	47%	12%	12%
UK	43%	56%	40%	45%
Total	26%	36%	19%*	25%*

* Includes Belgium and Luxembourg

Table 2.8 offers selective data on changes in scheduled air fares where competition has emerged.

The series of EU reforms also seem to have influenced the size of aircraft flown in Europe; Table 2.9 shows the slow decline in the average number of seats following the liberalization trend. This is in the face of increased infrastructure capacity problems (Chapter 4). This temporal pattern can in part be explained by the increased ability of airlines to compete in terms of service quality in a less regulated environment. Passengers put a premium on a high frequency of services. Linked to this, experiences from the 1978 US deregulation also suggest that hub-and-spoke operations can lead to the use of smaller aircraft. The growth of alliances (see also Chapter

7) has also provided the potential for carriers to make more efficient use of their fleets.

Table 2.8 *Scheduled airfares from Brussels (in Belgian Francs)*

	January 1993			January 1995			July 1995
Return fares from Brussels to:	IATA	SN	BQ	IATA	SN	BQ	IATA
Madrid	14570	11230	4600-9000	14500	8490	4600-9000	14500
Vienna	16290	17790	5600-9000	17790	6990	5600-9000	17790
Rome	18730	9990	5600-9000	20170	5600	5600-9000	20170

Source: Commission of the European Communities (1996). *Impact of the Third Package of Air Transport Liberalization Measures*, com (96) 415 Final.

Table 2.9 *Average size of aircraft used by AEA member airlines on European and domestic air services*

Year	Average Number of Seats	Year	Average Number of Seats
1973	106.5	1983	137.0
1974	109.5	1984	135.0
1975	113.0	1985	135.5
1976	120.0	1986	134.5
1977	124.0	1987	134.0
1978	123.0	1988	135.0
1979	125.5	1989	135.5
1980	131.5	1990	134.0
1981	136.0	1991	133.0
1982	139.0	1992	133.0

More recently the attention of the EU Commission has switched to the matter of the relationship between EU air transport policy and external relations. (Mencik von Zebinsky, 1966). The traditional right of airlines to negotiate bilateral air service agreements with non-EU states has been brought into question by the Commission[26]. The adoption of the offer of

[26]   This does not mean the EU Commission has not previously been involved in negotiating aviation agreements with third countries. The early agreement between the EU and Norway and Sweden which extended the scope of the EU air transport legislation to these countries is an example. The EU Commission was given permission in 1996 through the majority voting

Open Skies policies by the US and the *de facto* granting of anti-trust immunity to the airlines of countries that follow this course has led to divisions in the EU. In particular, the UK has traditionally opposed giving up negotiating rights with the US given the domination of Heathrow as the main trans-Atlantic hub.

2.4.5   Related EU policies

In addition to developments in explicit air transport policy a number of changes in other areas of EU industrial policy have played an important role in defining the way the aviation sector has developed. The EU's policy regarding monopolies and anti-competitive behavior has evolved over time.

The Rome Treaty quite clearly provides a power to control agreements – e.g. collusion in the form of collective price fixing. This is contained in Article 85 which is the Union's equivalent of Section 1 of the Sherman Act in the US[27]. Article 86 allows the Commission to attack abuses by enterprises that are in a market dominating position. Broadly it equates to the powers under Section 2 of the Sherman Act and to certain provisions of the Clayton Act – but not Section 7 thereof. What was less than clear initially was whether or not the Commission possessed a power to control mergers – i.e. a power on the lines of Section 7 of the Clayton Act. The desirability of having such a power was highlighted by the Commission as early as 1965.

In 1973 the Commission put forward a proposal for a regulation that would provide an explicit merger controlling power but it failed to find favor for many years. However, in the European Court of Justice (1973) the *Continental Can Case* provided an interpretation of Article 86 that indicated that it could be employed against mergers. In that case, Continental Can had acquired control of a major can producer in West Germany and was deemed to be dominant in the West German market. It then sought to acquire control of a leading Dutch can producer. The Commission then intervened seeking to ban the merger.

Because of inadequacies in the factual case it presented the Commission failed since the Court was not satisfied that the Commission had defined the relevant product market properly and had not identified all the relevant factors that determined the degree of market power enjoyed in the West

procedure to negotiate on behalf of all EU countries on soft-issues regarding aviation but did gain the unanimous support for taking over responsibility for hard rights.

[27]   The word 'equivalent' implies broad equivalence since Article 85 does not take a *per se* stance.

German market. In short, the Commission had failed to establish the market dominance that must be proved before any abusive act deriving therefrom is addressed. There was also a legal principle at stake – namely, did Article 86 in any case apply to mergers? On this the Court replied in the affirmative[28]. This was something of an empty victory since Article 86 requires the problem of market power to exist before it can be attacked but an effective merger law ought to be capable of preventing unjustified market power from coming into existence. The new power was little used.

The commitment to complete the internal market by 1992, contained in the 1986 Single European Act, came to the rescue. One of the measures that the Council agreed was essential as part of that program was the introduction of a specific power to control mergers. Such a power was approved in 1989. The regulation in question applies to concentrations of undertakings. It also becomes the sole instrument for controlling the concentrations in question – this implies that Articles 86 and 85 cease to be applicable in such cases. The regulation applies to concentrations that have a Union dimension. Two issues therefore immediately arise. What is a concentration and what gives it a Union-wide dimension?

A concentration is deemed to arise when either of two conditions are satisfied. Two or more previously independent enterprises merge. One or more persons controlling one undertaking acquire (by purchases of securities or assets, by contract or by any other means) direct or indirect control of another undertaking. Joint ventures whereby competitive behavior is coordinated but the enterprises involved remain independent are not caught by these definitions.

Such a concentration has a Union wide dimension where the aggregate worldwide turnover of all undertakings concerned is more than 5,000 million ECU; and the aggregate Union-wide turnover of each of at least two undertakings concerned is more than 250 million ECU. The latter point is qualified. If each of the undertakings concerned achieves more than two-thirds of its aggregate Union-wide turnover within one and the same state then its primary impact is national and would not be subject to Union control. Of course, it might be attacked by a member state.

---

[28]   The Court was of the view that:
There may therefore be abusive behavior if an undertaking in a dominant position strengthens that dominant position so that the degree of control achieved substantially obstructs competition i.e. so that the only undertakings left in the market are those which are dependent on the dominant undertaking with regard to their market behavior.

A concentration that satisfies these tests is subject to Commission control and will be declared incompatible with the common market if it creates a dominant position, or strengthens an existing dominant position, such that effective competition would be significantly impeded in the common market or in a substantial part of it. Concentrations have to be prenotified to the Commission. The latter has the power to suspend a concentration until it has investigated it. The power to ban is also accompanied by a power to order a divestiture.

3.   Is Europe Different?

3.1   DIFFERING ATTITUDES TOWARDS REGULATORY REFORM

Demonstration effects have played their part in forcing regulatory change. The past decade has witnessed considerable liberalization of transport and other markets around the world (Button and Swann, 1989; Button and Keeler, 1993). Perhaps, one could suggest the stimulus for much of the reform in policy lay in the success of the UK's 1968 Transport Act and its freeing of the road haulage industry from economic regulation. More realistically, however, the essential demonstration effect came from the US, particularly the 1978 Airline Deregulation Act.

There is a natural tendency to contrast the US domestic reforms that were essentially of the 'Big Bang' type and the more gradual, incremental developments in EU aviation policy. As pointed out in Chapter 2, the clear conclusion of the EU Commission is that European gradualism, although not yet leading to a new long term equilibrium, has been economically superior to the shock therapy adopted under the 1978 Airline Deregulation Act in the US. The view of the European authorities is clear on this, *viz*:

> The single market in aviation did not occur with a 'Big Bang': there was no spectacular reduction in fares nor any dramatic disappearance of the more important carriers. Liberalization has happened in a progressive way and without major upsets. This contrasts with the situation that the US experienced at the time of deregulation of the aviation market. The [European] Community has been able to find the correct balance between competition and control mechanisms. Competition and the consumer have both benefited (Commission of the European Communities, 1996)[1].

[1]   The Commission presented an analysis of the earlier packages of reform in Commission of the European Communities (1994).

The consideration of the respective merits of the two approaches, however, involves a number of different factors. These concern not only the particular features of the favoured paths, which others may not be able to replicate, but also the contexts in which the changes were made. The general conclusions of the EU Commission on the outcome of their packages is also open to questioning.

Initially it is helpful to look at the wider background of the reform movement and the fundamentals upon which comparisons can be made.

From a microeconomic perspective, the period since the late 1980s might appropriately be called 'The Age of Regulatory Reform'. The changes in Eastern and Central Europe that have followed the fall of the communist governments has initiated considerable moves towards free markets and private enterprise. In western Europe and North America a longer term series of less dramatic changes have been in train with liberalizing reforms to existing economic regulations and the privatization of many former state owned enterprises.

Both at the micro and macro levels these reforms have been the subject of considerable debate not least over the pace at which they should be initiated[2]. At the extremes are the proponents of the 'Big Bang' school of thought who favor rapid and radical change while at the other are those in favor of a gradual, more phased series of incremental regulatory reforms. This debate also bears on the much more limited reforms taking place in transport markets in the traditionally capitalist states.

The time paths of the costs and benefits of reform associated with the two philosophies are stylized in Figure 3.1. Essentially, the shock treatment approach has high initial costs of disruption to an industry and possibly consumers but a rapid move to a higher level of total economic welfare. In contrast incrementalism has fewer initial adverse implications but the benefits of change take longer to materialize.

At its simplest, this diagram highlights the importance of the social discount factor in selecting the desirable strategy[3]. Advocates of

---

[2]   The developments in Europe have stimulated an extensive literature looking at the merits of different approaches to market liberalization. See; Dewatripont and Roland (1992); Hayes (1992); Hoen (1996); Roland (1993).

[3]   A discount rate is used to weight the importance that is attached to current as opposed to future returns. For example, a market interest rate reflects how much a person is willing to pay to give up income today to have it later (plus the accrued interest). A social discount rate reflects society's preferences for having something now rather than in the future - a very low discount rate reflecting almost indifference between, say, current consumption and future consumption.

incrementalism implicitly have a lower discount rate. This implies less concern with the current costs of regulatory inefficiency and less interest in reaping the immediate benefits of liberalization. The diagram is also suggestive of the need to have a fairly accurate impression of the overall costs and benefits associated with the alternatives.

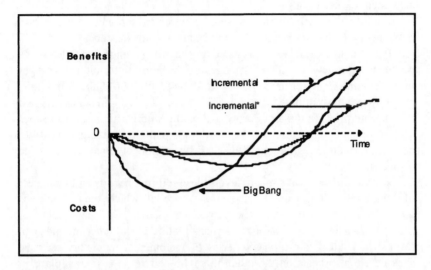

Figure 3.1 *The time paths of incremental and Big Bang policy effects*

This stylization hides important practical considerations. Reforms are seldom as straightforward as the diagram implies and, for instance as we have seen in Chapter 2, the EU liberalization of air transport services has represented a number of separate, often independent, liberalizing initiatives, not a series of pre-planned and advertised incremental changes. Equally, the US reforms were not totally of the Big Bang type, measures such as the Essential Air Services Program were the subject of subsequent periodic reviews as was the issue of mergers policy.

As drawn the diagram implies that ultimately there is a convergence in the paths of the alternative strategies but there is no reason to anticipate this happening. The incremental path could converge on a lower asymptotic benefit level than the Big Bang curve (e.g. path Incremental* converges to a lower asymptotic benefit curve than does the Big Bang path). An important factor can be the timing and intensity of external shocks on the market's path to equilibrium. Policies and their implementation are also the subject of a diversity of forces and an inevitable degree of regulatory capture occurs. This not only affects the possible distribution of the gains and losses of regulation changes but potentially their magnitudes.

An argument for sudden comprehensive change is that it gives actors in the market, particularly incumbent suppliers, less time to capture the reform process. This advantage can be lost, however, if incumbents play a significant role in defining the format of the Big Bang[4]. Conversely, incrementalism provides scope for 'learning-by-doing' and permits policy makers to modify and adjust the reform measures in the light of information gathered as market adjustments take place. Technically, it can also mean that existing hardware can be written down gradually with less physical wastage. It also, however, provides the opportunity for those affected to regroup and redefine their reactive positions; new controlling coalitions have time to emerge (Keeler, 1984).

Comparative assessments can be important in the review of policy changes. To be legitimate, however, there is the need to recognize that there can be important differences in background conditions that have to be taken into account. The US reformed its domestic air transport market in a specific way but also in the context of a set of geographical, institutional and economic conditions that were somewhat different to those pertaining in the EU. Further, the implications of changing economic regulatory structures are multidimensional involving complex temporal patterns of effects and a diversity of assessment criteria. While the incrementalism of the EU may have shown advantages in some respects it has been less successful in others.

3.2 LESSONS FROM THE US

Because of both the size of its air transport industry and its early progress to more liberal markets, the US is often seen as a benchmark in judging developments throughout other aviation fields of how market forces shape the supply of aviation services (Pryke, 1991; Button, 1996a).

US domestic aviation was heavily regulated from the late 1920s, initially as part of a policy to foster air mail services but subsequently on grounds of promoting safety and, from 1938, to seek economic efficiency. The responsibility for the economic regulation of interstate airlines services was exercised by the Civil Aeronautics Board (CAB) which controlled market access and, through the right of disapproval, fares. Safety and related issues came under the control of the Federal Aviation Administration from the early 1950s.

---

[4]   Outside of transport this was a demonstrable problem with the privatization of the UK energy sector. See Button and Weyman-Jones (1994).

A combination of forces brought about regulatory change in the late 1970s. A series of academic studies emerged and unfavorably contrasted the performance of regulated interstate aviation with that of some more liberal intrastate services such as those in California. The fresh intellectual ideas then emerging concerning regulatory capture and market structures brought a new questioning of the underlying rationale for controls. There were also demonstration effects from other network industries, such as UK trucking, that liberal markets could be workably competitive and stable. At the macroeconomic level, Keynesian policies seeking to reduce what was perceived as cost push inflationary pressures sought ways of lowering prices.

A number of *de facto* measures from 1976 preceded new legislation and the CAB began permitting discriminatory fare discounts and free access to selected routes. Restrictions on charter services were also relaxed. The subsequent 1978 Airline Deregulation Act was a big bang in the sense that a single act radically changed the way the domestic aviation market was regulated[5]. The move was not to an immediate free market but rather a time schedule for relaxation of price and entry regulations was established such that by January 1983 all fare and entry regulations were eliminated except that carriers must be fit, willing and able. The CAB was abolished in 1985 with its residual functions over such things as international aviation and mergers being transferred to other agencies (Borenstein, 1992a).

The experience of the US in liberalizing its domestic aviation industry demonstrated that the preceding period of extensive market regulation had stifled the natural development, led to excessive fares, fostered inefficiency and limited consumer choice. By the mid-1970s, it had become clear that such a regime was not maximizing economic efficiency. Particularly, it impeded the natural growth of 'hub-and-spoke' operations and meant that economics of density and scope could not be fully exploited. In contrast, costs can be considerably reduced in many cases by employing key hubs as consolidation points for flights with routes radiating out from them. Because of the indirect routings and probable changes of planes required at hubs, the replacement of linear direct services by hub-and-spoke operations increases journey times for the passenger, but it also reduces airlines' costs (and in a competitive environment, also fares) while increasing the range of available flight possibilities[6].

[5]   US domestic air freight transport had been the subject of liberalizing reforms in the previous year.

[6]   Many of the cost reductions were also a function of the savings brought about by making more efficient use of labor, e.g. in terms of hours flight crew worked.

While the conclusions are not unanimous, there is considerable support for the argument that the US liberalization of domestic air transport produced considerable net social benfits (Morrison and Winston, 1995)[7]. It is not surprising that it is often seen as a model to be followed.

Inevitably, the US experience and its fruits of lower fares attracted the attention of Europeans. Much of the interest lay in the dramatic reduction of domestic scheduled fares in comparison to the much higher levels prevailing in Europe. The UK House of Lords Select Committee on the European Communities (1980) pointed to instances of European fares being double those for comparable services in the USA, although these were extreme examples since differences in return fares were generally somewhat smaller. The Committee explained that,

> The interests of consumers appear to be sacrificed to the prestige of flag-carrying national airlines and the protected environment in which they operate.

Despite the overall economic gains from deregulation, US reforms have not been trouble-free, and the impressions gained in Europe may be seen as those viewed through rose-tinted spectacles. Airlines have responded to the new situation by trying to reduce the market competition edge. Because of a concurrent relaxation of anti-trust policy, mergers have occurred between airlines that limit competition between them on particular routes (increased hubbing is not necessarily between various origin and destination pairs) and over landing slots at some key hub airports. By purchasing Ozark Airlines, for example, TWA gained control of 83% of the traffic at St. Louis (Lambert) airport, while the merger of Northwest and Republic meant the resultant company provided 77% of the flights into Minneapolis and 62% of those at Detroit.

Mergers are not the only device to blunt the edge of competition. The details on computer reservation systems (CRSs) used by travel agents (but owned by airlines) that give customers flight information and booking seats were claimed to have been manipulated to favor the parent company. Even though one of the final acts of the Civil Aeronautics Board in 1985 was to initiate controls over such practices, some 60% of travel agents still wrote tickets on systems provided by United or American. Bonus schemes and other incentives also suggest that the resulting 'halo effects' bias the

---

[7] Initial results include average load factors per plane up from less than 55% in 1978 to about 62% in 1988, and passenger boardings up from 275 million to 455 million. Air fares, adjusted for inflation, fell by 21% over the period.

system, even if the information held within the CRS program is objectively presented. Frequent-flyer programmes giving extra flights to loyal customers have been deployed as a defensive weapon to encourage existing passengers to stay with the airline currently favored but can also act as an offensive device to attract flyers away from companies not offering such a perk.

Despite these difficulties, the general view seems to be that liberalization in the US, in overall cost benefit terms, has yielded a positive rate of return. While market imperfections exist and the post-reform market hardly corresponds to the ideals established as benchmarks for efficiency by traditional neo-classical economists, distortions are seen as less damaging than the government failures which accompanied the previous, heavily regulated regime (Keeler, 1990). Policy makers in Europe have seen this as a case for liberalization of their markets, albeit in a modified form, designed to contain the major problems which have arisen in the US.

Experiences observed in one market may, however, have limited relevance for what might occur elsewhere, so it is important to examine ways in which European air transport deviates from the US domestic sector .

3.2.1 Domestic/international traffic split

Essentially, the US market is domestic, while within Europe it is predominantly international in scope. In 1990, 52.9% of departures and 55.0% of passengers carried by EU registered airlines were international, compared to 15.4% and 8.9% respectively for the US. The vast majority of EU carriers are viewed as international airlines and tend to act as such. Historically, they have enjoyed the economic rent associated with regulated international aviation in some markets, and the natural inclination for rent protecting may take longer to erode than occurred in the US.

Table 3.1 provides comparisons between income per seat earned by European airlines on intra-European routes and comparable income for US domestic routes of a similar length. It is unlikely all institutional constraints will be removed by 1997, given the variety of economic, social and political objectives which underline nations' aviation policies. EU airlines also operate extensive external networks where bilateral controls and, *ipso facto*, rent extracting potentials remain.

Table 3.1 *Comparison of income per seat kilometer between international traffic in Europe and domestic traffic in the US during 1985*

Company	Average length per flight (kms)	Income per paid seat (cent/km)	US income per paid seat (cent/km)[1]
Air Lingus	530	17.25	13.10
Air France	748	15.06	10.63
Alitalia	906	14.36	9.46
Austrian	790	17.38	10.27
British Airways	796	13.46	10.23
BCAL	430	19.34	14.88
Finnair	1,017	14.09	8.82
Iberia	1,120	8.48	8.31
KLM	645	14.65	11.63
Lufthansa	751	14.93	10.60
Luxair	464	16.05	14.20
Olympic	1,769	6.70	6.30
Sabena	712	14.81	10.95
SAS	707	17.19	11.00
Swissair	732	16.13	10.77
Air Portugal	1,379	8.61	7.60
Weighted Average	824[2]	13.58[3]	9.44[4]

Notes

[1] based on the same travel length as the European carrier

[2] weights reflect number of passengers/total passenger for AEA companies

[3] weights reflect number of paid seat/total seat kms for AEA companies

[4] weights reflect number of seat kms/total number of seat kms for AEA companies

Source: Midttun (1992)

3.2.2 The non-scheduled market

Traditionally, European aviation has involved a large charter component. In 1985, about the time serious EU reforms began, 42 million of 162 million passengers carried within the 22 member countries of the European Civil Aviation Conference were by charter, compared with 3 million of 336 million domestic US passengers. The current compostion of scheduled and non-scheduled service patronage is set out in Table 3.2 Non-scheduled EU operators enjoy easy market entry, and many have relatively new fleets and an established market image. Unlike the US situation prior to 1978, strong countervailing forces exist in some air travel markets restraining excessive profit making by scheduled operations.

Table 3.2 *Composition of airline services in the EU*

Major Airlines (AEA)	114,791	31%
Medium and regional airlines (ACE)	25,384	7%
Medium and regional airlines (ERA)	24,075	6%
	(32,100)	
Charter airlines (ACE)	206,470	56%
APK (million)	370,720	100%

Source: Commission of the European Communities (1996)

The extent of the power of charter airlines should be put into context. Although inexpensive, charter services are not as flexible and less useful for business travelers. In many ways scheduled and charter services in Europe have served different market segments. Where markets for leisure travel are dominated by charter carriers, in many cases no scheduled services are offered. Of the 51 most significant city-air routes where there was charter traffic from the UK in 1987, 23 had no scheduled traffic. On the remaining 28 routes, only 23% of traffic was scheduled. Deregulation could permit a more efficient mix with lower costs and less stringent discount conditions and generate benefits not found in US markets. A pre-existing pool of experienced charter operators may also combat the 'economies of experience enjoyed by incumbent scheduled airlines, which limit effective market penetration by new carriers in the US.

3.2.3 Market size

The average route length in Europe was in the mid-1980s some 750 kilometers, whereas in the US it is 1300 kilometers. Of the top 75 routes in Europe, only 17 have flight times of two hours or more and ten of these the flight times is less than two and a half hours. Short flights offer less scope for hubbing since time spent changing planes takes up a relatively large part of the overall journey time. Indirect flights in Europe, even if fares are lower, seldom offer the effective competition to direct services occurring in the US.

Pryke (1991) finds that while liberalization in Europe is likely in the long term to reduce the degree of monopolistic power over many routes (e.g. on short-haul routes a single carrier supply will remain at about 48% of services, while the number of two carrier routes will fall from 32% to about 25% as multiple supply expands), eventual outcome will fall short of the

US situation (where only 38% of routes have one supplier and 25% have two suppliers).

The scale of the European market is also reflected in the actual size of the European Union's airlines. The merger of British Airways (46.3 billion scheduled passenger-kilometers) and British Caledonian (8.8 billion) in 1987 made it the largest European carrier in terms of passenger-kilometers. The situation has not changed significantly since that time and while there are some large European carriers (see Tables 3.3 and 3.4) the world's largest passenger airlines and cargo carriers as measured by conventional parameters are US based.

Table 3.3 *The world's largest passenger carriers (1995)*

Airline	1995 Revenue Passenger Miles (Millions)	Airline	1995 Revenue Passenger Miles (Millions)
United Airlines	111,539.0	Southwest Airlines	23,330.1
American Airlines	102,668.9	Cathay Pacific	21,949.6
Delta Airlines	85,108.5	Korean Air	20,991.9
Northwest Airlines	62,502.7	Alitalia	19,727.7
British Airways	58,323.4	Thai Airways	16,810.7
Japan Airlines	43,357.4	Air Canada	16,351.0
Lufthansa	38,278.9	Iberia Airlines	14,791.5
USAir	37,619.4	Canadian Airlines	14,757.4
Continental Airlines	35,512.8	Malaysian Airlines	14,587.3
Quantas Airways	32,231.6	America West Airlines	13,272.7
Air France	30,773.5	Varig Brazilian	12,972.7
Singapore Airlines	30,075.3	Swissair	12,256.7
KLM Royal Dutch	27,625.4	SAS	11,499.4
All Nippon Airways	26,629.4	Saudia	11,496.6
Trans World Airlines	24,905.3	Air New Zealand	11,012.9

3.2.4 Production efficiency

Production costs differ in Europe to those in the US for a variety of reasons. While it is difficult making direct comparisons, evidence suggests that Europe's scheduled airlines, while improving, use labor less productively. McGowan and Seabright (1989) show eight US majors enjoying 1.6 million revenue passenger kilometers per employee compared to 1.1 for the best European carrier (British Airways), with airlines such as Sabena (0.6), Lufthansa (0.8) and TAP (0.4) considerably less productive. Adjustments for differing stage lengths makes British Airways 65% as productive as its US majors. Oum *et al* (1994) confirm this and suggest that BA and KLM are only about 70% as efficient as their US counterparts[8].

Table 3.4 *The world's largest cargo only carriers (1995)*

Airline	1995 freight ton miles (millions)
Federal Express	5,070.0
United Parcel Service	3,377.0
Cargolux	1,329.0
Nippon Cargo Airlines	1,111.0
Polar Air Cargo	977.1
Emery Worldwide	935.2
American International Airways	767.6
Southern Air Transport	578.1
Airborne Express	485.1
Evergreen International Airlines	405.6

Part of these efficiency differentials are due to European government subsidies and the existence of niche markets (Good *et al*, 1993; Encaoua, 1991). European airlines, however, are also confronted with higher costs outside of their control than their US counterparts. The International Air Transport Association, for instance, has estimated that landing fees in the US represent 10% – 30% less than the European level. This is supported by data from individual airports (Table 3.5). Equally, Table 3.6 shows the

[8]   There are now two recognized methods of assessing the relative levels of technical efficiency of suppliers in a market; the econometric and the programming. Econometric studies (e.g. Oum and Yu, 1996; Ng and Seabright, 1995) specify a cost function, often in a flexible translog formulation, and decompose the resulting estimated error term into a random component and an efficiency component. The theoretical basis for the modeling being derived from standard microeconomic theory. The programming approach defines the, usually, non-linear boundary of efficient suppliers, generally deploying a data envelope method, and measures the extent to which actors' costs are outside of this boundary. The method is pragmatic rather than theoretical in its underpinnings. Both methods offer scope for a variety of variations but equally both also suffer in being relative measures – all active suppliers could be inefficient albeit to differing degrees. The alternatives can also give differing results especially in terms of the scale of the relative inefficiencies.

variations in fuel prices that are found on either side of the Atlantic and, again, European prices emerge as generally higher.

Table 3.5 *Landing costs (US dollars)*

City	DC-9	A320
United States		
Atlanta	17	26
Dallas	176	272
Detroit	281	325
Washington/Dulles	161	249
Orlando	175	259
Miami	104	161
Europe		
London/Heathrow	596	716
Paris/CDG	323	496
Copenhagen	438	649
Frankfurt	1,564	952
Athens	137	171
Gibraltar	887	1,377

Table 3.6 *Fuel costs (US versus Europe)* [9]

City	Fuel costs per US (US cents)
United States	
Atlanta	56
Dallas	58
Detroit	58
Washington/Dulles	58
Orlando	61
Miami	59
Europe	
London/Heathrow	63
Paris/CDG	65
Copenhagen	73
Frankfurt	65
Athens	72
Gibraltar	100

[9] Mid February quoted jet fuel price at each airport.

Even allowing for this, part of the reason for the higher costs stems from lower productivity rather than higher unit input prices. While US deregulation resulted in substantial reductions in labour costs, mainly through wage reductions, downsizing and changes in working conditions, it seems unlikely that different attitudes towards labour relations in most European countries, coupled with higher mandatory severance costs, would permit the same thing to occur, or at least not so rapidly[10]. Air France, for eaxmple, has experienced severe problems as it has sought to reduce labor costs since the mid-1990s.

Finally, most analytical work has focused on comparing the efficiency of scheduled carriers in the EU with those in the US. As we have seen, however, there is a very sizable charter market in Europe. These carriers often perform a similar function to some of the low cost US airlines. Comparisons of labor efficiency between these airlines and the scheduled EU carriers (Table 3.7) reveal them to be in general much more productive. Deregulating the scheduled EU services and comparing the outcome with the entire US domestic air transport network may thus provide misleading results.

3.2.5 Ownership of airlines and subsidies

The inherent public service attitude of many European countries means that traditionally ownership of large parts of the transport infrastructure and of the operating capital has been in state hands. Things are changing but at a slow pace. Consequently, while the US commercial airline industry is in private hands, there is only a gradual move towards public sector participation in the ownership of many European airlines (Meersman and van de Voorde, 1996).

Table 3.8 provides details of state ownership levels of European flag carriers. Despite repeated statements by the national government indicating a desire to privatise, Air France is essentially 100% government owned, as are Olympic, TAP, Aer Lingus and Iberia, with many other airlines having a majority of government holdings. This has historically been because in many EU countries, a 'preferred vehicle' exists for advancing a national aviation policy.

---

[10]   Evidence on EU airline labor cost changes is limited. Alamdari (1997) examining labor costs across EU carriers for the period 1991-95 found a fall of 38% per ATK with real wages per employee rising by 15%; the latter attributed to the outsourcing taking place leaving higher skilled labor within the airlines.

Table 3.7 *Labor productivity 1993: ATK/employee (000)*

Germania	1060
Monarch	930
Caledonian	919
Condor	857
Airtours	834
Excalibur	718
Air 2000	709
LTU/LTU Sud	654
Spanair	649
Aero Lloyd	597
Britannia	497
Hapag Lloyd	473
Air UK Leisure	433
KLM	378
BA	333
Lufthansa	329
Air France	306
Alitalia	305
Swissair	250
Iberia	192
SAS	188
Sabena	161

Theoretically, there are arguments that state ownership should not affect the efficiency of any undertaking if that undertaking is confronted by competitive pressures. State ownership of airlines would, however, seem to lead to high levels of X-inefficiency. Institutionally, it can also affect the attitude of negotiators at bilateral air transport talks who may seek to protect a national carrier rather than further the interests of the airline user. Although US carriers have gone bankrupt[11], public sector involvement inevitably affects the way an airline is treated, so it is difficult conceiving a government-owned European carrier going bankrupt. As pointed out before, the level of state involvement is now slowly declining albeit at a slow pace in many countries.

[11]   Chapter 11 arrangements in the US are less stringent than most European bankruptcy regimes and allows for existing management, under supervision, to restructure a company's finances rather than have the assets of the undertaking realized. Hence, airlines such as Continental have been through several bankruptcies in recent years.

Table 3.8 *State ownership interest in European airlines*

Airline	Financial Stake
British Airways	Fully publicly quoted
Lufthansa	51.42%
Air France	99.30%
Alitalia	86.40%
Iberia	99.80%
TAP Air Portugal	100.00%
Olympic Airways	100.00%
SAS	50.00% (through 50% state-owned shareholders in Sweden, Norway and Denmark)
KLM	38.20%
Sabena	61.80%
Luxair	23.11% + 13.41% state-owned bank
Aer Lingus	100.00%
Finnair	70.00% + 9.69% state-owned Neste-Oy
Austrian Airlines	51.90% + 15.00% Austrian public shareholders

One reason for this has been the changes in general EU rules that apply to subsidies. Although there has been a tradition of subsidizing European flag carriers (Table 3.9), recent changes in EU policy regarding state subsidies have been tightened and criteria have been made more explicit under which subsidies may be given[12]. Operating subsidies are not permitted but subsidies are allowed to permit an undertaking to restructure. State owned airlines must show that the level of capital subsidies awarded would be in line with the amount that a private airline in similar circumstances might expect to be able to raise from the private sector. Subsidies are also generally given only with the proviso that pre-specified targets are met by the airline.

The variety of protection afforded EU carriers in the past also means that, despite the subsidies that many airlines have enjoyed, they were able to extract higher fares from users than had been the case in US markets before the 1978 Act. Some indication of the comparative yields is given in Table 3.10.

[12]   The EU has no special legislation to deal with state aid to airlines but applies general principles under Articles 92 and 93 of the Rome Treaty. *Memorandum No.2COM (84) Annex IV (Guidelines on the application of the state aid policy to the air transport sector)* offers a set of general principles for the application of these rules. These guidelines were further refined in 1992.

Table 3.9 *Airline subsidies to EU carriers*

Year	Airline	Amount (million ECU)	Aid as a % of annual revenues
1991	Sabena	833	85.8
1991-92	Air France	843	20.3
1992	Iberia	929	37.4
1993	Aer Lingus	224	47.2
1993	Air France	228	4.9
1994	TAP Air Portugal	914	139.9
1994	Olympic Airways	1900	276.6
1994	Air France	3000	61.6
1995	Iberia	674	n/a

Table 3.10 *Yields (per kilometer)* [13]

Sector	Km	Lowest Sector fare $	Yield per km (cents)
United States			
Atlanta-Orlando	667	43.65	6.5
Atlanta-Washington/Dulles	917	52.58	5.7
Atlanta-Miami	1,000	47.62	4.8
Detroit WC-Orlando	1,037	48.61	4.7
Atlanta-Detroit	1,046	61.50	5.9
Atlanta-Dallas FW	1,185	63.99	5.4
Atlanta-Los Angeles	3,139	108.14	3.4
Europe			
Paris CDG-Frankfurt	463	72.20	15.6
Luton-Glasgow/Edinburgh	519	44.08	8.5
London Heathrow-Frankfurt	796	71.44	9.0
London HR-Copenhagen	1,083	91.20	8.4
London HR-Gibraltar	1,852	128.44	6.9
London HR-Athens	2,574	106.40	4.1
London HR-Moscow	2,778	224.20	8.1

[13] Based on fares 19 February 1996.

3.2.6. Intermodal competition

Substantial intermodal competition in Europe exists for medium distance travel in some corridors, especially where there are high-speed train services (such as the French TGV). Except for some services along the northeast corridor, US railroads are essentially a freight system. The geography of Europe makes high-speed rail more commercially viable – the French TGV service betwen Paris and Lyon covers its full costs. Rail, however, is still heavily subsidised in many EU countries which keeps fares down. Additionally, in many instances, it competes with air on the basis of door-to-door journey time for trips up to 500 kilometres.

Many EU countries are now working on high-speed train programs, and are at various stages of development. In 1983 the French national railway introduced Europe's first high-speed train service[14] from Paris to Lyon; Germany has opened its IC-Express network and there are high-speed rail projects in Italy, the Netherlands and Belgium. The ability of high-speed rail to attract air passengers has been seen in France, where the opening of the TGV service between Paris and Lyon contained air traffic growth on this route. A similar picture emerges on the Paris-Geneva service. The rail services through the Channel Tunnel have exerted a major impact on several short London-Continental Europe air routes.

3.2.7 Infrastructure availability

There were a significant number of bottlenecks in US air infrastructure at the time of deregulation and the period following, with limited airport capacity and out-of-date air traffic control systems[15]. As liberalization has proceeded within the EU, the scale of infrastructure constraints has become substantial and the mechanisms for dealing with them more cumbersome.

Although the measurement of capacity lacks exactitude, there is some agreement that airport capacity in Europe is rapidly being reached at many major terminals. More than 50% of traffic passes through 24 airports, and all of these will, according to most forecasts, find their capacity stretched by the end of the century. Although figures are somewhat subjective on the issue of airport capacity, of the 46 largest airports in western Europe, 12 are already operating at or around capacity, and a further 11 will, on projected traffic levels, have reached capacity by 2000. In 1988, a special task force of the International Air Transport Association identified problems at seven of Europe's airports as critical (i.e. Heathrow, Gatwick, Munich, Dusseldorf, Frankfurt, Linate and Fiumicio).

---

[14]   The term high-speed rail is a relative one and has changed with the years. The definition has also varied across countries to meet the need for enhanced national prestige.

[15]   For more details see Chapter 4.

Unlike domestic US aviation where there has been centralization, air traffic control in Europe has traditionally been a national concern. The system comprises a patchwork, while the US has less than half the number of centers and standardized mainframe computers. Additionally, flight paths in Europe are severely constrained by the demands of military aviation which again has tended to fit in with national priorities. There have been particular problems, for instance, in routes involving several countries in the core of Europe. This has been relaxed somewhat since the end of the Cold War. It still seems probable that Europe will suffer more from capacity constraints than the US in the past, although the latter still needs an upgrade to its ATC computer systems.

3.2.8 The wider international context

When the US deregulated its interstate aviation as part of a wider package of domestic reform, it also took place in a vacuum since international air transport was still the subject of strict bilateral agreements. The EU reforms are in the context of broader liberalization measures under the Single Market and political union initiatives (Commission of the European Communities, 1985) but are also occurring at a time when pressure exists for wider international actions to deregulate aviation (Button, 1992). Indeed, several EU members, alongside the US, are part of this movement. Given this combined action of intra-EU reform and external developments in the World's aviation markets, it is unlikely that the outcome will necessarily replicate the US experience.

3.2.9 Advantage of hindsight

EU policy makers have the US as an example to guide them against some of the difficulties encountered. The Directorate General for Competition of the EU, for example, is fully aware of the potential problems airline mergers may cause and the latent market power which exists through flight code sharing and domination of CRS systems. Implementation of policies to counter these will itself cause reaction among the operators themselves as they seek shelter within the more competitive environment. Given the different institutional constraints confronting them, airlines may act differently than their US counterparts. This was one reason for discussions in early 1993 involving KLM, Swissair, SAS and Austrian Airlines as they explored the possibility of forming a joint holding company rather than seeking direct takeovers.

3.3 REFORMS ELSEWHERE

While the focus has been on comparisons between the US and European aviation, policy changes elsewhere should not be ignored. These other changes, while attracting less attention have interesting features of their own and offer insights into the policy reform process. Space precludes a detailed discussion and an indepth account would be moving away from the main thrust of the book. Therefore, only some brief comments are offered.

The Canadian aviation situation has historically had some features similar to those found in Europe. One of its major carriers, Air Canadian, was traditionally state owned and heavily protected in terms of both fares and market access. The path of reform has also been similar to the EU in that it has been incremental (Button, 1989). There are, however, also important differences. The Canadian market is essentially linear, east-west. The scope for hub-and-spoke operations is thus limited[16]. There are vast areas in northern Canada that are only effectively accessible by air and social and political cohesion requires that adequate services are offered in such areas.

The initial changes began in 1979 with removal of all access controls in the long distance Canadian market and the allowing of CP Air to compete with Air Canada. It also introduced the charter carrier Wardair into the scheduled market. Limited fare discounting was permitted. A series of other minor changes led in 1987 to the National Transport Act that, in effect, cut the Canadian domestic market in two. The northern part remained protected with some directly subsidized services while there was effective US style deregulation in the southern part. The state owned Air Canada was committed to act commercially and was subsequently privatized (Gillen *et al*, 1989). There has been a considerable amount of merger activity among smaller, regional carriers and acquisitions in the Canadian market since deregulation.

In 1996 the Canadian and US governments agreed on a phased relaxation of their bilateral agreement that after three years would effectively integrate their air transport markets[17].

The result of the Canadian reforms has been increased efficiency in terms of airline costs although, after an initial phase of market entry, mainly by regional carriers into the national market, there has been

[16]   One of the pressures leading to reform in Canada was that high cost/high fare Canadian carriers were losing business to cheaper US carriers that competed along the border and could exploit input lower costs and, in many cases, the economies associated with hub-and-spoke operations.

[17]   This was outside of the North American Free Trade Agreement that governs many other aspects of US-Canadian trade.

rationalization and financial restructuring. US carriers have begun to integrate their activities with Canadian airlines through equity holdings and code-sharing. For example, American airlines has an equity stake in Canadian. Nevertheless, econometric studies (e.g. Oum *et al*, 1994; Oum and Yu, 1996) consistently show that they remain about 10-25% less efficient than the US majors.

In the early 1980s, both Australia and New Zealand had separate, tightly regulated airline markets. In spite of the remoteness of the two countries and the close economic ties between them, each had a distinct domestic aviation market and, in the case of Australia, there was no integration of the international and domestic markets, which were served by different airlines (Forsyth, 1991, 1996). Domestically, the Australian market was served by two airlines (the 'Two Airline Policy'); Ansett, which was privately owned and the state owned Australian. Qantas enjoyed a monopoly in terms of international services. The state owned Air New Zealand enjoyed monopoly powers in both domestic and international markets.

By the mid-1990s, the aviation markets of both countries have undergone extensive change. Domestic markets have been deregulated, and there is scope for open competition, although the actual number of competitors is not large. New airlines have attempted entry in both markets. There has been some progress towards forming a single aviation market covering both countries, although this has been on hold for the last year or so. At the same time, there has been considerable change at the corporate level. All the main airlines are now private, and all have been affected by mergers and strategic alliances[18]. It is likely that, in the near future, there shall be seen two major airline groups competing in an extended, deregulated market, consisting of the domestic markets of both countries, along with the market between the two countries.

This raises the question of how much has really changed in Australia. While there are only two airline groups, there is more possibility of competition between them, and there is scope for others to enter. The disincentives created by regulation have been removed, even if there is greater scope for the airlines to use any market power they have. There is evidence of better performance by the airlines. In the transition to the present, governments have been ambivalent about their commitment to competition. In the earlier stages, the later 1980s, they were willing to open up markets to maximize competition. In more recent times, they have

[18]   The market within Australia remains dominated by the older carriers. Efforts by a new entrant, Compass Airlines, failed in large part because of managerial weaknesses but also because of difficulties in gaining good access to airports (Nyathi *et al*, 1993).

encouraged mergers which have lessened potential and actual competition. There is a trade-off between consolidation and competition, and governments have lately favored consolidation. This poses the question of whether the gains from consolidation have been real and whether there is sufficient competition to enforce efficient performance from the airlines.

3.4 SOME CONCLUDING THOUGHTS

Comparative assessments of policy public reform are often very insightful. To be so, however, there is the need to recognize that there can often be important difference in background conditions that have to be taken into account. When the US reformed its domestic air transport market it did so in a specific way. But it also did it in the context of its particular geographical, institutional and social conditions that were somewhat different to those pertaining in the EU at the same time. The same can be said of countries such as Canada, Australia and New Zealand that have also been the subject of recent deregulation studies.

Further, the implications of changing economic regulatory structures are multidimensional involving complex temporal patterns of effects and a diversity of assessment criteria. Hence, while the incrementalism of the EU may have been shown by the Commission to advantages in some respects, for instance in terms of the level of market entry and exit, it has been less successful in others, most notably in improving the economic efficiency of many carriers.

There is also a much broader question: the EU Commission's claim for the superiority of its incrementalism cited at the beginning of the chapter implies that there was some kind of grand design behind the path to liberalization in Europe. This seems a rather strong stance. The Commission does seem to have a case that it was at the forefront of pressing for change but its effectiveness took time to emerge. Many of the changes that have to date impacted most have involved the unilateral actions of individual EU States, or bilateral actions outside of the Commission's remit. Legal judgments also played their role in bringing about reform.

Finally, and returning to the earlier quotation from the EU Commission, the EU aviation market has still to generate the levels of consumer benefits associated with US reforms. Incrementalism by its nature takes time to produce a new equilibrium. Nevertheless, it is twenty years since the Big Bang was initiated in the US and the results to date in Europe imply that the Commission must employ an extremely low social discount rate to contend that the costs of avoiding the disruptions of the US market in the early 1980s have been worthwhile. This is particularly so in the case of maximizing the economic efficiency of the major airlines.

In summary, to adopt the quaint Scottish legal verdict, the case for favoring incrementalism in air transport deregulation as advanced by the experiences of the EU is 'Not Proven'.

4.   Infrastructure Policy

4.1   EUROPEAN AIRPORT NETWORK

Air transport is dependent upon an extensive and sophisticated infrastructure[1]. This network of hardware and software includes airports and air traffic control and navigation systems. One might also add to this list the financial institutions and various regulatory agencies that control the sector; the administrative infrastructure. We largely ignore this temptation. For the EU Commission's notion of interoperability to be realized, air transport infrastructure should be efficiently used and investments be optimal[2].

This poses a range of problems. Infrastructure generally has associated with it indivisibilities that make marginal changes and adjustments difficult. It is also generally long lived and this can lead to a divergence between its economic life and its technical life. Much air transport infrastructure is expensive, the British Airports Authority was floated in 1987 for £1.3 billion, which poses challenges for financing. Efficient pricing principles are often problematic partly because of the extent of common cost allocation issues but also because of the multifaceted nature of much infrastructure.

These inherent economic and technical complexities are often made more difficult in the context of European air transport because of the legacy of institutional arrangements that govern the way infrastructure is provided and access is granted. Public ownership is common and systems have primarily been created to meet national needs.

A particular economic problem is to decide exactly how much infrastructure capacity should be provided. Given the indivisibilities inherent in most forms of infrastructure, optimal capacity will mean periods when a

[1]   There are a wide variety of issues surrounding the definition and measurement of infrastructure (Lakshmanan, 1989). These are avoided here and a rather general definition is used.
[2]   Doganis (1992) is a standard reference on the economics of airports while Ashford and Moore (1992) cover airport finance.

facility may be technically at or above capacity. Its use will be at its engineering capacity and, unless there are correct economic charges in place, there will be a latent, unfulfilled demand for its use. Investment in a new piece of infrastructure only becomes justified when the benefits of expansion or new facilities exceed the costs. How costs are defined in this case depends on the institutional framework concerned. Financial accounting forms the basis of commercial decision-making but public policy may also take into account a range of social costs such as environmental intrusion[3].

[3]   Technically, a purely commercially run airport will, in the absence of a budget constraint, accept investments when the financial net present value is positive, that is,

$$NPV_f = \sum_{n=1}^{K} \left\{ \frac{P(R_n) - P(F_n)}{(1+i)^n} \right\}$$

where: NPV_f is the financial net present value;

$P(R_n)$ is the probable social revenue that would be earned in year n from the investment;

$P(F_n)$ is the probable financial cost of the investment in year n ;

$(1+i)^n$ is the rate of interest reflecting the cost of capital to the undertaking; and

K is the anticipated life of the investment;

In contrast, if overall economic efficiency is assessed – including such factors as environmental damage, accident levels, the social costs of capital and so on – using some form of cost-benefit analysis then, in the absence of a budget constraint, this suggests accepting airport investment schemes with a positive social net present value. This is when the following calculation is postive:

$$NPV_s = \sum_{n=1}^{k} \sum_{m=1}^{j} \left\{ \frac{P(a_m B_{mn}) - P(b_m C_{mn})}{(1+r)^n} \right\}$$

where: NPV_s is the social net present value;

$P(a_m B_{mn})$ is the probable social benefit to be enjoyed by individual m in year n as a result of the investment's completion. B_{mn} is given a weighting a_m to reflect society's welfare preference;

$P(b_m C_{mn})$ is the probable social cost to be enjoyed by individual m in year n as a result of the investment's completion. C_{mn} is given a weighting b_m to reflect society's welfare preference;

$(1+r)^n$ is the relative social weight attached to a cost or benefit occurring in a given year;

It should also be noted that there will be periods when a facility is used at less than its engineering design capacity because indivisibilities mean that apparent surplus capacity is justified in the short term to meet an anticipated increase in effective demand in the longer term. There are opportunity costs involved in having this idle capacity that must be contrasted to the congestion implications of having too little.

Interoperability does not, therefore, mean infinite capacity for all users at all times but rather that capacity is efficiently used and invested in. In this sense, airports, air traffic control and other elements of air transport related infrastructure can represent technical barriers to interoperability. In practice, however, given the nature of air transport, it is generally the legal and institutional arrangements governing access and use of air transport infrastructure that pose the greatest problems[4].

Modern airports provide a range of services that not only allow the coordinated provision of air transport services but are substantial intermodal interchange points[5]. The scale and activities of major airports pose important environmental challenges associated not only with the direct intrusions caused by the movement of aircraft but also from the surface traffic going to and from them and the ground vehicles needed to serve passengers, cargo and airplanes within airport perimeters. These factors complicate the pricing and investment decisions of air transport infrastructure operators.

Airline services also rely extensively on sophisticated navigation and air traffic control systems. Some of these are on-board aids but most are dependent upon a common infrastructure to be fully effective. The provision of this infrastructure across an extensive international network of air services poses problems of coordination to ensure that differing systems and operating practices do not impinge on safety and at the same time provide efficient services to the airline operators. While airports and air traffic control are generally treated separately they interact. The flow of traffic to an airport is an important consideration in determining its effective capacity and the number of airport movements determines the scale of the air traffic control system that is required.

k is the anticipated life of the investment; and

j is the total number of individuals affected.

[4]   This is perhaps less so in some areas of infrastructure provision given the issues surrounding air traffic control in Europe but even here the question is generally one of overall capacity rather than conscious efforts at market distortion.

[5]   Airports are also big business and in Europe airport charges amount to over $3.4 billion per annum.

In the short term, even allowing for existing capacity and planned capacity expansions, the forecasts are in general agreements that the situation regarding airport capacity is not only difficult now but will inevitably get worse as continued traffic growth takes place into the next century (Table 4.1)[6].

Table 4.1 *Predicted airport capacity problems at selected German airports*

Airports	Capacity in 2000 (annual flight movements)	Capacity demand in 2000 (Annual flight movements)	Percentage utilisation in 2000
Frankfurt	370,000	406,000	110
Munich	375,000	268,000	71
Düsseldorf	185,000	196,000	106
Hamburg	210,000	166,000	79
Cologne / Bonn	250,000	154,000	61
Stuttgart	185,000	153,000	83
Hannover	305,000	103,000	34
Nüremberg	170,000	90,000	53
Bremen	140,000	68,000	49
Saarbrücken	120,000	35,000	29
Münster / O,	140,000	60,000	43

Source: Baum and Weingarten (1992)

Airport congestion across Europe, therefore, represents an increasing barrier to entry at a large number of major air terminals. The nature of the problem is not uniform but varies considerably between airports. Munich airport, for example, was in 1994 almost at its apron capacity during peak

---

[6]   Measuring infrastructure capacity is notoriously difficult. This in part stems from fact there is no single measure of the output of aviation infrastructure together with the fact that there are many possibilities for changing the ways pieces of infrastructure are used (e.g. regarding airports this could involve the types or size of aircraft allowed access). There are also often various ways in which the different elements of infrastructure may be used (e.g. aprons can be used as stands). Pricing influences the way airlines use airport capacity.

hours while its terminal was only at about 73% of its declared capacity. This is because of the diversity of activities that make up airport operations (Figure 4.1)[7]. Many of these are of a technical kind involving the movement, servicing and parking of planes and the loading and unloading of passengers and cargo. Others, such as immigration and customers, have more to do with institutional arrangements[8].

The effective capacity at any airport is determined by the constraints imposed by the most congested element in the chain of throughput components set out in Figure 4.1[9]. In many cases this involves landing and take-off limitations and constraints posed by other design features of a facility, but increasingly there are also mounting problems of surface traffic congestion limiting access to airports.

As we have seen, various potential constraints exist, including shortages of runaway capacity, terminal capacity, aircraft stands and problems of surface access. The capacity problem at airports can extend across a national system of facilities. Heathrow in the UK, for example, suffers from all four types of constraint to some degree and, as a result, is now full throughout the operating day. The number of slots available in the summer of 1993, for example (including just seven departure slots throughout the busiest week), were at random times of day and would not allow a new entrant or an incumbent to mount a new daily scheduled service. Because of this, airlines are having to use existing slot portfolios in order to introduce new international scheduled services. While Gatwick, also owned by the British Airports Authority, is currently not so slot constrained as Heathrow, it still has difficulties in meeting demands in peak periods.

[7]   Since European airports generally have extensive international activities, issues of infrastructure design and space for immigration control, customs and security take a more prominent position than in, say, the US.

[8]   Increasing commercialization also means that many European airports effectively serve as major shopping centers as well as transport interchange points. Concessions and rentals now form a large part of many airports' revenue flow. This leads to further complexities and trade-offs in terms of the way physical capacity is allocated between functions.

[9]   This diagram should very much be seen as a simplification of the activities that go on at any major airport. If one takes ground handling as an example, the IATA subdivides this into: ground administration and supervision, passenger handling, baggage handling, cargo and mail handling, ramp services, cleaning, fueling, aircraft maintenance, flight operations and crew administration, surface transport, and catering services.

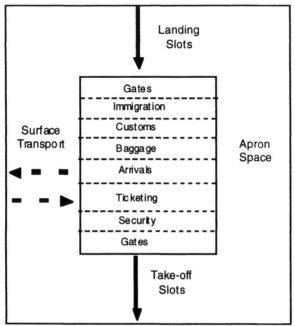

Figure 4.1 *Elements of airport infrastructure.*

The development of hub-and-spoke operations by airlines also poses particular problems of peaking. While it is true that many of the major European airports have capacity problems throughout much of the day these are compounded where airlines bank flights so as to maximize their economies of scope and density (Doganis, 1992). The large number of long range international flights to and from European gateway airports and the requirements of these to meet certain time slots can further concentrate demand.

Technical developments have allowed for some enhancement of capacity without major new constructions. The number of hourly allocated runway slots to airlines for both arrivals and departures, for instance, has been gradually increased at Heathrow over the last fifteen years, from 69 movements in 1978 to a maximum 79 in 1993. This has been possible because of refinements in the methods to calculate runway capacity, technical developments and a greater willingness on the part of airlines to accept delays. Further increases in declared capacity may be possible over the next few years, but given the current operating environment, these are likely to be only modest.

A number of other Union airports face constraints. According to IATA, airports with runways close to saturation or full most of the day in Summer

1992, included Athens, Berlin, Dusseldorf, Frankfurt, Heraklion, Madrid and Milan (Linate). Fourteen additional airports were classified at near saturation in peak periods - Barcelona, Brussels, Copenhagen, Corfu, Geneva, Helsinki, Lisbon, Manchester, Oslo, Palma, Paris (Charles de Gaulle and Orly), Stockholm and Zurich. In terms of terminal capacity, Berlin, Madrid, Milan (Linate) and Rome had serious problems, while Lisbon a shortage of apron capacity. Taking all these factors together, only Amsterdam (among the ten busiest international airports in Europe) was relatively unconstrained.

A report published by IATA in 1990 concluded that without further enhancements, capacity of 16 European airports would be severely limited by the turn of the century with Madrid, Frankfurt, Heathrow, Gatwick, Barcelona and Milan (Linate) worst affected. Even if potential measures helped to increase capacity, other than new runways put into place, 13 airports would still remain constrained by 2010.

The lack of a high quality network of airports and the mounting levels of congestion is costing money - British Airways estimates that every minute one of its Boeing 747s is stacked, it costs them $1,500. Lost time is also important to passengers, and this has been valued on the average at about $21.50 per hour in Europe. The overall impact is put into context by Lufthansa which calculates that its aircraft are stacked for over 5,000 hours a year over Frankfurt and Munich alone.

Several of the busiest airports in Europe have embarked on programs of expansion or have announced plans to develop the following:

- Amsterdam aims double capacity to 34 million passengers by 2003, including a new runway and taxiways.
- Brussels is to increase capacity by more than double to 22 million by 2020. 60% of a new terminal was completed by 1993, with the remainder in 1994.
- Frankfurt opened a new terminal in 1994 for 10-12 million passengers. Terminal 1 will also be expanded.
- Paris (Charles de Gaulle) opened module C of Terminal 2 in June 1993, providing capacity for an additional 4 million passengers. In 1996, phase 1 of Terminal 3 added a further 6 million. Charles de Gaulle's planned capacity is 60 million passengers. A new airport for Paris is planned to be located at Chartres.
- Rome is planning for 30 million passengers by 2005 and 60 million by 2030. Runway capacity is thought to be sufficient until 2005.
- Apart from Amsterdam and Paris (Charles de Gaulle), new runways are in the master plans of Athens (in place of Hellinikon), Helsinki, Madrid, Manchester, Oslo, Rotterdam (a replacement) and Stockholm.

4.2   ALLOCATION ISSUES

It is not just capacity *per se* that poses problems but also the ways in which it is allocated. This involves the way rights at airports are given to the various airlines. There are a number of issues but two principal problems exist, namely access to landing slots and the right to handle.

4.2.1 Landing slots

In general, landing and take-off slots are allocated according to a set of administrative principles. The underlying principles of traditional slot allocation are simple; fundamental is the concept of grandfather rights, which lays down that an airline using a slot in one traffic season is entitled to its use in the same traffic season the following year. Secondary criteria include such things as size of aircraft, curfews at other airports and the need for a mix of services.

This approach has been criticized by economists because of its evident anti-competitive aspects, serving to advantage incumbents over would-be new entrants. Its defenders point to the inability so far of the system's critics to come up with a superior alternative.

The EU Commission, in an attempt to reduce the protection afforded incumbent carriers, initiated measures in 1993. Council Regulation 95/93 set out to establish a process based on, 'neutral, transparent and non-discriminatory rules' and '...to facilitate competition and to encourage entrance into the [Union air] market.' To this end the state is obliged to play a role in the allocating process and the rules are binding[10].

It effectively codified the existing system of administrative procedures with the aim of co-ordinating the actions of the parties involved and ensuring that the process is not excessively elongated. The desired features of a slot allocation process are:

- Sufficient flexibility to allow negotiations to take place and trade-offs to be made to reach an agreed allocation of slots,
- Participants have a strong incentive to reach agreement amongst themselves.

[10]   The EU also recognizes that there are problems in handling slots under Articles 85 and 86 of the Rome Treaty. The Commission, for example, has never attempted to use Article 86 presumably because it would be difficult to show that simply holding a slot constitutes a dominant position or that its use constitutes the abuse of such a position. Article 85 may be more germane but block exemptions have removed this from short term debate.

At congested, fully co-ordinated airports the Regulation requires the establishment of a co-ordinator (who acts in an independent manner and is responsible for slot allocation and information dissemination) and a co-ordinating committee (made up of airport users, airport representatives and air traffic control bodies, to advise the co-ordinator) together with the conducting of a capacity analysis.

The reliance mainly on grandfather rights as the prime allocative criteria reflects the traditional IATA approach outlined below[11]. The important new element being the effort made to allow new entrants to take up under-used slots or new slots[12].

The system is often seen as being limited (Castles, 1997) in that:

- there is a lack of clarity over what is being allocated (i.e. the rights and obligations that accompany the holding of slots);
- the administered rules are inefficient in allocating scarce capacity to highest value use;
- the distinction drawn between new entrants and incumbents is arbitrary if the balance of policy objectives remains undefined;
- there is declining effectiveness of the new entrant measures with shrinking slot pools at highly constrained airports;
- there is unresolved conflict between the need for flexibility to reflect local conditions and the need for consistency to meet the objectives of the EU.

The system, also, seems to have had minimal impact. There are few available slots at the most heavily congested airports, and those that do become available are often at unattractive times. Even the acquisition of a slot may be of little use to a carrier that requires a threshold number of slots to initiate or develop a viable service. At London's Heathrow Airport, for example, in the summer of 1994 new entrants only took up 20% of the 'EU pool', incumbents took another 40% but 40% went unused because they were unattractive. The pool itself was small, amounting to 7% or 8% of the total.

What should be noted, however, is that for the first time, save for exceptions laid down in the Regulation, slots are the property of the airlines and could be freely exchanged between them or their use transferred between

---

[11]   The IATA code is set out in *IATA Scheduling Procedures Guide*.

[12]   In practice IATA had required a proportion of unclaimed slots to be set aside for new entrants since 1990. Under Council Regulation (EEC) No. 95/93 of 18 January 1993, an airline holding more than 3% of daily slots at an airport or more than 2% of the slots in an airport system cannot be a new entrant.

types of service[13]. This is a novel concept in most European countries. It, therefore, introduced a fundamental change to the allocation process.

In the past the Commission has also been pro-active in intervening to limit the concentration of slots when airlines have merged. This was done when British Airways took over British Caledonian and in the cases of Air France/UTA, KLM/Transavia, Air France/Sabena and British Airways/ TAT[14]. The merged airlines were forced to give up slots to allow new entry.

The actual use an airline will make of its slot allocation will be influenced by the price it must pay. Economic pricing of airport facilities is not practiced in Europe[15]. Charges have traditionally been centered on a landing fee based on aircraft weight, together with a fee for each passenger, with a minor contribution from charges for aircraft parking. This conforms very closely to the type of pricing policies for airports favored by organizations such as IATA and ICAO (Table 4.2). The underlying principle is the accountancy one of cost recovery but deviates considerably from a charging structure that would make efficient use of the capacity. The

---

[13]   There is some legal dispute in the EU, however, over whether they may be bought and sold. The main advantage of property right allocations is that it allows markets to develop to ensure efficient use is made of scarce resources.

[14]   The latter two were examined under the Merger Regulation.

[15]   The optimal pricing policy under conditions of fixed capacity is to equate the marginal cost (MC) of using an airport with the marginal benefit (taken to be effective demand – D) of making use of it. The marginal cost in this context represents the additional cost to all users of the facility rather than simply that perceived by the carrier involved. The carrier will view costs purely in terms of the existing average cost of use (AC) without taking cognizance of the additional delay costs its actions imposes on other aircraft. This means that in terms of the diagram, fees should be set at F so that use is limited to Q_0 rather than Q_a which is the level where no account is taken of congestion effects.

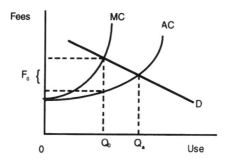

components of the charge are seldom based on separate cost calculations but are adjusted periodically to conform to airports' revenue needs[16].

Table 4.2 *ICAO and IATA recommendations on airport charges*

ICAO	IATA
1. Should be simple	Agree
2. No discrimination against foreign airlines or between them	Agree
3. Landing fees based on weight	Agree
4. No differentiation for inter-national flights or by stage distance	Agree
5. A single charge where possible	Agree
6. Landing fee to cover lighting and radio aids	Agree
7. Passenger charges acceptable but collected from airline	May be economic necessity but collect from passenger
8. Security charges only to cover relevant costs and if non-discriminatory	Not justified; it is government responsibility
9. Noise surcharge only to cover noise-alleviation measures	Not justified
10. Fuel throughout charge to be considered as concession fee	Only if covering costs of fuel facili-ties; not justified as concession fee
11. -	Peak-period surcharges not justified

An important point regarding the situation at congested airports is that while there is no effective congestion charge levied by the airport, the airlines themselves effectively cover the costs of congestion by charging higher fares themselves (Starkie, 1997)[17]. There is thus no major incentive

[16]   The system is not universal and different ones are used outside of Europe. In the US 'use agreements' are drawn up with charges based on capital and operating elements derived from accountancy calculations. Passenger facilities are dealt with by space rentals.

[17]   In terms of the diagram, in order to limit runway use to its capacity the airport would impose an economic rationing price of ab above the accountancy cost of 0b. The airport would then earn a profit of abcd. Without this price the quantity demanded, d*, would exceed the available capacity of the facility. If, however, the airport does not impose such a charge but simply allocates capacity on an administrative basis, then the airlines would still have to contain the demand for the seats that it can offer. They would have to limit seats so that

for airlines to either push for economic slot charges or to give up slots to new entrants.

It can also mean that many of the slots are not used optimally in the sense that carriers that could extract greater benefit from them are excluded. A system of secondary trading can help to reduce this problem once an allocation of slots has been made. Allowing the price mechanism to lubricate the trading process has been demonstrated in many markets to minimize transactions costs and produce a more efficient outcome.

Even where there have been efforts to bring landing fees more in accord with economic principles (e.g. as with London's airports – Table 4.3) the emphasis has been on the accounting notion of costing rather than the economic theory. In the London context, passenger charges were introduced in 1972 at Heathrow and have subsequently been refined with the creation of a peak period runway movement charge at the busiest time of the day in

runway use stays within the capacity. To do this they would charge fares of 0a (or with yield management, discriminatory fares down the demand curve to the point where capacity is fully utilized). The airlines holding slots thus enjoy the scarcity rent, abcd that would go to the airport with effective slot charging.

The fact that there is a capacity shortage also means that the slots are not well used. The extreme case can be illustrated in the diagram if we consider the dd* shortfall in capacity would have been used by marginal services if it had been available. If these services are instead still provided as part of the administered allocation (i.e. d**d is set equal to dd*) then there would be an efficiency loss equal to the shaded area. In other words, less demanded services would be replacing more demanded services. The illustration is an extreme one since the carriers with runway output d**d would have an incentive to make good use of it although there may be some other institutional constraints preventing this from being completely realized.

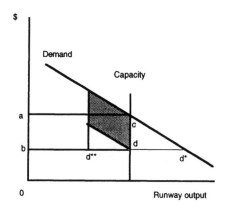

1976[18]. Passenger peak period charges were implemented at Gatwick in 1976. Stanstead also has differential fees. As can be seen from the table the degree of differentiation between peak and off-peak varies between airports reflecting pressures on airport capacities.

Table 4.3 *Landing fees at London's airports 1991 (in £s)*

Peak Period (GMT)	1986 (1000-1459)	1987 (0900-1529)	1988 (0900-1529)
British Airways			
BA 215 Boston	1515	1600	1600
BA 600 Vienna	0900	0855	0850
Air Algerie			
AH2055 Algiers	1500	1530	1530
Cyprus Airways			
CY 327 Lamaca	0900	0900	0830
El Al			
LY316 Tel Aviv	1515	1530	1545
JAT			
JU231 Rijeka	1500	1615	1610
Olympic Airways			
OA264 Athens	1520	1520	1545
Royal Air Maroc			
AT915 Casablanca	1515	1515	1615
TWA			
TW755 Philadelphia	0955	0930	0855

The fee is based on a calculation of the long run marginal cost of occupying a runway and this cost is independent of aircraft size[19]. The aim

[18]   There are also differential aircraft parking charges at Heathrow to reflect limited stand capacity.
[19]   The main guiding principals of the regime were based on the ability to pay and incremental cost. This is seen by the authorities as the long run marginal cost including compensation for the capital invested. The structure and implementation of the charges has not been without its critics (see Toms, 1994).

of such pricing has been to transfer demand from peak to trough periods so as to make better use of facilities; to reduce aircraft delays and to demonstrate to airlines the costs of adding capacity to meet peak demands.

The Commission of the European Communities (1995) issued a very general discussion document with the objective of establishing more efficient principles for allocating scarce airport capacity.[20] The stated aim is that real costs should be reflected in transparent charges. Price discrimination is allowed once they are operated in a consistent manner. Variations in the basic cost-related concepts are permitted with regard to peripheral or remotely located airports. While the proposals, which are meant to be supported by ICAO ideas, clearly cover some aspects of airports service provision, such as landing and parking, it remains unclear how such things as security, passenger charges and some other items are to be charged. The proposals also are at the individual facility level and it is unclear what implications this has on a system of inter-related airports.

4.2.2 Handling costs

The costs to airlines of using the ground services at airports in Europe have traditionally differed considerably between terminals and these variations cannot be explained away purely in terms of differences in national labor costs (Doganis and Lobbenberg, 1994). These costs, which embrace a variety of services ranging through refueling, baggage handling, aircraft servicing, cleaning and passenger services[21] are also significantly higher in Europe than those found in the US (Table 4.4).

The higher cost airports found within Europe in 1994 were generally associated with monopolies over ramp handling (i.e. Athens, Bilboa, Düsseldorf, Faro, Frankfurt and Madrid). The Association of European Airlines has in the past estimated that costs are about 30% higher at airports where there is no competition (UK Civil Aviation Authority, 1993). Because of local market conditions and the nature of individual airports, the nature of the service offered does differ between airports, as do the input

---

[20]   Reynolds-Feighan (1997) provides a critical assessment of the EU's position.
[21]   Ground handling is a term which is often used generically. IATA, however, in its Standard Ground Handling Agreement isolates specific components: - ground administration and supervision; passenger handling; baggage handling; cargo and mail handling; ramp services; cleaning; fueling; aircraft maintenance; flight operations and crew administration; service transport; and catering services.

costs involved, but it seems unlikely that this can explain the generally higher costs found at monopolized terminals (Table 4.5).

Table 4.4 *Handling costs; US versus Europe (US dollars)*

City	DC-9	A320
United States		
Atlanta	700	800
Dallas	750	850
Detroit	700	800
Washington/Dulles	750	850
Orlando	800	900
Miami	800	900
Europe		
London/Heathrow	1,071	1,530
Paris/CDG	3,175	4,762
Copenhagen	1,754	2,632
Frankfurt	2,721	4,286
Athens	1,758	3,823
Gibraltar	765	1,148

Table 4.5 *Airport and handling charges (1993 ECU) for a scheduled A320-100 service*

Airport	Airport-related charges per turn-around	Handling costs per turn-around, adjusted to reflect labor cost differences	Airport-related charges and handling cost per turn-around
Amsterdam	1,953	1,372	3,325
Athens	2,003	2,815	3,629
Bilbao	847	1,883	2,463
Brussels	1,612	1,611	3,210
Dusseldorf	1,671	1,582	3,389
Faro	1,391	4,468	3,124
Frankfurt	2,052	2,656	4,936
London Gatwick	1,145	1,030	2,160
Madrid	986	2,053	2,748
Manchester	1,952	943	2,881

As competition in the industry grows, so does the ability of airlines to secure what they regard as proper standards of handling. Airports usually restrict these rights, often on the proposition that space is too restricted to allow for the levels of equipment that would accompany unlimited handling rights or for reasons of security. Too often, the result has been that it becomes restricted to one company, frequently the national carrier or the subsidiary or associate of the airport operator.

In the UK, this problem has been diminishing. There have long been a number of competing handling companies, both airside and landside, at Heathrow and Gatwick. Following the intervention of the UK's Monopolies and Mergers Commission, multiple airside handling will be in both terminals at Manchester. Given this precedent, it is highly probable that multiple handling will be introduced, when necessary, at airports where it is absent. Elsewhere in the EU, the tradition of monopoly handling has tended to continue. This is despite efforts by the Commission to open up ground handling to competition in the mid-1990s.

In the wake of the conclusion of the Comité des Sages (1994) that '...ground handling services at European airports must be fully liberalized as soon as possible...', the Commission had produced a Consultation Paper setting out its ideas[22] followed by a Ground Handling Directive[23]. The legal basis for the latter being Article 84(2) of the Rome Treaty. The broad underlying principle being that full liberalization should be focused on ground handling activities that come into some sort of contact with passengers with partial liberalization of other services. The reason for this was the diversity of services involved and the concern that the primary focus should be on areas where an airline's brand image seemed to be important.

The liberalization process is to be phased in until 2003 with larger airports being the early movers. Self-handling will be liberalized less rapidly than third party handling[24].

4.2.3 Ownership of European airports

The ownership of European airports varies considerably both between and within countries (Table 4.6). In particular, there are important differences in the degree of central government, local government and private sector ownership. Moving away from the static picture, there has been an increased interest in private sector financing of airports. This stems mainly from a

[22]   OJ 1994 C41/2.

[23]   COM 994) 590.

[24]   Details of the measures are found in Soames (1997)

shortage of public sector funds required for capital investments but also reflects a move to a more commercial approach to airport management in Europe.

Table 4.6 *Ownership structure of selected European airports*

Airport	Owned by
Amsterdam (Schipol)	Dutch government (75.8%); municipalities of Amsterdam (21.8%) and Rotterdam (2.4%); no privatization or change in shared structure planned.
Birmingham International	Public limited company owned by public shareholders in the form of seven local shareholders.
Copenhagen	Independent company, with 25% private ownership.
East Midlands International	Airport assets transferred from local authority ownership to a new airport company, owned by Coach Operator National Express (1 April 1987).
Leipzig/Halle	100% publicly owned (leasehold agreements).
Lisbon	ANA, an autonomous public corporation.
Riga International	State-owned, financially independent of the government.
Turin	Limited company (SAG AT) for the running of the airport, on behalf of the City Council of Turin.
French airports	Most French airports belong to the state but are entrusted to concessionaires with a number of financial guarantees.
Vienna	Republic of Austria (17.38%), City of Vienna (17.38%), Province (7.38%), private shareholders (46.86%), Amsterdam Airport Schiphol (1%).
Warsaw	Polish airports state enterprise.

The question of ownership often overlaps that of both handling and slot allocation. Public ownership of an air terminal offers a theoretically stronger leverage to manipulate the market for airline services. This can violate EU competition policy rules. In the past, for example, the European Commission in 1995 pointed to the landing tax at Brussels/Zaventem airport as favoring the Sabena group. With regard to handling, similar problems of potential bias can arise. Again at Zaventem, the Belgium Court of Justice has began to open up the handling at the airport beyond the duopoly enjoyed by Sabena and Belgravia.

4.3 AIR TRAFFIC CONTROL AND NAVIGATION SYSTEMS

Although the physical elements of radar and telecommunications are vital, the control and navigation of air traffic involves perhaps the ultimate software infrastructure in aviation. Essentially, pilots of aircraft need to know their location, what lies ahead and feel confident there are no other aircraft in the immediate area. At present, this is largely achieved through ground control systems. The overlapping networks of area controls, navigation aids and corridors is, however, far from comprehensive in terms of what is possible in modern aviation.

At one level, there is a growing gap between navigation technology on board aircraft and that used on the ground. ATC requires aircraft to limit themselves to relatively narrow corridors, whereas modern, on-board navigation technology would permit much greater flexibility in routing. This could reduce flight times and fuel consumption. In the past, the US has experimented with area navigation (RNAV), whereby exclusive use of more great circle routes, independent of ground navigation, is adopted. But it was not a success and subsequently was abandoned over much of the system.

New satellite navigation systems such as the global positioning system of the US are now available and workable, although there remain problems of making them operational for Europe before the end of the century[25]. The use of collision-avoidance devices that alert crew to aircraft encroaching on their air space is still being discussed in Europe.

Since the capacity and efficiency of a software system is governed by the quality of its weakest link, ground traffic control currently acts as the major constraints on the system. Hardware and software used for navigation and controls varies between countries, but since air traffic is passed from one Air Traffic Flow Management Unit (ATFMU) to another, the capacity of one system is determined by the poorest of another. As the EU Commission stated in a report on Air Traffic Control,

> European national ATC systems are heavily interdependent. As such, the weakest link creates repercussions throughout the system. If the overall system is to be improved, available resources need to be channeled toward the weakest links.

Radar quality, for example, determines how closely aircraft may safely fly together; in Northern Europe, systems permit spacing of five to ten

---

[25]   There is also some concern about putting too much reliance on a system reliant on a US military satellite system.

nautical miles, but in Greece and parts of the Southern Mediterranean, it is 60 miles. Estimates by IATA suggest this simple difference in radar alone reduces the potential capacity of the system by about 25%.

One of the major underlying problems leading to software differences is the organizational fragmentation of air traffic control in Europe. Unlike the US, there exists only a limited degree of coordination between the various regional ATC centers in Europe. The difficulty is that short term national interests have tended to discourage countries from giving up any sovereignty over their air space and, therefore, the operational network, despite some elements of joint action, remains extremely fragmentary.

Therefore, European air traffic control is effectively a patchwork of 31 systems operated out of 54 en-route control centers, using 70 different computer languages. The result is a huge and cost-ineffective fragmentation of civil airspace.

Some limited coordination does exist. In 1966, Eurocontrol was established to coordinate research, national plans and training, execute studies and research, collect user charges and define objectives in the field of air navigation. It runs the combined civil-military Air Traffic Control Center at Maastricht. All members of the EU belong to it except Denmark, Italy and Spain. Its actual power, however, tends to be limited by the reluctance of some members to hand in its control of the overall ATC system in Europe. Indeed, its role in the past was mainly one of collecting revenues for use made of the various ATC systems.

In terms of day-to-day operations, traffic passes through a number of Air Traffic Flow Management Units. Prior to take off, a clear path must be established. Direct links between ATFMUs are poor, with only Frankfurt, Paris, London, Madrid and Rome linked by a telecommunications system. They are essentially mismatched and under-funded. This point was forcibly made by the secretary of the Association of European Airlines. Centers operate with different levels of performance and technology, with no commonly agreed standard and a lack of compatibility between the systems.

The control itself involves verbal contact between ground control and pilots. While this is used in the US with success, Europe has a multiplicity of languages and inevitable conservatism must be exercised in controlling aircraft movements in the face of possible misunderstandings. Automated control systems are available, but the necessary network of computerized infrastructure is still missing.

Recent years have also been plagued by staff problems within the ATC system. In 1988, the European air traffic system encountered this due to industrial action which, in retrospect, was a symptom of a more serious underlying malaise. There are now suggestions that shortages of experienced air traffic controllers can arise due to cohort effects, e.g. as in the past when about 40% of West Germany's staff retired between 1988 and 1990.

While differences in equipment and training add to geographical inflexibility, it is not clear that more will improve the overall ATC network. An ATC system is at its most inefficient point when a controller in charge of one section hands it over to a colleague in charge of a contiguous one. Use of more controllers requires a rise in the number of sectors and hence greater inefficiency in some respects.

Reduction in the number of centers is an obvious step forward. While major differences exist in the nature of respective traffic, it is interesting to observe in the Continental US, the ATC is a unified system based in 20 centers, less than half the European number. The FAA already has a unified system of computers up and running, while in Europe, the UK has adopted smaller computers since no physical space exists to locate the large machines.

By the late-1990s, it is planned that a new Central Flow Management Unit (CFMU) will become operational so that an overview of flights can be obtained. This will increase the network's capacity by about 30%, but it will not be capable of handling the predicted long term traffic growth. Furthermore, a Future European Air Traffic Management System (FEATS) is proposed for the year 2010 which would embody coordinated technical planning. Eurocontrol will pay a much larger role in this new structure.

Actual investment, however, is much slower in coming. The UK has a five year program costing some £0.6 billion, but this is perhaps the firmest plan for investment. Recent reports indicate tentative plans for a further £2.2 billion to be spent by other European nations, but this is not definitely committed. This could be compared with the large scale research and investment program in the US where about $4.0 billion has been spent on automation alone, and at least a further $16.0 billion of investment is planned.

Put another way, members of the 22 nation European Civil Association Conference plan to spend about $13.75 per annual boarded passenger on new hardware, compared with $24.00 in the US. Such investment is cost effective in the long run; while both the US and Europe spend annually about $1.6 billion guiding aircraft over their respective territories, the US system deals with nearly three times as many flights.

Delays due to air space limitation, a function of both ATC systems and corridor capacity, have been growing. In 1986, some one in ten flights were delayed over fifteen minutes. In 1988, this had risen to one in five, and in 1989, it was one in four (although the figures for the peak months of June and July were nearer one in three).

While efficiency may require some congestion existing in the system, especially at peak times, the current situation may be seen as economically costly. At any one time, this means there are some 100 aircraft waiting for take off, while another 100 are stacked waiting to land. This broadly equates to an aircraft fleet about the combined size of Air France and Lufthansa.

The financial cost of these delays, according to calculations by the Association of European Airlines, amounted to some 4.19 billion ECU per annum. In another study, time lost due to air traffic delays in Europe was placed at 33,000 hours per annum by the German Air Space Users Association in 1989, with associated costs of $970 million to airlines each year and $540 million to air travelers. While new equipment may be costly, initial capital outlays would soon seem likely to be recuperated in the savings generated.

Access to air space is a related issue. As pointed out earlier, substantial parts of European air space are still reserved for military use, thus concentrating civil aviation in limited corridors and causing problems for air traffic control. In France, 40% of air space is controlled by the military, while in Germany, until recently, almost all north-south traffic had to pass through a corridor between Frankfurt and Munich to avoid air space reserved for NATO aircraft. In the UK, problems exist flying from Manchester to Brussels because the most direct route over East Anglia is in Ministry of Defence air space. Therefore, traffic must pass through the already crowded London area.

Another problem is also the division of tasks and cooperation between the military and civil aviation authorities, especially in upper air space. It is very likely that the end of the 'Cold War' – with its cuts in defense budgets – will also mean a reduction of military flights and a restructuring of military airspace. At present, the military situation is very unclear, given the ongoing process of economic, political and military fragmentation of the former eastern Europe.

As a result, the average aircraft in Europe flies some 10% further than on a direct route and many even more (e.g. Brussels to Zurich is 45% more). This could be compared with the fact that military flights account for just 4% of flights in Eurocontrol's central route charges office but 50% of air space; military use is therefore very inefficient. Problems are compounded that much of the demand for air travel in Europe is concentrated on particular routes. The economic cost of inefficient use due to the lack of a suitable civil corridor network was estimated in 1989 by the German Air Space users Association at $1.27 billion to airlines, and $510 million in wasted passenger time.

4.4   SURFACE ACCESS

4.4.1 Local access

All air transport movements involve accessing and leaving the air terminal. Air movements pose one set of problems but there are also mounting difficulties associated with ground movements. Accessing Europe's major airports is becoming increasing difficult as surface traffic congestion grows. The emerging edge city pattern of urban land-use is compounding the problem as local traffic becomes entwined with that using the airport. The problems are often most acute for users traveling from central city sites who have to make radial trips out to air terminals along heavily used commuter routes. Most movements to and from airports are by private car and the forecasts are that even with the international trend towards policies involving traffic constraint, car ownership and use will grow.

Land transport movements also pose severe environmental problems, inflicting noise and fumes on those living on access corridors. This is increasingly leading to public pressures to limit the construction of new road access links.

Mass public transport offers one possible methods of more efficiently moving the forecast number of future air travelers. Some airports already have extensive public transport access. In some cases airlines have also been proactive in attempting to ease the problem for their users by operating public transport services. This has, for instance, been a policy of Lufthansa at Frankfurt where the airline's 'Airport Express' has provided train services to nearby urban areas.

In many cities there are plans to either introduce new public transport systems to improve access or to up-grade existing ones (Table 4.7). Nevertheless, fixed track transport involves considerable capital investments and in many cases such as Heathrow the forecasts suggest that new capacity will merely slow the increase in car traffic growth, not reverse it. The geographical configuration and historic pattern of land use in many European cities also poses serious planning problems that can often only be resolved using expensive technologies such as tunneling.

4.4.2 The inter-urban network

Fixed track public transport is particularly attractive if it links not only an air terminal to its parent urban area but also ties it into a region's larger public transport network. Linking high-speed rail and air transport in this way also takes some of the strain of slot congestion at airports by allowing airlines to use more of their capacity for medium and long haul services.

The openings of the Paris-Lyon TGV and the Channel Tunnel linking the UK to continental Europe are illustrative of this type of effect. Part of the traffic making use of these links has been diverted traffic from the London-Paris air services.

Outside of the EU, the Swiss have already established a precedent by having a mainline rail station located under each major airport and travelers' baggage may be checked-in and delivered at any Swiss railway station. The development of the French TGV system and its extensions into the low countries is involving joint rail/air terminals at Charles de Gaulle and Schipol airports.

Table 4.7 *Rail links at selected European airports*

Airport	Rail link
Amsterdam	Regional, urban and intercity rail links in place. Potential for high-speed link.
Cologne-Bonn	Intercity and urban rail link.
Copenhagen	Regional and urban rail link planned. Potential for high speed link.
Dusseldorf	Intercity and urban rail link.
Frankfurt	Intercity and urban rail links. High-speed rail link planned.
Geneva	Inter-city rail link.
Hamburg	Metro connection planned; timing depends on funding.
London/LGW	Urban rail link.
London/LHR	Underground link in place. Heathrow Express under construction.
London/Stansted	Urban rail link.
Manchester	Urban rail link.
Milan/Malpensa	New high-speed link to city centre plus links to regional rail system.
Munich	Urban rail link.
Oslo	New high-speed link to city centre under construction.
Paris/CDG	Regional and high-speed rail links in place.
Paris/ORY	Urban rail link.
Vienna	City centre link to be improved. Possible future intercity connection.
Zurich	Inter-city rail link.

The idea that the EU airport network should be linked with the wider EU inter-urban transport network formed one element of the Commission's approach to developing the trans-European transport network. The guidelines for developing air transport infrastructure priorities include not only the enhancement of existing airport capacity; the development of airport capacity; and the enhancement of environmental compatibility but also the development of access to the airport and interconnections with other networks.

5.   Airline Alliances and EU Air Transport

5.1   THE CONCEPT OF AIRLINE ALLIANCES

There are a variety of operational issues concerning EU aviation that are current and are likely to remain so in the immediate future. One that transcends a number of sub-issues is that of airline alliances.

The notion of airline alliances is one that has come under public scrutiny in the wake of several publicized efforts by a number of major international airlines to link their operations[1]. The nature of ties differs between groupings, as the success of partners in gaining both official ratification and the way they operate and manage their alliances.

Although the formation of the International Air Traffic Association by six European carriers in 1919 might be seen as an early example, alliances in aviation can be traced back as far as 1945 when the International Air Transport Association (IATA) was established by the world's leading air carriers to coordinate international air fares. The bilateral structure of agreements following the inability of the 1994 Chicago Convention to initiate free international aviation markets focused on regulated fares, routings, schedules, designated carriers and revenue pooling. The primary aim of the immediate post-war structure had been to protect non-US carriers when, as a result of the Second World War, the US had built up a dominant fleet of aircraft that could be transferred to commercial uses. Subsequently, the IATA was often used to protect economically inefficient state-owned carriers from the rigors of market competition.

---

[1]   The majority of the airline alliances that have attracted most public interest have involved one or more European carriers joining with a large US airline. Alliances are certainly not unique to air transport, nor indeed to transport in general, but are one of the most rapidly growing forms of business practice.

The US domestic market first used alliances in 1967 as a way for jet and commuter operators to jointly develop markets in an era of tight economic regulation. The late 1980s and early 1990s saw growth of new forms that embraced somewhat different characteristics and served different purposes. Alliances have been less institutionalized, as they have generally been formed by privately owned commercial airlines outside of governmental or inter-governmental agency initiative. Growth has primarily occurred in international alliances.

These alliances are also in a continual state of flux. According to the *Airline Business* survey, the Spanish carrier Iberia reduced its alliances from 27 in 1995 to 13 by May of 1996 (Gallacher, 1996a). Over the same period, Austrian Airlines canceled six agreements and added four new ones, and Swissair added six agreements and dropped three. Similar patterns emerge for other carriers, and these changes are part of an overall tidying-up process as carriers formulate more coherent network strategies for their needs.

The exact number of existing alliances is unclear, not only because of the dynamic nature of the arrangements but because the term 'alliance' is generic, with no precise definition (Tretheway, 1990). In a strict legal sense, in some countries it can mean some degree of equity ownership of one carrier by another, but more often it is interpreted, in looser terms, to embrace such things as code-sharing agreements, interchangeable frequent flyer programs and coordinated scheduling of services. Equally, airlines are often involved in a large number of different alliances embracing a single partner, but it may involve several others carriers. Increasingly, a more relevant feature is several major carriers linking activities in so-called 'galaxies'.

An annual survey by *Airline Business* attempts to track these major alliances and reports changes in some of their main features (Table 5.1). Growth is immediately obvious as is the relatively small quantitative importance involving an equity stake and their slow growth in numbers. The data is not definitive, and the *Economist* (1995), for example, produced figures claiming 401 alliances in 1995, double the number it estimated four years earlier. The overwhelming conclusion, though, is that the number of airline alliances is large and increasing.

The North Atlantic market embraces a number of alliances involving code-sharing and cooperation in other ways across a large number of routes so as to strategically link networks. This type of strategy dates back to the Global Excellence alliance formed by Swissair, Singapore International Airlines and Delta in 1989.

Other airline alliances, such as between Continental and Alitalia and United and British Midland, are regional in orientation and involve specific code sharing restrictions. However, the vast majority of 'point-specific' alliances are relatively minor, targeted affairs which usually generate few controversies. Blocked-space agreements are often a feature, with airlines purchasing and reselling seats on each others' flights. This often benefits participants, particularly if they allow new routes to be serviced more effectively or make withdrawing an aircraft from one easier.

Table 5.1 *Airline alliances 1994-1997*[2]

	1997	1996	1995	1994	% change
Number of alliances	363	390	324	280	29.6
With equity stakes	54	62	58	58	-6.9
Without equity	309	327	266	222	39.2
New alliances	72	71	50	-	-
Number of airlines	177	159	153	136	30.1

Source: Airline Business June 1977

In their various guises, point specific alliances can lead to fears of monopoly domination of an individual route. Multifaceted, strategic alliances are now often seen as potentially posing challenges of a greater magnitude. Figure 5.1 provides a simple schema of the links involved for Swissair in the Global Quality alliance in 1994 showing that alliance structures can be very complex. Such complexity poses problems for policy formulation across countries that may have quite diferent forms of competition policy.

In broad terms, the types of feature characterizing an airline alliance can be divided into distinct categories. These features are not necessarily unique to aviation, and many can be found in other network sectors where collusion has been allowed. Shipping conferences and consortia provide a close parallel to airline conferences, and comparisons can be made between deferred rebates and EDI systems in shipping and frequent flyer programs and CRS systems in air transport. Conferences are also concerned with setting and coordinating frequencies of integrated services. These types of arrangement are often long standing but involve parallel commercial and policy considerations to alliances in aviation.

[2]   New alliances are those entered into since around May of the previous year and not then listed as planned. Alliances restricted to frequent flier co-operation were included in 1994, but excluded in 1995-96. The actual number of alliances in 1994, the first year *Airline Business* compiled information, was marginally higher than stated as some alliances went unreported. However, some domestic regional operators owned by majors were included in 1994, but excluded in 1995-97.

5.1.1 Mergers

Full mergers were a feature of the US domestic market following the 1978 Airline Deregulation Act as the initial period of instability moved into one of consolidation and rationalization (Morrison and Winston, 1995). There have also been significant merger activities within the Canadian market and Europe in recent years (Hanlon, 1996)[3].

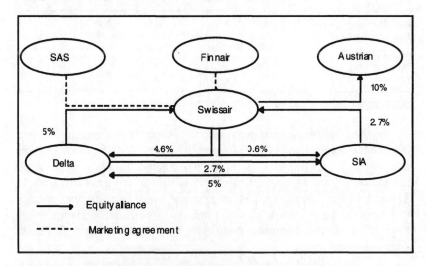

Figure 5.1 *Swissair and the Global Quality alliance 1994.*

Mergers of this type are the most extreme form of alliance and traditionally a way that carriers coordinate operations and other activities. They enjoy the advantage of complete control in the hands of a single board with resources that can be allocated more effectively (Carlton *et al* 1980). There may be benefits of improved information flows within a single structure as well as cost savings where duplications in administration and service provision can be avoided.

In practice, though, mergers are not always successful. As with failed mergers in any sector, some have simply been ill conceived, badly planned and ineptly executed. A few general principles seem to emerge regarding successful mergers. Generally, linking overlapping networks in any transport industry offers fewer economies than combining interfacing

---

[3]   The first cross-border takeover in the EU was when Maersk Air acquired the balance of shares in Birmingham European in 1993.

networks (either in geographical terms or with respect to types of service offered). In some instances, problems also arise because those involved have miscalculated the costs of transition which, in a sector where each operator often has developed its own character, can be quite considerable.

Mergers generally involve the need to obtain institutional approval from various authorities. In virtually all cases cross-border mergers have not been possible in the past because national regulations limited the degree of foreign ownership in an airline. A notable exception to this is SAS. Cross-border mergers also pose problems in terms of implications for international air transport agreements, since the nationality of a carrier can become blurred under these circumstances. Within the EU, for example, there is now no notion of national ownership of a carrier but in terms of external bilateral agreements constraints may still be relevant.

Even within countries, mergers are often controlled, at certain levels, by national governments. Within the EU, European countries have taken a variety of positions; mergers such as British Airways with British Caledonia and Air France with UTA have only gained approval by the airlines when routes or slots are relinquished[4].

5.1.2 Cross equity holdings

Other than the extremes of direct mergers or takeovers, the strongest form of airline alliance is either unidirectional (as with the former USAir/British Airways and on-going Northwest/KLM alliance) or cross-entity (as with Delta/Swissair/Sabena/Austrian alliance, depicted in Figure 5.1) share holdings.

While mergers still take place, there has been a recent tendency for the level of control through equity holdings to fall short of a full merger, especially when airlines are from two separate countries and national laws limit the extent of foreign ownership. Such forms of airline investment have grown considerably in recent years, and Table 5.2 provides details of some of the major examples in 1995 (see again Table 2.6 for details of European airline foreign ownership). What is not shown is the degree of control equity holdings afford an airline. Particularly, voting rights are often less than the relative amount of capital involvement.

Both the absolute and the relative importance of airline alliances involving equity stakes has been declining. *Airline Business* recorded less than 15% of agreements in May 1997 involving investments compared with 18% in 1995 and 21% in 1994. Nevertheless, this does not imply there has not been a large increase in their overall importance; other surveys indicate

[4]   See again section 2.5 for a brief review of EU competition policy.

that from 1992, ownership stakes above 20% have predominated (Lindquist, 1996).

Table 5.2 *Foreign ownership of major airlines*

Country	Airline	%	Country	Airline	%
	Europe			North America	
Austria	Austrian	20	USA	America West	
	Lauda	40		Continental	20
Belgium	Sabena	49		Delta	20
France	TAT	49		Hawaiian	10
Germany	Deutsche BA	49		Northwest	33
Hungary	Malev	30		US Air	24
Luxembourg	Luxair	13	Canada	Canadian	22
Russia	Air Russia	31			33
UK	Air UK	45		Australasia	
	BMA	40	Australia	Quantas	29
			New Zealand	Ansett NZ	100

Source: Airline Business, December 1995

Equity holdings have the advantage over looser alliance arrangements discussed above because they show stronger commitment on the part of the carriers for greater periods of time. It also acts as a device to prevent other carriers from forming alliances with those involved. Additionally, holdings prove prudent investments if the synergy effects from an alliance meet or exceed expectations. This is the case with KLM's stake in Northwest Airlines (Gallacher, 1996b). The holder earns a commercial return on the investment. It is less clear that British Airways enjoyed such gains from its venture with USAir.

One difficulty with such holdings is that they represent a commitment which, if the alliance fails to deliver anticipated benefits, can prove costly to reverse. The second bankruptcy of Continental Airlines in 1991 was so for its equity partner, SAS. In many cases, regulations over controlling an airline also means that foreign carriers cannot obtain the level of governance commensurate with a particular level of holding.

5.1.3 Code sharing

Individual travelers have traditionally suffered a dearth of information regarding their air transport options. This problem has compounded since the late 1970s as fare deregulation and adoption of yield management techniques by airlines introduced a massive array of continually changing alternative fare options. The computer reservation systems (CRSs) now generally provide the interface between carriers and potential travelers. These systems have become a powerful marketing tool for carriers (Humphreys, 1994a).

This ability of individual airlines to control information flows is recognized by many governments (Humphreys, 1994b)[5]. It is on this basis that CRSs have been the subject of regulation in the US since 1984, in Canada since 1989 and in Europe for a number of years, with a Code of Conduct established in 1991 by the ICAO to govern standards of information display and access. These aim to limit exploitation by CRS-controlling airlines.

One major problem in the past has been national discrimination. The increased internationalization of ownership of CRSs has tended to reduce this (Table 5.3). More recently, the General Agreement on Trade in Services (GATS) has sought, in its Annex on Air Transport Services, to bring regulatory regimes covering CRS systems within a wider multilateral framework.

Although historically important, halo effects (booking practices favoring CRS-owner airlines) are diminishing. They are already considerably less in European markets where multiple airline ownership of systems has been more long-standing. Rapid advances in computer technology, the development of the Internet, and the potential for passengers to book directly through personal computer systems or by telephone (e.g. the self-service systems developed by SAS and Lufthansa) are also likely to diminish the power exercised by the incumbent owners.

With respect to the US and the EU, the recent high-level studies of aviation policy do not consider the halo issue an important impediment to entry (US National Commission to Ensure a Strong Competitive Airline Industry, 1993; Comité des Sages for Air Transport, 1994).

Airlines are increasingly combining to make use of CRS information channels in a somewhat different way by stimulating joint traffic flows. This involves code-sharing which is now seen as the main feature of any modern airline alliance, with the number growing considerably in recent years.

[5]   These codes were initially devised at a time when it was felt airlines owning a CRS system would, by the way information was shown up, bias bookings against competitors or use information in a system regarding the activities of other carriers using it to gain an unfair competitive advantage. Code-sharing was very limited when these codes were initiated.

Table 5.3 *Ownership of CRS systems*

Abacus[1]	Galileo International	Sabre
All Nippon Airways	Aer Lingus	American
Cathay Pacific	Air Canada	
China Airlines	Air Portugal	Sertel
Dragon Airlines	Alitalia	Aero Mexico
Eva Air	Austrian	Mexicana Airlines
Garuda	British Airways	
MAS	KLM	Skycall
Philippine Airlines	Olympic	Japan Air System
Royal Brunei Airlines	Swissair	
Silk Air	United	System One
Singapore Airlines	Swissair	Continental
Amadeus[2]	Gemini[3]	TIAS
Air France	Air Canada	Quantas/Australian
Iberia	Canadian International	Ansett
Lufthansa		Air New Zealand
Axess	GETS	Worldspan[5]
Japan Airlines	SITA	Delta
		Northwest
	Infini[4]	TWA
	All Nippon Airways	

[1] Worldspan owns 5 per cent of Abacus.
[2] Amadeus now owns a majority of System One.
[3] Gemini has now been replaced by Galileo Canada, wholly owned by Air Canada, which distributes Galileo International in the Canadian market.
[4] Abacus owns 40 per cent of Infini
[5] Abacus owns 5 per cent of Worldspan

Technically, a code-share is a marketing arrangement between two or more carriers allowing them to sell seats on each other's flights under their own designator code. In the case of connecting flights of two or more code-sharing carriers, the whole flight is displayed on a CRS system as a single carrier service. From a customer's perspective, it gives the impression of an on-line service or, at the very least, features such as single check-in, common frequent flier program and coordinated flight schedule.

Code-shares can be across a wide range of services as with major strategic alliances, but numerically more often, it is a single or small network of services. The latter can be attractive to smaller carriers wishing to expand their networks but whose own does not ideally dovetail with any other single airline. The tendency, however, is that small network code-shares are short lived as new coalitions of interests emerge in a dynamic market place.

A stronger form of code sharing involves blocked space arrangements. In this case, one carrier buys space on another airline's aircraft which it then sells under its own name and designator code. This can allow for the use of larger aircraft on routes and thus generate economies of density for a carrier. It may also permit better use of slots at congested airports.

5.1.4 Scheduling

Hub-and-spoke operations, particularly the 'banking' of flights as an effective concomitant, can be more efficient if carriers coordinate their flight patterns. By allowing traffic to be consolidated and transshipped between flights, hub-and-spoke operations can enhance load factors and allow airlines to reap any economic benefits of existing economies of scope and density. By coordinating schedules, airlines can increase the potential amount of traffic across their combined networks. Coordination of this type can be particularly useful to airlines that individually have small numbers of slots at airports and without co-ordination of schedules with another carrier would be unable to provide a fully integrated service to potential customers.

5.1.5 Franchising

Franchising has been a tradition in sectors such as hotels, fast food and clothing. In aviation, it allows major carriers to spread their brand name and generate revenues on thin routes without a commitment of major capital investments. It can also funnel traffic to slots at constrained airports where carriers cannot increase their own frequencies. The franchisee gains from increased market recognition as well.

Franchising is now a growing alliance form in international markets, especially in Europe where British Airways has been successful developing their activities (see Table 5.4). In March 1996, they had six arrangements that carried an estimated combined total of 3.4 million passengers and generated revenues of more than $77.7 million. British Airways' franchises now extend beyond Europe, and since October 1996 includes the South African Airline Comair (Jones, 1996).

Other carriers have been less enthusiastic about franchising arrangements and much slower to adopt them. Air France is moving cautiously, for example, with Brit Air and Air Littoral. And although the management at Lufthansa has a limited number of franchising agreements, it has indicated that potential labor problems exist if the franchisee pays lower wages. Further, not all arrangements are long lived. The Irish carrier

CityJet, for instance, broke away to operate under its own name from Virgin Atlantic after 30 months.

Table 5.4 *British Airways' franchisees*

Airline	Number of routes	operated as
British Mediterranean Airways	3	British Airways
Brymon Airways	19	British Airways Express
CityFlyer Express	12	British Airways Express
Comair	9	British Airways
GB Airways	16	British Airways
Loganair	33	British Airways Express
Maersk Air	7	British Airways
Manx Airlines	28	British Airways Express
Sun-Air	11	British Airways Express

From a policy perspective, regulatory authorities to-date have tended to monitor rather than react against existing franchising arrangements in Europe. If anything the European Commission's (1996) assessment of franchising in its overall review of the Third Package is that it has fanchising as practiced by British Airways has many virtues. It has advantages for customers in terms of the company looking after problems arising as part of a journey; to British Airways in terms of developing its operations at near zero cost; and to the partners in terms of image and management inputs (e.g. the handling of frequent flier programs and the control of cash receipts).

5.2   THE MAJOR TRANS-ATLANTIC ALLIANCES

The term airline alliance should, therefore, be treated as a generic concept embracing a variety of differtent forms of cooperation. While there are many different variants on airline alliances, however, several involving large international EU carriers on mainly trans-Atlantic routes are seen of particular importance and have attracted notable attention[6]:

[6]   The coverage here is far from comprehensive and, given the fluidity of alliances, will become quickly dated. The aim is to provide some factual background to the nature of strategic alliances involving EU carriers and to highlight the dynamics of most alliances.

5.2.1 Continental/SAS (formed 1988)

This early code sharing involved flights from Newark to Copenhagen and beyond, with SAS taking equity holdings in Continental. Between 1987 and 1991, SAS moved its New York terminus for two trans-Atlantic services from JFK Airport to Newark, Continental's hub. Service expansions of the airlines predominantly involved hubs of the other firm. Their alliance ended in 1991 when Continental went into bankruptcy and SAS wrote off an investment of $100 million. Continental subsequently formed an alliance with Alitalia – code sharing flights from US cities to Rome and Milan via New York/Newark – and, since 1997, Virgin Atlantic.

5.2.2 Northwest/KLM (formed 1989)

This formed at a time when Northwest experienced severe financial difficulties and considered Chapter 11 bankruptcy. The alliance involves (Worldwide Reliability) not just code sharing, frequent flyer programs, and joint flights but also a 33% equity holding after an initial investment of $400 million (that was written down in 1993) by KLM in Northwest. Code-sharing and joint marketing began in 1991 when Northwest secured block space and code sharing agreements on KLM flights between Amsterdam and Minneapolis. The signing of the US/Netherlands 'Open Skies' agreement in 1992 allowed for unlimited code sharing.

This was the first major international strategic alliance given anti-trust immunity by the US. The five year immunity granted in November 1992 allowed the alliance full protection from civil or criminal charges of collusion, as well as cooperation in fare setting and promotions. Particularly, it permitted fare setting on double-connect routes (such as those behind Amsterdam to beyond Detroit) which would otherwise have been determined by IATA fare constructions. Getting official individual acceptance for such routes would have imposed severe transaction costs on the airlines.

Concern that the Dutch carrier would take control of Northwest caused the US firm in 1996 to limit voting powers of any share holding block in the company irrespective of the scale of the equity holding.

5.2.3 British Airways/USAir (formed 1993)

This alliance formed after the partnership between the British carrier and United Airlines ended in 1991 when United began its own overseas services. British Airways took a 24.6% equity stake of $300 million in USAir when it was in serious financial difficulties[7]. Further investment of $450 million was possible under the agreement but never took place because of the poor financial performance of USAir; even in 1996, British Airways wrote off half of its existing investment. In addition to USAir, British Airways has significant equity stakes in Qantas, TAT and Deutsche BA as well as some smaller UK carriers.

Subsequent code sharing between British Airways and USAir was largely unidirectional, with many USAir trans-Atlantic flights taking British Airways' designator codes. This allows British Airways to display flights to 64 US cities as joint flights, although it physically serves few of these points.

Some USAir flights accessed British Airways codes in 1996 as part of a bilateral agreement which allowed the British carrier to tender contracts in travel markets by US government employees. No blocked space arrangements existed in this situation but instead, both airlines drew seats from a common USAir pool.

In 1996, British Airways' efforts to form an alliance with American Airlines led to relationship problems with USAir, with the decision reached to end their alliance in March of 1997. British Airways sold its remaining shares in US Airways (as it was renamed) later in 1997.

5.2.4 United/Lufthansa (formed 1993)

This alliance formed in June 1994 during a period when the US and Germany had trouble renegotiating bilateral air service agreements. It was intended to help Lufthansa to perform better and for the airline to establish a presence in the North American market. Yet unlike other alliances, significant competition existed between the two carriers on several important routes.

The alliance currently involves extensive multiple code-sharing, especially on flights through Frankfurt into Europe, Africa and Asia. They share a common frequent flier program with no equity swap, and Lufthansa moved to the United Airlines terminal at Chicago O'Hare to further integrate their operations.

The alliance has enjoyed anti-trust immunity in the US since the acceptance of a liberal bilateral air service agreement between the US and Germany. This immunity extends to the tripartite alliance involving SAS. The carriers also have a number of individual two party pacts with, for example, Thai Airways and Air Canada.

---

[7]   British Airways also held 3 seats on the 16 member board.

5.2.5 Delta/Swissair/Sabena/Austrian (formed 1996)

Delta Air Lines traditionally forms alliances with smaller carriers to fill gaps in its international network rather than partner with a single firm. This alliance grew out of longer standing ties between Delta and Swissair since 1989 and included the Global Excellence alliance involving Singapore International Airlines and a small equity exchange. The airline purchased 4.7% of Delta's equity and 2.77% of Swissair. Delta purchased 2.7% of SIA's shares and acquired a 4.5% holding in Swissair. In turn, Swissair bought a 0.62% equity holding in SIA and a 4.6% stake in Delta.

In 1996, Delta linked into a wider-ranging partnership with a group of European carriers (Swissair/Sabena/Austrian) that share important equity and alliance cross-ties. Arrangements involve a variety of code-sharing and other plans designed to integrate the trans-Atlantic operations of all its partners. The alliance enjoys anti-trust immunity in the United States.

Additional linkages have allowed Swissair to acquire a 49.5% stake in Sabena. Managerially their ties are strong, with Swissair largely responsible for appointing one of their own, Paul Reutlinger, as Chief Executive Officer of Sabena.

5.3   THE RATIONALE BEHIND ALLIANCES

Since it is difficult defining an airline alliance, it is inevitably hard to account for the reasons they have existed, both past and present. There are many elements, and the underlying motivation of agreements has varied. Further, since they have effects on demand and supply sides of an operator's activities, it is inevitable that trade-offs are made when deciding on specific strategies. Youssef (1992) argues there are two broad reasons for airline alliances. First, there is the improvement in technical economic efficiency which accompanies scale, the creation of optimal networks, and coordination of services. And second, alliances create market power and limit competition. This, however, is somewhat of a simplification and alliances are often formed for a complexity of commercial and operational reasons.

While not unique to the aviation sector, alliances are one of the fastest growing features of contemporary business. From a historical perspective, their current forms take a number of distinct conceptual types.

Horizontal alliances embrace undertakings that serve the same market, vertical alliances link specific activities, and external (or diversification) alliances involve agreements with suppliers in other industries.

Traditionally, the international aviation system of agreements within the IATA framework involved revenue pooling, fare controls and service frequency coordination fit within the framework of horizontal alliances. The development of more liberalized international aviation markets, however, has reduced this form of alliance in air transport.

More common instead are vertical forms of alliances. Within the confines of international aviation itself, agreements exist between carriers providing complementary services (e.g. feeders to hubs served by major trunk carriers). Abutting these strict aviation activities are a number of alliances between airlines and complementary services. Over time, British Airways has partnered with hotels such as Marriott and the Ritz-Carlton Group and Son, car rental agencies such as Hertz, and charge card companies such as Diners Club. Airlines in the US and Australia have become involved in terminal ownership, although public ownership of airports precludes this in most EU countries.

External alliances have generally involved hiving-off specialized activities to outside companies such as catering. Neither management science nor economic theory can provide an uncontroversial specific reason why airlines unite.

5.3.1 The economic theory of airline alliances

Traditionally, the concern of anti-trust authorities is that alliances concentrate market power and exploit monopoly advantages that partner airlines forge. The result may be a reduction in supply and higher prices for users. This judgment, however, may not be automatically because merger or cooperative behavior can often increase economic efficiency. Where there are potential economies of scale, density, or scope, the public policy challenge is to ensure these advantages are maximized without suppliers extracting all the economic rents. Equally, alliances may circumvent the economic problems of market instability that can exist in network industries as well as offering a mechanism of avoiding the worst excesses of any other intervention failures.

In basic terms, an airline alliance can impact the demand for a carrier's services and its cost structure. The ultimate effect on customers will depend on characteristics of the market where the airline alliance operates; if an alliance forms but is only a small part of a large competitive market, the incentive for carriers to maximize efficiency and keep prices low is likely to produce considerably different results to when the carriers dominate a market and erect barriers to new entry.

Because of the diversity of forms that alliances take and the ways potential elements can be combined, it is dangerous to generalize. Some broad points, however, can be made with a simple diagrammatic representation of a specific air transport market.

In Figure 5.2, D1 and C1 represent the demand and cost curves confronting a carrier on a particular route. They are linear, and the cost curve horizontal is simply for presentational clarity. If the airline joins with one or more competitors, then:

- by virtue of joint marketing, code-sharing, common frequent flyer programs, coordinated scheduling and so on, the demand for an airline's services would move out (e.g. to D2) and
- because of the potential for rationalizing services, the scope for reducing ground costs and so on, costs would fall (e.g. to C2).

In this framework, it is assumed the market is stable and viable prior to any alliance being formed. In practice, an alliance may keep loss-making carriers in a market, but this is not dealt with here.

The extent and nature of these shifts in demand and cost schedules would depend not only on the details but the response of carriers outside the alliance. If the alliance results in other, non-partner carriers becoming more cost conscious, cutting fares or improving services, then the demand curve in Figure 5.2 would not shift or only slightly move out. Equally, pure code-sharing alliance may have minimal effects on costs. For purposes of exposition, very simple cases are shown in the diagram.

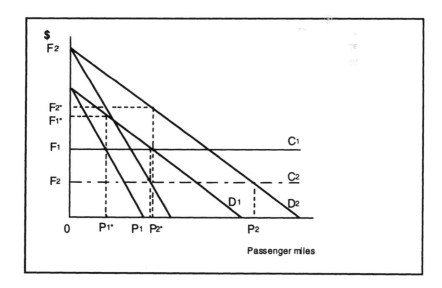

Figure 5.2 *Fares and passenger miles associated with an airline prior to making an alliance and after making an alliance*

Making matters more realistic only strengthens the case that predicting full economic implications of any alliance is extremely difficult. A number of possible outcomes emerge from this simple framework:

- If the market is initially competitive and the alliance has no significant effect on conditions (e.g. two small players enter a large market), full benefits of any cost reductions and service improvements (reflected diagrammatically in enhanced demands) will be passed to consumers. In other words, fares will fall from the old cost related level of F1 to the new cost level of F2, and passenger seat miles will rise from P1 to P2.
- If the market is initially monopolized and the alliance, through a blocked space arrangement[†], brings new players into the game, then both fares may fall and passenger miles increase. Initially, the fare level would be F1* if there was no price discrimination, but it would fall to F2.
- If the alliance gives partners monopoly power on a route previously competitive (associated with all capacity in an international bilateral agreement over landing slots, dominant frequent flyer program, etc.) and they seek to maximize profits, then the outcome will depend on the strategy both adopt. If a single fare approach is used, conventional monopoly theory indicates that fares charged by the airline under review will change to F2* and passenger numbers to P2*. The ultimate fare level may be higher or lower than the original competitive level, depending on the extent the alliance results in cost savings. Equally, the number of passengers may be higher or lower than P1, depending on the elasticities of demand involved.
- Widespread practice of yield management, however, enables carriers 'to price down demand curves' rather than charge a single uniform fare. If there is perfect price discrimination, then the airlines would price differentially to the point where demand meets cost, to a level where it carries P2 passengers. (This gives the same number of passenger miles as the competitive final outcome but all the surplus that users enjoy with competition is translated into airline profits.) In this case, fares would vary between F2[†] and F2. The airline would also benefit by generating additional revenues equal to the area under the demand curve above C2 and to the left of P2.
- The alliance carriers may decide not to maximize monopoly profits from the arrangement as managerial slack emerges (so-called X-inefficiency[8]). In this case, the carrier's cost function may not fall

---

[8]   Technically monopoly can lead to allocative inefficiency (when monopolists whilst managing their undertaking efficiently keep prices above

114

entirely to C2, and the pricing decision not exploit the full potential of price discrimination. The result would be less passenger miles than previous scenarios with reduced revenues going to the carrier.

- While enjoying short term monopoly power, the airline alliance may be concerned that excessive profits could encourage new entry that is difficult to combat. Alternatively, these profits may bring policy responses from the government that might influence their actions. In this case, fares may be set below those associated with the single price monopoly or of yield management[9]. The extent to which this deviation would occur depends on the degree of risk aversion felt by carriers in the alliance.

The above is a gross simplification of reality, but it illustrates some of the problems associated with assessing the implications of alliances, especially from an anti-trust perspective. The situation in practice, however, is more complicated; particularly, aviation is a network industry, and any effect on one link impacts elsewhere on the network[10]. Shifts in demand and costs should also be treated in this matter.

Linked to this are problems in defining the relevant market for analyzing alliances. This issue was not explored in the diagram, but from an anti-trust policy perspective, this is a matter of crucial importance. In many cases, individual routes may have alliance carriers providing services but not enjoying any significant monopoly advantage. There may be competition from a variety of indirect alternatives, or the service itself may act only as one element in a wider complex network where many different routings exist.

Figure 5.3 is a simple illustration of the types of issues in assessing the economic effects.

If an alliance involves carriers operating between A and B which results in a monopoly position along this route, then the actual degree they can exercise power depends on a variety of factors. For example, if there are indirect services between A and B via C or D or even F, then airline demand services will be conditional on what happens along these alternatives.

---

the competitive level or output below it); Posner inefficiency (when monopolists use their rents to protect their positions, for example by lobbying or holding under-used slots) and X-inefficiency (when a supplier does not manage the undertaking so as to minimize costs at each potential level of output).

[9]   This is known as 'limit pricing'.

[10]   The economics of networks is complex; for a survey see Economides (1996).

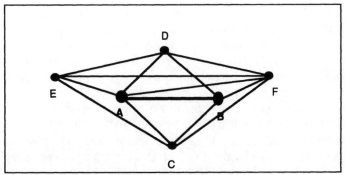

Figure 5.3 *Network implications of airline alliances*

If the link between A and B forms only part of many longer trips involving travel between A and F for example, then the number of options to travelers becomes even larger. They may avoid the link by a direct flight from A to F or on other, alternative indirect routes via C or D. If the services between A and B are used frequently in more complex travel patterns involving several inter-changes as one link in a trip from E to F, the number of possible, competitive options is increased.

The situation in Figure 5.3 relates to a point-specific route alliance (namely between A and B). A strategic alliance poses more complex problems in defining relevant markets for public policy purposes. By co-ordinating activities across a network, airlines forming in a strategic alliance may be in a position to influence fares and service quality on the indirect routes that potentially compete for traffic in A to B services. This could occur, for example, if partners were dominant hub carriers at these two airports.

Whether such an alliance is against the public interest would depend if efficiency gains outweigh efforts by the airlines to extract supernormal profits (i.e. those beyond a normal rate of return on an investment). In turn, this is often determined by the exact details of an alliance. If it is the blocked space variety where each carrier buys space on the other planes, then even if the alliance were a monopolist in a market, competition between members within the aircraft themselves could keep fares to a level of workable competition[11].

Strategic alliance arrangements involving a degree of market segmentation where, despite prior hub dominance, competition existed

---

[11]   Workable competition involves an imperfectly competitive situation but one that cannot be improved upon for such reasons as high transactions costs or inadequate knowledge by government intervention.

before are less likely to provide consumer benefits. These will not occur unless the activities coordinated by the airlines significantly reduce costs or there is significant countervailing power exercised by potential new market entries or the threat of government regulations tempers the strategic alliance's fare setting strategies.

Even if a threat of entry remains, cooperative undertakings may contain competitive implications when actions reduce their costs. By adopting limited price strategies below what small, independent suppliers can offer, it still is in excess of their own costs. In other cases, undertakings may set prices to attain a reasonable return for shareholders, but, at the same time, not maximize them; essentially, management aims to create conditions subject to less competitive stress.

There is also a theory suggesting that airline alliance cooperation introduces stability into markets where excessive competition would discourage adequate supply. The commitment to provide scheduled services encourages them to price down short-run marginal costs, although this does not allow them sufficient income to cover fixed costs. Knowing this, many otherwise efficient carriers will not enter the market.

5.3.2 Airlines and alliances

In terms of specific advantages for engaging in alliances, a listing would embrace such factors as:

- Access to new markets by tapping into a partner's under-utilized route rights or slots;
- Traffic feed into established gateways to increase load factors and to improve yield;
- Defense of current markets through seat capacity management of the shared operations; and
- Costs and economies of scale through resource pooling across operational areas or cost centers, such as sales and marketing, station and ground facilities, maintenance and purchasing.

Such lists, however, often hide the more detailed reasons for airlines cooperating.

5.3.2.1 Cost savings. Many elements of a strategic alliance involve a degree of coordination between carriers' activities that, in turn, can lead to cost savings. This was the driving force behind aircraft maintenance alliances developed in Europe in the late 1960s and subsequent consortia formations to develop CRSs. Cost savings are also a major factor in alliance development from the west and in other developing parts of the world (e.g. LufthansaÕs links with Air China and British Airways with China Southern). The far eastern countries sought quick and cost effective methods of improving their air transport industries, while the Europeans wanted to gain new market penetration.

Airline alliances motivated by cost reducing considerations may be viewed as a way for carriers to reap economies of scale, density and scope without the rigidities and uncertainties that accompany full mergers. Savings may result from the sharing of common ground facilities and improved scheduling. Bulk purchasing by the Global Excellence Alliance (Singapore Airlines, Delta and Swissair) are estimated to generate up to $21 million a year in savings for them. Many smaller airports, for instance, have excess baggage handling and check-in facilities that can be utilized by a larger operation.

Blocked space arrangements, whereby airlines consolidate flights and sell space on each other's planes, can lead to lower unit costs by utilizing better an aircraft's seating capacity or rationalizing the number of flights required to carry a given number of passengers. Even without this, scheduling changes reduce the number of required flights to provide a certain level of service. After forming their alliance, United Airlines and Lufthansa consolidated their trans-Atlantic services into fewer flights.

Yet there are more difficult trade-offs when considering mergers rather than the looser forms of airline alliances. While mergers offer efficiency from reduced managerial overheads and tighter controls over duplicated costs, initial transaction costs can be high because of such things as redundancy pay to staff. Mergers also take up liquidity in payments for equity holdings, which weaken balance sheets and pose problems if the sector moves into recession.

5.3.2.2 Market penetration and retention. Strategic alliances are also seen as important on the demand side. Carriers view the economies of market presence as a strong contributor to the revenues they enjoy. A traditional argument is that a carrier's profits increase faster than its market share, so by combining their assets, partners may therefore anticipate a rise in their combined revenue.

Additional traffic resulting from lower fares may accompany lower costs associated with an alliance, as Northwest and KLM has claimed (Gellman Research Associates, 1994). More importantly, a wider range of options, in terms of both flights and final destinations offered, provides potential consumers with a large number of products to choose from. Seamless schedule coordination and the *de facto* service image created enhances their

118

effect, as does the availability of common airport lounge facilities and joint frequent flyer programs.

In practice, strategic alliances benefit from network values because of the range of options offered to potential travelers. The USAir/British Airways alliance created a network which, in theory, could serve 17,000 city pairs, and the Northwest/KLM alliance created a network of 36,450 city pairs. Equally, the Singapore International Airlines/Delta/Swissair alliance can serve 300 cities.

Predictions of future demand patterns suggest that alliances may also serve a second market penetration in terms of allowing airlines to expand out of geographical markets where growth is forecasted to be slower (mainly North America and Western Europe). Global reach becomes important in this context, and alliances permit this process to be pursued in a flexible manner. From a negative perspective, the fear exists that not being a member of a global alliance leaves individual carriers isolated and at a competitive disadvantage. This is an important consideration in an industry where profit margins are notoriously thin.

There is also a question of image. Smaller airlines, such as British Midland, have been developing a wide range of code-sharing alliances to give the impression they are a much larger carrier. Franchising is a more direct way of tying a small carrier to one with an established reputation. On the other hand, Delta, after taking over Pan American's Atlantic routes, lacked the image of its predecessor, so it rapidly entered into alliances with better image European operating partners that enjoyed dominance in their own markets. In a way, these alliances are acting to help some carriers develop a counterbalance for the lack of their own established image.

5.3.2.3 Financial injections. A number of major alliances have come about when one or the other partners were experiencing financial problems. Thus a mechanism was provided, whereby a partner could enjoy a financial injection. The funds made available by SAS to Continental in 1988 allowed the latter to continue its operations until bankruptcy overtook it.

More recently in the formation of the KLM/Northwest and the British Airway/USAir alliances, the European carriers added significant financial contributions to their respective US partners. Within Europe, Swissair assisted the Belgian carrier, Sabina (amounting to Bfr10.5 billion, see Hill, 1996), and in North America, American Airlines injected money to Canadian Airlines. In some cases, the funds came as part of the privatization, as did the 25% stake that British Airways took in the Australian carrier Qantas and the 30% Iberia took in Aerolineas Argentinas.

The introduction of foreign capital into US carriers such as Northwest and USAir also circumvented problems that might have arisen if other financial plans had been pursued. Particularly, if KLM or British Airways had been US carriers, domestic US anti-trust laws would have been considered, and the eventual outcome may well have not been allowed.

5.3.2.4 Infrastructure constraints. As seen earlier in Chapter 4, airport congestion is a problem expected to become worse, especially at major international hubs where traffic is forecast to grow rapidly (see Table 5.5)[12]. A study of European airports by the Stanford Research Institute predicts that by 2010, there will be considerable capacity problems at about half of Europe's airports. While technological developments, investments, and expanded facilities will increase the physical capacity of the infrastructure available, factors such as environmental and safety concerns means that overall growth will likely be slower than demand. Given these constraints, the 50% increase in airport capacity by the end of the century envisaged in the Outline Plan of the Trans European Airport Network is unlikely to materialize (Commission of the European Communities, 1993).

Table 5.5 *Forecast use of top ten airports by 2005*

Airport	Number of passengers (millions)	
	2005 forecast	1995
Hong Kong International	82.0	na
Dallas/Fort Worth International	81.3	56.5
O'Hare International	78.6	67.3
Heathrow	68.1	54.5
Los Angeles	60.2	53.9
Rhein/Main	47.9	38.2
Kimpo International	43.4	30.9
Logan International	42.0	24.4
San Francisco	40.5	36.2
Charles de Gaulle	39.5	28.4

As we have seen, the way in which infrastructure itself is managed is also usually not very helpful. Airports generally have administrative rather than market-based mechanisms for allocating source capacity, especially at their available landing and take-off slots. This poses problems for new entry

[12] Congestion is not in practice a definitive condition. Technical developments, innovative management techniques, changes in pricing and marginal investments can lead to increases in capacity. Much also depends upon how capacity is measured, e.g in terms of passenger or aircraft movements.

and carriers wishing to expand their existing activities. Even if the market indicates their services are the most efficient (as shown by the prices carriers are willing to pay for slots or gates), there are limited ways in which to gain that access. Additionally, there is less incentive for an incumbent carrier to maximize slot use if it is protected from competition. As we have shown, at many European airports, there has been a tradition for ground handling services to be provided on a monopolistic basis, often by the dominant-based airline. This pushes up costs, and in Europe the expense of handling a charter 737-400 varies from 600 ECU to over 2,400 ECU.

The EU has attempted to reduce such problems. It introduced limited measures requiring independent companies to run local scheduling committees, and for slots not used for 80% of the time to be put back for reallocation, with 50% available to new entrants (Council Regulation (EEC) 95/93). It has also sought to introduce more competition into ground handling as well.

Alliances allow entry to capacity constrained markets by permitting new carriers to buy blocks of space on incumbent aircraft or schedule services using fewer, larger aircraft. Not only does this allow more competitors to service a particular route, but by taking competition inside rather than between planes, it stimulates the use of larger aircraft and reduces the number of plane movements for any given passenger flow[13].

5.3.2.5 Circumventing institutional constraints. While reforms are taking place, international aviation is still largely controlled by a series of bilateral agreements between national governments, with approximately 1,200 at present. While Member States of the EU, for instance, have effectively given up their rights to control air traffic with partners and opted instead for a regional multilateral system and others, especially those involved with the US, have very liberal external bilateral agreements, in many other markets bilateral agreements are still extremely restrictive, reserving rights for specific carriers and controlling fares. Many alliances allow partner carriers to offer services to cities to which they often do not have traffic rights. This can apply to direct services but is also applicable to traffic that goes beyond an initial gateway airport.

Bilateral controls are often supplemented and reinforced by limitations whereby foreign ownership is permitted in national airlines. Within the framework of allowable foreign investment, there are limits on governance

---

[13]   This is one reason why British Airways and American Airlines were willing in 1997 to make some concessions regarding giving up Heathrow slots in their arguments to the UK and US authorities concerning their code-sharing proposals.

that non-nationals may exercise over airline control in which they have invested.

In addition to limitations directly existing in bilateral service agreements and foreign ownership, there are a range of other institutional factors involving such things as ground handling rights, slot access and operational controls that directly impede entry or make it costly into aviation markets. Code sharing and similar alliances with airlines based in countries with such restrictions can help reduce the problems involved in such instances.

This bilateral structure of agreements, combined with the inability to conduct cabotage in many countries and other market entry impediments, has led airlines into seeking ways to circumvent institutional barriers to trade (Kasper, 1988). Entering into an alliance with a carrier who has significant restrictions on its ability to serve the markets permits, at the very least, the opportunity to more fully utilize the capacity that is allowed. Indeed, the reason for many international alliances is to circumvent those institutional barriers.

5.3.2.6 Market stability. Air transport, particularly the provision of extensive scheduled services, is a network industry. As such, it exhibits features suggesting it might be inherently prone to instability and, at the very extreme, to under supply (Telser, 1994).

Essentially, once a service has been scheduled, there is every incentive for the airline to fill their seats, provided the marginal cost of carrying extra passengers is exceeded by the revenue generated. However, this can mean there is insufficient revenue contributing to the long-term costs of the aircraft and other assets. As a result, services will eventually be withdrawn. In the extreme theoretical case, carriers would have perfect foresight and not even bother entering the market and thus, insufficient capacity would be offered by the airlines. Technically, economists refer to this idea as the empty core case.

To remain in network markets where the potential for such instability exists or to even enter in the first place, carriers may try insulating themselves from the extremes of competition. Frequent flyer programs or corporate discounts may be a way of trying to retain customers. By uniting with other carriers, problems with excessive competition may be reduced even further. Extending networks and service attributes with the introduction of code sharing allows capacity to be filled more completely and with greater certainty. Blocked space arrangements offer the greatest flexibility on the supply side.

Isolating the types of environment where alliances are formed for combating market instabilities rather than market exploitation is difficult.

To date, analysis has relied on indicative and almost anecdotal evidence (Button, 1996b; Smith, 1995). This issue will be explored further in Chapter 7.

5.4   THE PUBLIC POLICY RESPONSE

International airline alliances have only been possible because of the actions, or sometimes inactions, of national governments. These have on occasions actively assisted in the formation of an alliance, while in other cases, they have removed particular obstacles. The situation has not, though, been universally positive and in some cases governments have acted to prevent an alliance forming or to radically restructure a proposed alliance.

Airline mergers have posed particular problems for the authorities, although, in general, their attitude has been sympathetic. Following the US 1978 Airline Deregulation Act, the US Department of Transportation, who took responsibility for mergers policies, did little to contain the airline rationalization which took place. In 1984, for example, 90% of the US domestic market was operated by 15 carriers, but by 1989, this number had dropped to only 8. A similar story of concentration also emerges from Canada.

The European situation has been slightly different; a combination of flag carriers protected by national governments and by the competition policies of the EU and national authorities has acted together to limit mergers.

Where mergers have taken place, it has generally involved airlines of the same country (e.g. British Airways and British Caledonian, and Air France, UTA and Air Inter). But even those mergers have been limited by public policy as newly merged undertakings are denuded of certain routes if others feel it leads to the potential of monopoly power being exploited. In the French situation, the Commission of the EU insisted that 8 domestic and 50 international routes be transferred to other carriers, Air France divest itself of the 35% stake it held in TAT European Airlines, and slots be made available at Paris' Charles de Gaulle Airport for independent carriers wishing to serve domestic markets.

As highlighted earlier, cross-border mergers are rare due to strong institutional barriers, while cross-equity holdings are much more common. In many cases, there are strong institutional barriers to cross-border mergers of airlines. The US allows a maximum 25% voting share holding in any American airline, and two-thirds of the board must be US citizens. Within the EU, the third package of liberalizing measures reduced this problem for intra-European aviation. Difficulties, however, extend beyond these strict legal limits of ownership. Existing international bilateral agreements often involve clauses specifying the nationality of carriers, and mergers between different nationalities invalidates some of these agreements.

As with mergers, the emergence of strategic alliances, especially code-sharing, has brought an explicit public policy response. Since 1987, the US Department of Transportation has required all code-shares be registered for annual agency approval[14]. In practice, however, few agreements have been rejected, although some were reviewed by the Department of Justice.

Much of the early concern about code-sharing centered on the need to protect consumers from being misled by a code-sharing alliance and codes-of-practice were investigated to ensure that potential passengers were aware of the carrier actually transporting them (Shenton, 1994; *Avmark Aviation Economist*, 1995).

More generally, public policy efforts have ensured that code-sharing arrangements do not misinform or disadvantage passengers. This involves not only issues where individuals have information on exact airlines traveled, but it extends to such things as responsibility for missed connections, directions to connecting flights and ensuring appropriate information systems are available at airports. To prevent 'screen padding' on CRS systems, the EU limits code-shared flights to being displayed twice. The US has no such policy, but what they do is inform passengers, via airlines, of the actual carrier on which they travel. The European Civil Aviation Conference (ECAC) has a similar code for disclosure, but it is not legally binding on member states.

Another feature of the alliance movement, the gradual globalization of the international airline industry, poses particular problems in the formulation of public policy. Despite the existence of several international agencies, it is still largely conducted on a national basis. Even where regional blocks have emerged, most notably in Europe, external aviation still remains within the domain of individual countries. Bodies such as the ICAO have been effective in improving and maintaining technical standards in civil aviation, but they have exercised limited powers over the function of these international air transport markets. Equally, GATS coverage can be marginal at best.

---

[14]   This stems largely from a code-sharing alliance between United Airlines and British Airways that proposed code sharing on United flights in the Chicago-Seattle market as an extension of its London-Chicago service; British Airways already having route authority on the London-Chicago-Seattle route. In fact the US Department of Transportation granted exemption early in the following year.

Public policy towards airline alliances will continue being difficult because of the poor data available to public policy makers. Even if alliances are generally beneficial to travelers, public authorities require monitoring development, as with any other rapidly changing sector of the economy. There is also a need to keep the public informed about trends in an intermediate industry that has important knock-on effects on sectors such as tourism and on trade and location matters.

Obtaining necessary information in a consistent format requires national initiatives and international cooperation. It must also be accomplished efficiently to minimize the burden on the air transport sector itself. Initially, this means it should be clear just exactly what policy issues are relevant. In anti-trust terms, the parameters of any concern, such as definitions of the market area under consideration, must be clearly identified. In the international context, though, this is often not the case; not only are there national variations in anti-trust controls, but even within countries, divergent views exist between responsible agencies on these matters.

More recently, a number of important events at the international level have resulted in a complex set of public issues and pressures developing regarding air transport:

- Rapid growth, combined with widespread measures of market liberalization, has meant that international airline alliances are being used by carrierss as a mechanism to circumvent remaining institutional constraints on their activities. While sound theoretical economic reasons may exist for removing many long-standing restrictions embodied in bilateral air service agreements, public authorities are concerned that alliances in some markets may affect the nature and speed of institutional changes in other places. Policy makers must consider distribution implications as well as pure efficiency criteria in their actions to make sure alliances do not have major adverse distribution implications.
- Increasing alliances of more than two carriers leads to problems of jurisdiction and policy conflicts. As in the case of aviation and elsewhere, policy formulation generally becomes more difficult as the number of interested parties increases.
- Some recent alliances have embraced very large actors. The early days of code-sharing linking smaller carriers with larger ones has extended into mega-carrier alliances. This poses larger problems and naturally attracts more public attention. Large airlines who oppose those formed by other major carriers have greater resources to make their case vocally heard. The actions of Virgin Atlantic in late 1996 against British Airways and American Airlines provides testament to this.

- Code sharing has become more complex and extends across a wide range of interactive relationships. This introduces complicated policy questions, not only in terms of the effects of each new element in an alliance, but also their combined effects as well. This can complicate more traditional concerns about consumer protection as it did concerning anti-trust immunity for some US alliances.
- For the first time, freer trade has embraced explicit consideration of matters pertaining to international aviation. This can be seen in the, albeit limited, number of air transport topics covered by the World Trade Organization's remit under the General Agreement in Trade in Services.

Despite this surge of interest, policy response has still generally been favorable until recently. The situation has been changing as the alliance movement has become more widespread and complex. For example, strategic alliances, particularly those involving EU carriers with significant North Atlantic activities, are seeking more anti-trust immunity from US authorities. Such immunity has only been given in a limited number of cases. Even then, conditions are attached - see Table 5.6.

Equally, the European perspective is changing. While the initial strategic airline alliances caused some concern to the EU authorities, especially when they embraced on a unilateral basis the introduction of the US-inspired Open Skies bilateral agreements, their scale was relatively minor when contrasted with the recent efforts of British Airways and American Airlines to initiate code sharing. The more extensive alliances also have greater implications for infrastructure policy within Europe.

The announcement by British Airways and American Airlines in June, 1996 that they intended to form a code-sharing alliance the following year brought with it a somewhat confused set of policy signals.[15] The UK-US market with 12 million passengers annually is also twice the German-US market and three times the size of the France-US market (Table 5.7). It is therefore a very important market *per se*. The large size of the airlines, their market share on North Atlantic routes (about 60% of scheduled passenger

---

[15]   The alliance would involve: (i) the coordination of passenger and cargo activities between the US and Europe, with revenue pooled according to the profitability of routes; (ii) code-sharing, where permitted, across both airlines' global network of about 36,000 city pairs; and (iii) the establishment of a fully reciprocal, worldwide frequent flyer program. There would be no exchange of equity or other forms of cross-share holding. The arrangement would be for at least six years.

traffic between the US and UK[16]), the importance of Heathrow as a hub airport, combined with complex interrelationships with bilateral air service negotiations, made the issue even more challenging.

Table 5.6 *Conditions attached to international alliances by the US Department of Transportation*

United/Lufthansa
- No coordination of certain fares and capacity for local US point of sale passengers on Chicago-Frankfurt and Washington-Frankfurt.
- Withdrawal from all IATA activities affecting prices on US-Germany routes, US-Netherlands routes and routes between the US and home bases of other " immunized" carriers.
- Requirements to file subsidiary and subsequent agreements, plus O&D survey.

Delta/Swissair/Sabena/Austrian
- Limitations on integration of service and fare coordination on Atlanta-Brussels, Atlanta-Zurich and Cincinnati-Zurich (however, promotional and most restricted fares are not limited).
- Review within 18 months, and in coordination with the Department of Justice, competitive operations on New York-Brussels, New York-Zurich, New York-Geneva and New York-Vienna.
- Withdrawal from all IATA activities affecting prices on US and home bases of other "immunized" carriers.
- Worldspan/Galileo activities excluded from immunity.
- Requirement to file subsidiary and subsequent agreements, with five-year review of alliance agreements, plus O&D survey.

American/Canadian
- Restrictions on fare and capacity coordination on New York-Toronto until February, 1998 (when all carriers gain open entry).
- Exclusion on services to third countries and all-cargo services.
- Tentative approval for CRS coordination.
- Requirement to file subsidiary and subsequent agreements, with five year review of all alliance agreements, plus O&D survey.

The objections of actual and potential UK and US competitors together with some other European carriers serving trans-Atlantic routes, but most notably involving Heathrow, were vocal from the start. Smaller carriers objected on the grounds that the alliance would squeeze them from the market, while other major carriers argued their lack of access to Heathrow Airport would make effective competition impossible. The existing UK/US bilateral agreement (Bermuda II signed in 1977) only allows American

---

[16]   The extent to which such an alliance would dominate actual trans-Atlantic flow of passengers may be much smaller because of the nature of hubbing (*Avmark Aviation Economist*, 1996).

Airlines and United to operate from the main London terminal, and capacity is severely limited.

Table 5.7. *Trans-Atlantic passenger traffic*

US to	Number of Passengers	%
United Kingdom	12,543,084	37.9
Germany	5,865,141	17.7
France	3,866,468	11.7
Netherlands	2,874,381	8.7
Italy	1,921,831	5.8
Switzerland	1,227,504	3.7
Spain	1,130,704	3.4
Ireland	1,037,778	3.1
Belgium	691,290	2.1
Denmark	449,454	1.4
Greece	403,518	1.2
Portugal	327,773	1.0
Finland	381,941	0.9
Sweden	244,666	0.8
Austria	142,516	0.4
Norway	69,525	0.2
Luxembourg	4,556	-
TOTAL	31,785,101	100.0

A number of abstract policy approaches can be isolated.

The UK authorities referred the protected alliance to its Office of Fair Trading to see if the Monopolies and Mergers Commission needed to rule on it.[17] The House of Commons Transport Committee (1996) conducted investigations. The EU Transport Commissioner invoked Article 89 of the EC Treaty that allows examination of actions that could damage competition within the Union. The Commission works with national authorities on the issue. The UK's President of the Board of Trade also concluded that he had a duty under Article 88 of the Rome treaty to investigate possible abuse of dominant power and restrictive agreements. Various US Senate Committees looked into the matter. The UK and US re-opened negotiations on an air service agreement to replace Bermuda II. These

[17]   Under the 1973 Fair Trading Act, a merger in the UK need not involve equity exchanges but concern companies actively becoming indistinct.

negotiations focused on links between possible anti-trust immunity for the alliance and the adoption by the UK of an Open Skies agreement.

Equally, a number of possible compromise solutions have emerged. The UK Office of Fair Trading argued that in order to ensure that what it considered a reasonable degree of competition would emerge, British Airways and American Airlines should relinquish a number of their Heathrow slots. The number suggested was 168 a week. Ninety-eight would be sold, and the others leased or returned to British Airways when other slots became available. This divestiture would affect a total of 12 services, and the result was that the combined US traffic handled by British Airways/ American Airlines would fall to about 50%. The stance of the EU Competition Directorate, however, has been that the alliance would be anti-competitive and therefore automatically violate EU competition policies. It also objects to the idea that airport slots should be sold or leased, arguing that they should, under EU laws, be relinquished.

The US General Accounting Office (1997) looked at the number of additional slots required by competing US airlines to ensure that there would be sufficient competition after the formation of the alliance. While not specifying an exact number the Office argues that at least 23 additional round-trip services would be needed linking Heathrow to various US airports. While some of these slots would be made available through normal allocation mechanisms some would have to come from British Airways and American Airlines' current holdings.

6. Alliances and Markets

Considering the scale and the controversy often surrounding the formation of international strategic airline alliances, relatively little rigorous empirical analysis has been completed in looking at real world implications[1].

What has been done tends to focus on North Atlantic strategic alliances and short term implications for the carriers involved and immediate competitors. An early assessment is found in Oster and Pickrell (1986), but the main body of work includes two major US studies (Gellman Research Associates, 1994; US General Accounting Office, 1995), analysis by the UK authorities (UK Civil Aviation Authority, 1994) and several academic studies (Pustay, 1992; Dresner *et al*, 1995; Dresner and Windle, 1996; Youssef and Hansen, 1994).

Much is US in origin, reflecting both the country's tradition of undertaking quantitative analysis as part of its policy making processes as well as an explicit concern about the position of its aviation sector traditionally seen as a dominant force in world markets[2]. However, the performance of its carriers in the trans-Atlantic markets has been variable since the adoption of an Open Skies philosophy (see Table 6.1).

The vast bulk of the limited empirical information available on airline alliances relates to the large strategic alliances. More common, point-specific ones have been ignored, although for individual markets these may be important. Equally, an airline with a number of individual alliances over a range of routes could potentially have more control over its market than if

---

[1]   There is, however, a growing number of what might be termed adversarial studies produced for public hearings regarding airlines alliances (e.g. regarding the British Airways/ American Airlines alliances, see; UK House of Commons Transport Committee, 1996).

[2]   There is also the data consideration that the US has traditionally collected a significant amount of information from its carriers. The situation varies considerably across EU states and Eurostat is only now developing a consistent data base.

it were involved in a single alliance. A many-carrier alliance, however, is less transparent, and for this reason, is likely to have received the same attention as the larger ones.

Table 6.1 *US airlines' share of European-US traffic*

	1980	1984	1988	1992
United Kingdom	55%	61%	56%	46%
Germany	46%	48%	53%	57%
France	48%	54%	62%	68%
Netherlands	7%	7%	11%	21%

One reason for an overall lack of empirical analysis is that assessment is seldom simple. As we saw in Chapter 5, alliances are often multi-dimensional, with wide-ranging spatial and temporal effects that impact differently on many groups. While an aggregate assessment of the economic implications of airline alliances can be important, it is the incidence of costs and benefits, particularly on groups or geographical areas, which affects public policy the most. Distribution effects can also be cut in several ways. Policy concern may revolve about relative benefits and costs affecting consumers as opposed to airlines, but equally, it may also be influenced by the combined implications for a nation's own air carriers and passengers.

6.1   THE AIRLINES

Strategic alliances can affect participant incumbent carriers, competitors outside an alliance, and potential market entrants. While overall societal implications could prove positive, an alliance may be deemed undesirable because of distribution implications among the airlines, particularly so if adverse effects are felt by initially weak carriers.

One particular concern is that an alliance can result in airport domination to the detriment of new entry and other, incumbent carriers. The situation in the US is that many of the hub airports have since 1978 become dominated by a single carrier (see Table 6.2). International terminals in most countries are somewhat different to the domestic hubs in the US. Since most international traffic has grown up under rigid bilateral air service agreements, the incumbent national carriers seldom have 50% of the available capacity.

Table 6.2 *Share of enplanements of the dominant carrier at concentrated US hub airports*

Airport	1978		1993	
	Share	Carrier	Share	Carrier
Atlanta	49.7	Delta	83.5	Delta
Charlotte	74.8	Eastern	94.6	US Air
Cincinnati	35.1	Delta	89.8	Delta
Dayton	35.3	TWA	40.5	US Air
Denver	32.0	United	51.8	United
Detroit	21.7	American	74.8	Northwest
Greensboro	64.5	Eastern	44.9	USAir
Memphis	42.2	Delta	76.3	Northwest
Minneapolis-St. Paul	31.7	Northwest	80.6	Northwest
Nashville	28.5	American	69.8	American
Pittsburgh	46.7	Allegheny	88.9	US Air
Raleigh-Durham	74.2	Eastern	80.4	American
St. Louis	39.4	TWA	60.4	TWA
Salt Lake City	39.6	Western	71.4	Delta
Syracuse	40.5	Allegheny	49.5	US Air

Source: Calculations from enplanement data in Federal Aviation Administration, *Airport Activity Statistics of the Certificated Route Air Carriers* (US Department of Transportation, various years).

Since strategic alliances affect both traffic generation and traffic distribution, predicting the ultimate traffic share enjoyed by any alliance at a hub airport is difficult. The estimates that have been made involving the major alliances suggest, however, that the eventual outcome will not result in the degree of concentration that has taken place at US airports. Table 6.3 offers some estimates.

Studies of the North Atlantic alliances, especially those involving government agencies instead of academics, have paid close attention to distribution implications since they involve carriers from the US and Europe. They have inevitably focused on the effects of existing alliances on their carriers and existing competitors.

The earliest studies, undertaken by academics, explored the implications on the structure of the industry and, to a more limited extent, sought out the elements that lead to the creation of successful alliances. More recent work tends to be more case specific with, for example, Dresner *et al* (1995) focused on the Continental/SAS, Delta/Swissair and Northwest/KLM equity alliances up to 1989.

Table 6.3 *Proportion of scheduled passenger departures at main base airports (1995)*

Airline	Airport	Share of Departures	With Alliance*
British Airways	London Heathrow	38%	42%
Lufthansa	Frankfurt	59%	63%
KLM	Amsterdam	41%	59%
Air France	Paris CDG	44%	53%
SAS	Copenhagen	53%	63%
Delta Airlines	Atlanta	56%	74%

* Figures are the total number of departures of the airline, its alliance partners and code-sharing arrangements.

Source: Official Airline Guide, 1995.

A number of hypotheses were tested by Dresner *et al* (1995). They were concerned with; examining the extent partners strengthened an alliance when adjusting their international route structures to emphasize hub-to-hub routes, the extent to which an alliance would draw passengers from non-aligned competitors, and the effects of alliances on load factors. Differing features were isolated that characterized each alliance (Table 6.4), and it was found that those associated with the Northwest/KLM arrangement generated the greatest advantages in terms of increasing load factors, market share and realignment of strategies.

The US Department of Transportation awarded a contract to a consulting firm, Gellman Research Associates (GRA), to examine international airline code sharing[3]. Their study looked at the USAir/British Airways and the Northwest/KLM alliances. The approach adopted involves an econometric model that attempts to reflect the way consumers select an

[3]   This study should be set in the context of mounting criticism of the degree to which the US Department of Transportation was then evaluating alliances. For example the US General Accounting Office (1995) contains this assessment of the US position:

Our work over the past few years indicates that DOT [Department of Transportation] has not collected nor analyzed the information necessary to conduct sufficient economic analysis of proposed deals that revise bilateral agreements or to monitor the changing competitive conditions in the international market place. This has occurred largely because of several data limitations as well as the fact that DOT in the past placed little value on conducting economic analysis prior to key negotiations.

airline[4]. The model's parameters were estimated for the first quarter of 1994, a time when the Northwest/KLM alliance had matured but also when the implications of the USAir/British Airways alliance were still evolving.

Table 6.4 *The impacts of the early strategic international airline alliances*

	Continental/SAS	Delta/Swissair	Northwest/KLM
Carriers realigned their route networks to take advantage of alliance partners' hubs	Yes	No	Yes
The traffic increase for the alliance was greater than the average North Atlantic traffic growth	No	Yes	Yes
The traffic increase for the alliance on routes between the US and the partner's country was greater than the overall market growth between the US and the alliance partner's country	No	Yes	No
Load factors increased for both alliance carriers overall on trans-Atlantic routes	No	No	Yes

Source: Dresner *et al* (1995)

The results were estimates of the impact of alliances on the revenues, costs and profits of the partner carriers involved and other airlines serving common routes (see Table 6.5). GRS concluded that alliances generated benefits both for the airlines involved and for passengers as well. It was calculated that USAir/British Airways and Northwest/KLM increased their market shares on code-sharing routes by 8% and 10% respectively. In the case of British Airways, this represented $27.2 million of additional net revenue, and for USAir, $5.6 million. For Northwest, the strategic alliance was estimated to benefit them by $16.1 million annually and KLM by $10.6 million.

[4]   A standard discrete choice model was used at the level of the individual decision-maker to examine the probability that an individual will select a particular airline. It was applied to 117 markets in which code sharing was practiced on 76; including 37 by Northwest/KLM and 22 by USAir/British Airways. Logit models were deployed for estimation purposes.

Table 6.5 *Estimated implications of the USAir/British Airways and Northwest/KLM code sharing arrangements in 1994 ($ million)*

Airline	Revenue	Cost	Net Profit	Consumer Benefit	Social Benefit
USAir/BA alliance					
USAir	7.9	-2.3	5.6		
Other US carriers	-41.7	14.9	-26.7		
US total	-33.8	12.6	-21.1	4.9	-16.2
British Airways	45.8	-18.6	27.2		
Other non-US carriers	-1.3	0.5	-0.8		
Non-US total	44.5	-18.1	26.4	5.4	31.8
Grand total	10.7	-5.5	5.3	10.3	15.0
Northwest/KLM alliance					
Northwest	24.6	-8.5	16.1		
Other US carriers	-25.6	9.9	-15.7		
US total	-1.0	1.4	0.4	13.0	13.4
KLM	18.6	-8.0	10.6		
Other non-US carriers	-16.5	7.9	-8.6		
Non-US total	2.1	-0.1	2.0	14.1	16.1
Grand total	1.1	1.3	2.4	27.1	29.5

Source: Gellman Research Associates (1994)

While the study concluded that the benefits enjoyed by the alliance partners and passengers in terms of lower fares and improved services was the result of efficiency improvements, there were distributional implications of other carriers losing traffic and revenue.

A later study by the US General Accounting Office (1995) took a somewhat different approach. Rather than attempt to produce a detailed econometric model of the market, accountancy and other data over relevant sub-markets was combined with interview information and insights. The approach was broader, although lacking in the technical detail of the earlier analysis.

Table 6.6 provides a summary of the General Accounting Office study. As with the GRS analysis, those airlines participating in alliances have benefited, albeit to varying degrees. Some gains came from generated traffic, but a significant amount of transfers came from non-alliance carriers. In the Northwest/KLM alliance, for instance, Continental Airlines lost about $1 million in revenue in 1994 as a result of having to compete.

The GAO study also points to a number of new (or reintroduced) international services as a result of alliances involving US carriers. These include non-stop services between Zurich and Cincinnati (Delta/Swissair); European services to Memphis (Northwest/KLM), non-stop services between Houston and Rome (Continental/Alitalia) and direct services between Vienna and Washington (Delta/Austrian Airways).

The study also highlights that some alliances, by coordinating services of member airlines, now offer more choice of carriers and routes. Three alternative services available between Indianapolis and Lyon were cited by way of illustration.

Table 6.6 *General Accounting Office estimates of the impacts of US alliances*

Northwest/KLM
- $125 million to $175 million in increased revenues to Northwest Airlines in 1994 as a result of the alliance, representing 1/3 of Northwest's trans-Atlantic revenues and 5% of its international passenger revenue.
- $100 million in increased revenues to KLM in 1994 as a result of the alliance, representing 18% of KLM's trans-Atlantic revenues and 3% of its international passenger revenues.
- An increase in combined trans-Atlantic market share to 11.5% to 7%, attributed to the alliance.

US Air/British Airways
- $20 million in additional revenues to US Air in 1994 due to the alliance.
- $100 million in increased revenues to British Airways between April, 1994 and March, 1995, representing 5% of its revenues to and from the US and 1% of its international revenues.

United Airlines/Lufthansa
- An increase in traffic to United of 600 passengers per day attributed to the alliance.

United Airlines/Ansett Australia
- An increase in traffic to United of 120 passengers per day, representing $14 million in additional revenues due to alliance, accounting for less than 1% of United's trans-Pacific revenues.

United Airlines/British Midlands
- An increase in trans-Atlantic passengers to United of 30,000 per year and to British Midland of 25,000 per year, attributed to the alliance.

Source: Dresner and Windle (1996)

6.2 SOCIAL COSTS AND BENEFITS

6.2.1 Environmental concerns

While the question is asked from the perspective of individual carriers, national governments, and alliances of 'who gains and who loses?' wider social implications exist about overall efficiency matters and the impact of alliances on non-users of air services.

Aviation, as with other economic activities, has environmental repercussions. The degree and impact to which air transport impinges on the environment is still far from fully understood, but some initial observations can be made. As a mode of passenger transport, air transport is slightly less fuel efficient than the auto but offers significant benefits in terms of time savings over longer distances (Table 6.7). By consolidating one or more carriers' traffic, alliances can increase the load factors of aircraft and lead to using larger planes over any given route. This will reduce average fuel costs per passenger and may be one factor to help cope with the forecasted future traffic volumes without a massive increase in flight frequency.

Consolidation of flights may also prove beneficial for those living around airports. Because of the noise of take offs and landings, they are focal points for environmental concerns, and the ability to expand capacity in the face of environmental lobbies and financial constraints has already proved difficult in many countries (Perl *et al*, 1997).

These wider, less direct industrial effects of airline alliances have been seldom explored to date, but they may take on a much more significant role, given public concerns regarding environmental protection.

Table 6.7 *Relative fuel consumption of air transport*

	Energy per pkm (MJ/pkm)	Average Speed (km/hour)	Energy use per travel hour (MJ/hour)
Aviation	2.2	500	1100
HSR	0.7	150	106
Intercity train	0.7	80	56
Car	1.5	50	75

6.2.2 Safety issues

Mainly because of the potential severity of any major incident, aviation safety attracts a considerable amount of public attention. The incentive for any airline is to provide safe services, since business would suffer if the accident rate (perceived or real) exceeded the net benefits. Safety is one attribute potential customers and investors consider when making decisions. This inherent market pressure is boosted by regulations and codes of conduct imposed by EU national governments and international agencies. Their involvement is justified since market imperfections make it impossible for potential passengers to understand fully the risks. Even if information is adequate, passengers have insufficient market power to ensure levels of safety are optimized.

One way of looking at air transport safety is to consider it in terms of incentives that influence the actions of those providing air transport services. Essentially, the function takes the form:

$$S = f(E, G, I) + \varepsilon \tag{6.1}$$

where:
- S reflects the safety standard level adopted by an airline;
- E reflects the private economic incentive to be safe (e.g. reputation, insurance premiums, lost business, share price and the interest of flight personnel);
- G represents government safety codes and policies (e.g. aircraft safety features, maintenance standards and crews' working hours and conditions); and
- I represents infrastructure considerations (e.g. airport design and air traffic control).

There is an additional random element in the function ε, indicating the risk of something else, such as a missile or bomb, causing the accident (Moses and Savage, 1990)[5].

As for safety, there is no reason to assume it is socially desirable for an airline to be 100% safe even if that were technically possible. Opportunity costs are associated with devoting resources to safety. It is apparent from individuals' choices considering such things as how fast they drive and their choices regarding car versus air travel, that they continually make trade-offs

---

[5]   While the variables that fit in the right side of the equation may be expressed as independent factors, in practice, they will exhibit some degree of correlation. The nature of infrastructure provision is inevitably linked to the safety regulatory regimes adopted by authorities. Internal economic incentives influencing an airline's pursuit of safety cannot be completely separated from the institutional regime within which the carrier operates. Nevertheless, a three-way division is helpful in tying together implications of globalization and strategic alliances associated with aviation safety considerations.

of safety against other attributes of travel such as speed or costs. Indeed, many have argued that aviation is excessively safe, and if better information were available about relative safety records, society would focus less resources into it (Kahn, 1988).

In equation 6.1, changes in the structure of the industry, including the creation of strategic alliances, can have an influence in terms of operations and the ways authorities respond to them. What is not at present is a body of empirical evidence linking alliances to safety questions. Alliances are too new for detailed statistical analysis, and short term fluctuations in accident rates involving small incidents does not make for easy econometric work. What must be relied on instead are parallel aviation development experiences influencing the sector's structure and anecdotal evidence from the experiences of alliances to date.

6.2.2.1 Aggregate air travel demand. As claimed in a number of studies, significant consumer benefits are generated when alliances are controlled within an appropriate, possibly minimalist, economic regulatory regime. The economies enjoyed by carriers, combined with service enhancements and lower fares for users, have led to more air travel, a reflection of enhanced consumer surplus. This occurs when carriers do not excessively exploit monopoly powers associated with market strength that alliances could potentially generate.

According to arguments presented by Boeing in 1996[6], additional air travel will in the future lead to more aviation accidents. The economic efficiency associated with many alliances and the accompanying new traffic generated also inevitably increases the potential for even more incidents simply by virtue of there being more people at risk. Public policy (G in equation 6.1) inevitably responds to this type of situation. In the US, for example, the Federal Aviation Administration (FAA) has begun releasing more information in an effort to better inform the public, although the complexity of safety issues suggests that such information, in practice, does not offer great insights.

In terms of I in equation 6.1, the provision and use of aviation infrastructure may be changed as alliances go. We know that many EU airports and air traffic systems are working at or above their design capacity and often use out-dated technologies. There will be pressure, both from an air transport perspective and safety standpoint, to ensure existing infrastructure is better used and new infrastructure provided where justified.

[6]   The Boeing forecasts of traffic are mainly extrapolative with some scenario analysis to improve their sensitivity. They do not explicitly allow for the growth in alliances, although the latter may lead to more traffic.

This type of response is related to the number of incidents, however, rather than the existence of alliances *per se*.

There is, however, another perspective. The opportunity cost element is missing from many calculations on the implications of increased demand for enhanced safety. If individuals did not travel by air, they would engage in other activities with an attached safety aspect. Therefore, it is not altogether clear that more air travel would necessarily result in more deaths and injuries in aggregate.

Little empirical work has been conducted into this aspect of airline safety. What limited amount there is relates to US domestic airline liberalization after the 1978 Airline Deregulation Act. On many routes where US airlines compete with automobile travel, the diversion effect as the result of improved services offered by airlines reduced the number of road deaths. Inherent problems in defining counterfactuals make the calculations difficult, but Bylow and Savage (1991) estimate some 275 highway fatalities were avoided by the modal switches to air travel.

Not only are US estimates tentative for technical reasons, but the extrapolation to strategic alliances poses its own difficulties. While alliances involve new fare structures, services and modal transfers along routes involving EU carriers, focus is on long distance travel (often over oceans) where commercial aviation is the only viable transport option. What alliances do within these narrow confines is induce travelers from carriers outside of alliances. This was seen in the studies of the North Atlantic market cited earlier where KLM/Northwest and British Airways/USAir demonstrably took traffic from competitors. From a safety perspective, the issue becomes one of discovering whether carriers are safer than their non-alliance counterparts. This issue will be addressed later on.

Unlike the US, the internal EU context has a viable rail network effectively competing with air transport for medium distance journeys. European railways are generally as safe as air travel, and to transfer from rail to air under these circumstances would have a limited implication on safety.

6.2.2.2 Consumer information. Airline alliance structures affect the information travelers receive regarding the actual carrier they fly with. It is not difficult understanding why someone booking a multi-segment flight with Swissair under the Global Quality alliance arrangements, as depicted in Figure 5.1, could be puzzled at being carried by Delta Airlines. Blocked space agreements, as well, are potentially even more confusing.

In terms of safety, this raises two important questions for the consumer – concern of carrier identity in taking the passenger and the type of aircraft used for the actual flight.

Although variations are small, airlines have differing historic safety records, not only in terms of accidents experienced but also regarding the degree to which negligence has been attributed to them. As well, airlines have different frequencies and qualities of service. In a perfect world, potential passengers would make trade-off of carriers' various attributes when selecting the airline they wish to fly. In the case of alliances, however, it is difficult knowing exactly the various portfolios available since the actual carrier providing the flight is not immediately transparent.

Public policy efforts have been made to ensure alliance code-sharing arrangements do not misinform or disadvantage passengers. This involves not just direct issues concerning exact information, but it extends to responsibility for missed connections, directions to connecting flights and appropriate information systems available at airports. To prevent screen padding on CRS systems, the EU limits codeshared flights to being displayed twice. The US has no such limit. Their rules require that passengers be informed by US airlines of the actual carrier traveled with. The ECAC has a similar disclosure code, but it is not legally binding on member states.

Not only do airlines have differing safety records, but the same is true for commercial aircraft as well. Arguments exist that travelers' perception of safety is dependent on the different types of commercial aircraft that a carrier uses. This offers an argument for ensuring that this type of information should be transparent. The existence of an alliance could result in this information on aircraft types being less easily accessible for passengers. The extent to which this is a valid view is not, however, certain.

The evidence on consumer preferences regarding perceived safe or unsafe aircraft is limited and mainly indirect. The most documented case of an aircraft crash and the commercial impact on its producer is McDonnell Douglas and their DC-10. The producer's share prices significantly fell in 1979 and that could only be accounted in terms of lower anticipated sales. Karels (1989) extended this analysis to look at share prices of airlines (such as American) that also flew DC-10s. He found their share prices were also adversely affected after the incident. In 1989, however, a DC-10 crash seemed to have no long-term adverse effects on McDonnell Douglas. No evidence exists that share prices of Boeing or Lockheed fell significantly after the accident, suggesting that the impact of the 1979 DC-10 crash was atypical (Chalk, 1986).

6.2.2.3 Alliance versus non-alliance carriers. One vocal concern expressed during the 1978 liberalization of the US market was that free markets would force some carriers to cut corners to safe operations in order to keep fares competitive. The argument was again resurrected in the mid-1980s after a

141

series of accidents and fines on a number of US domestic carriers who violated maintenance and safety regulations. In this case, the evidence indicates that market changes had little effect on the overall level and trend of accidents in the US (Morrison and Winston, 1988).

What experience exists highlights US domestic air transportation, and there have been variations in the way airlines channel their resources into safety features. The US National Transportation Safety Board expressed concern that budget constraints might restrict maintenance, although this may reflect actual safety regulations already in place for such operations. Following deregulation, a number of studies produced evidence of reduced expenditure on potentially safety-related activities such as maintenance and training in some segments of the market (Lederer and Enders, 1989). Even if this did not immediately produce more incidents, an argument prevails that in the longer term, a legacy effect would result in accidents. Assessing this validity is not easy. Technical advances, especially in jet engines, have reduced maintenance needs and made it difficult isolating this shift in the maintenance cost function from the impact of institutional changes.

There is another set of findings of importance, linkages between the actual financial position of an airline and an airline's accident record. Rose (1990) finds in US domestic carriers that there was a one year lagged positive effect on accident rates of higher operating profits, although the effect is negligible amongst the largest carriers.

Where does this lead in regard to strategic alliance growth? Evidence obtained on North Atlantic routes indicates that alliances attract passengers from non-alliance carriers. A question to consider relates to financial pressures on alliance carriers: are market incentives to cut corners on maintenance or to employ cheaper and less experienced crews greater for such carriers? When mergers or equity holdings are involved, alliances have a larger resource base and are less prone to liquidity difficulties. As in the case of many (e.g. British Airways/USAir and KLM/Northwest), significant financial injections were made by one partner to bolster a flagging position of the other. This suggests, *a priori*, that many are in stronger financial positions than they were when operating in isolation. Overall, however, safety may not be improved, even if a strong financial performance correlates with fewer accidents; non-alliance carriers would be the subject of greater financial pressures.

Comparisons between alliance and non-alliance carriers brings two other elements into consideration.

First, biocked space alliance arrangements (where a carrier buys capacity on another plane) and coordinated scheduling (by code-sharing partners) can lead to using larger aircraft on the routes involved. The evidence available suggests that these tend to be safer than smaller ones (Oster and Zorn, 1989).

Second (and to complicate matters), when alliances 'rationalize' the use of a partners' capacity, this frees up the market and allows new entry. This may occur for commercial reasons or else is driven by institutional factors. In several European carrier mergers, for example, slots were relinquished by partners to meet anti-trust requirements. Similar arrangements appeared in British Airways and American's efforts to form a strategic code-sharing alliance. A question raised is whether new entrants are safer than incumbents. From US experiences, there is little difference in the safety record of established carriers and incumbents in terms of accidents (Rose, 1989).

Airline switch effects are far from clear. It does not appear that there are strong forces that will lead to reduced safety as a result of the way traffic switches occur between airlines; if anything, the changes would instead have a positive effect on safety.

6.2.2.4 Managerial incentives. There are other ways that the E component in equation 6.1 may change as a result of alliances being created. Does the establishment of an alliance influence a partner's management incentive to change their approach to safety? Available evidence is not altogether conclusive as to the implications of airline accidents. Much depends on the circumstances involved and how they manage the crisis.

One argument claims that accidents will discourage people from using the carrier, even after the immediate impact has passed. Measurement of this effect is difficult as carriers adversely affected in this way often lower fares to keep their market share.

An alternative perspective is to analyze the impact of accidents on an airline's financial status. In eye-balling the share prices of ValuJet and TWA, Button (1997) shows significant declines in respective share prices (actual and against a moving average) following the ValuJet crash in May 1996 and the TWA accident in July, 1996. The contrast is particularly clear when compared to American Airlines in 1995. Although it did experience a major crash during this data period (the loss of a Boeing 757 in Columbia) this tragedy did not adversely affect American's smoothed share value index. The difference between American and TWA and ValuJet lies in the location of the crash and in the perception of who was at fault.

The uneven pattern of stock market fluctuations is in conformity with more rigorous studies completed that looked at the financial implications of airline crashes. In this context, there has been work on a number of themes, much of it concerned with US experiences but relevant to the EU situation.

Because all carriers are extensively and excessively insured, an accident seldom costs in terms of immediate payments. What may happen, however, is there may be an effect on an airline's image, thus adversely impacting future insurance premiums it must pay. Mitchell and Maloney (1989) looked at rate adjustments after crashes and brand name recognition and found that falling share prices can be attributed to both projected future costs of higher insurance and the name effect associated with at-fault attribution.

In contrast, Chance and Ferris (1987) acknowledge an immediate dip in share price. Although it is extremely short lived, there is no impact on the industry in general. Golbe (1986) in his study of US domestic deregulation concluded, 'There does not seem to be a statistically significant relationship between safety and profits.'

Again, in contrast, Borenstein and Zimmerman (1988) found airlines suffered an equity loss of about 1.0% as a result of an accident. The picture is, therefore, not entirely clear.

Where do alliances fit into this picture? Much depends on their nature. If the structure is extremely loose, then little reason or pressure exists for any carrier to change behavior patterns. Where there is a closer relationship, especially involving equity holdings, there may be grounds for expected partner airlines to monitor each other's safety performance, especially if each fears any diminution in reputation of one affecting the other. Empirical evidence is not currently available, as strategic airline alliances are still too new and their structures vary too much to allow any sort of detailed testing.

6.2.2.5 Lobbying power. In addition to looking at the implications of alliances and their internal effect on safety, airlines often exercise considerable political power with large carriers, generally having more influence than smaller ones. In addition, alliances effectively change supply conditions, and this potentially has implications for the G component of equation 6.1.

One possible way of systematic analysis is to treat those involved supporting any aviation policy as a coalition (Keeler, 1984). Following this approach, alliances serve the interest of a number of different parties. To alter government policy, an analysis must be of factors motivating those in the 'ruling coalition'.

There appears little reason for aviation users to try and reduce safety standards unless they felt them to be excessive. From a competitive perspective, no compromise of standards is needed since larger carriers generally have solid safety records and thus a comparative advantage over non-alliance rivals. An exception is when an alliance has a monopoly position, and it is the combined advantage of partners to reduce overall safety standards for the sake of costs. There are few incentives for the responsible safety authorities to compromise on existing standards since this would reduce bureaucrats' power and influence. Equally, airline producers' attitudes would be little affected concerning safety and their lobbying positions not changed by the formation of a strategic alliance.

What can be concluded is that there are unlikely to be any significant changes where alliances manipulate public policy in a way detrimental to current safety conditions.

6.3.   PREDATORY BEHAVIOR

Linked to the issue of market power is predatory behavior. Conventionally, it is seen as a distortion to competition within the market (Hanlon, 1994). A number of studies have highlighted the potential for predatory behavior in the aviation industry. This is an example of an anti-competitive activity. The firm suffers a loss in the short term with the expectation this will induce exit so that it can recoup short-term losses of profit by improving its longer-term market position (Dodgson *et al*, 1991).

Economists have had a difficulty defining predatory behavior and in distinguishing it in practice from competitive behavior. It is also not only active predatory behavior that is the problem. A reputation for predatory conduct on the part of the incumbent may be an impediment to efficient market entry. Potential entrants, which consider coming into a portion of an existing network, may be deterred if they fear incumbents are likely to significantly cut fares or initiate large capacity increases on contested routes. The threat is latent in the sense that potential entrants base their decisions on expectation rather than action. Power of incumbency *per se* can limit the actions of potentially more efficient newcomers, but it can also distort the market. It is generally agreed that predatory practices should be regulated where clearly shown to exist, but latent behavior action is particularly difficult to handle.

Predatory behavior in aviation might take a number of forms. One is pre-cutting, where the firm charges prices below short-run marginal costs with the expectation of driving competitors out of the markets and recouping such costs in the long run. Alternatively (or in tandem), the carrier may expand output or service levels beyond short term profit maximizing levels. Airlines might also reschedule services by matching their competitors' schedules at times which would not be profit-maximizing.

A number of reasons exist why predatory behavior is legally difficult to detect. The first is distinguishing it from the effects of normal competitive price reductions or service quality improvements. One would need to know what the competitive response would be in a particular situation. Under some circumstances, an airline's actions might be predatory but in others, sound network economies may exist. As important is the need to avoid the prevention of competition under the guise of protecting against poorly defined predation, the Committee on Competition Law and Policy of the Organisation for Economic Cooperation and Development has recommended that allegations be subject to an analysis which would, in practice, screen out most claims.

A second difficulty in detecting predatory behavior is that competition agencies have generally been conscious of the need to protect firms against actions by powerful rivals that might go beyond competitive responses. Therefore, if predation is outlawed in one way or another, firms will usually only engage in this activity if they are not expected to be detected and possibly punished.

It is perhaps for these reasons there are few fully documented cases of predatory behavior involving airlines. In the case of UK carrier, Laker Airways, the US Department of Justice initiated and later dropped proceedings alleging that several US and foreign airlines had conspired to drive Laker out of business. Laker brought forth a private anti-trust suit that was later settled.

In Europe, a number of investigations involved behavior of this nature as well. In 1992, the charter carrier Britannia had a complaint rejected against British Airways regarding predatory pricing because aircraft used on weekly domestic shuttle services were being deployed weekends on international routes. The UK Civil Aviation Authority judged that the increased service frequency offered by British Airways on its London-Edinburgh service would make it and the competing Loganair unprofitable. The number of flights British Airways could provide were reduced. There have been other investigations by the European Commission which may eventually see the light of day, but generally in Europe, few formal instances of alleged predatory behavior have occurred, in part because of the previously tight regulation of the industry.

These experiences indicate the difficulties of investigating and distinguishing predatory responses from genuinely competitive ones. Detailed data is required on the patronage, revenue, costs and cost structures of both the incumbent and entrant firms. Additionally, investigations need to consider the question of what alternative outcomes were possible in the market under consideration, particularly whether a profitable entry opportunity was available and what sorts of actions by an incumbent would convert it into an unprofitable one for the entrant. An important issue is whether the incumbent, by its actions, gave up profits it could have earned in the competitive situation. Another consideration is whether entrants' losses were due to their own actions since, in a world of asymmetric information, entrants cannot be expected to behave as if they have perfect information.

A survey of the airline industry reveals a number of cases where informed industry experts thought that predatory behavior existed in the industry (Dodgson *et al.*, 1991). In particular, this includes instances where predatory conduct seems to be a plausible explanation of what occurred, but where the allegations have not been tested by a full published investigation and judgment. In other cases (such as the British Airway-Loganair dispute), judgments have been imprecise as to whether predatory practices existed. Indeed, there appear to be no full-fledged investigations ruling that successful predation took place in the EU airline industry.

Despite the lack of case studies, alleged predatory behavior should not be ignored. Of particular concern is the response of national airlines, which are backed up by substantial amounts of state aid, to the operations of low-cost carriers in the newly deregulated European market.

At the time of new entry, it is often hard for regulators to distinguish between pricing to maximize profits (or minimize losses) while moving to change competitive conditions, fill empty seats, and reflect falling costs due to enhanced efficiency and pricing to drive new entrants out of the market. Latent predatory power is even more elusive. Entrants fear that incumbents with accummulated fighting funds will, in the short term, reduce prices below costs or introduce large amounts of additional capacity.

Combined with the natural pressures for efficiency existing in a strongly competitive market, these have led some commentators to question whether it is worth trying to contain predatory activity in liberalized aviation markets where other entry barriers are low. With the existence of subsidies and other imperfections, however, the potential remains. Monitoring possible occurrences of predatory practices must be maintained using conventional national competition policy instruments.

Where regulation has been attempted, one way to contain the problem is the Bright Lines approach. Specific rules are indicated as to what constitutes predatory behavior (e.g. looking for prices set below a reasonable estimate of the relevant cost). An alternative favored by the EU is the Rule of Reason approach that looks at each case in its context. However, application of these concepts to aviation is limited.

Finally, it should be noted that where action is taken, investigations need to be reasonably speedy, otherwise they will not be completed before predatory practice has successfully occurred. A complication is that individual victims have little incentive to complain if the investigations do not protect them (especially if they receive no compensation when predatory behavior is proven after their demise). Regulatory agencies and courts of law

147

also need to be very wary of unsuccessful entrants who plead predatory practice as a source of self-inflicted woes stemming from their own commercial mistakes. In addition, new entrants cannot expect existing firms to acquiesce to their presence without a competitive response.

6.4 DURABILITY OF ALLIANCES

While considerable expansion has occurred in the number and types of international airline alliances, historically the record points in one direction, longevity among them is poor.

A recent Harvard Business School case study found that code-sharing alliances last an average of five years (Jennings, 1996b). Similarly, data from the Boston Consultancy Group (BCG) reveals double the number of alliances between 1992 and 1995 but a low survival rate (Table 6.8). The chances of an international alliance surviving over this period were approximately one in three. From this data set, those with equity investments would appear having the best survival rate[7].

What also emerges from these surveys, in part because of the absence of regulatory impediments coupled with operators' desire to manage feeder traffic, is two-thirds of alliances in BCG's 1995 survey involved equity investments in national markets and consisted of wholly-owned subsidiaries.

Table 6.8 *Airline alliance survival rates*

	Alliances 1995	Alliance survival rate 1992-95 Non-equity	Equity
Domestic	92	n/a	65%
Regional	176	36%	80%
Intercontinental	133	23%	77%
Total	401	26%	73%

The table also reveals a marked increase in regional airline alliances. In part, this may be accounted for by the changing regulatory environment in the European Union and the liberalizing of bilateral agreements within North and South America, thus making it easier to coordinate activities.

[7] The number recorded by the *Avmark Aviation Economist* is smaller than *Airline Business* due to differences in definitions and data bases used.

BCG's finding of a high failure rate for alliances, also pinpointed by recent surveys in *Airline Business* (Gallacher, 1996a), appears surprising since most of the major studies to-date have shown airline alliances, by and large, have benefited the parties directly involved.

One explanation for fluctuation is that airlines have changed attitudes towards alliances. American Airlines initially opposed them but now has a major link with Canadian International Airlines, has tried linking up with British Airways since late 1996, and has code sharing arrangements with British Midland, BWIA International, Gulf Air, Singapore International Airlines and South African Airways among others.

One way to approach the volatility of the alliance system is to examine the topic in terms of coalitions (Sharkey, 1986; Keeler, 1984)[8]. There is an argument from an institutional and structural perspective that for an alliance to form and survive, there must be a dominant coalition of interests supporting it[9]. In the case of airline alliance, it might embrace airlines, airports, employees, suppliers, passengers and public policy makers.

A coalition may well involve the combined interest of parties, not only from the supply side sector but also users of the services. This is perhaps most apparent when considering the structure of international aviation. Airlines' objectives are not always commercial, although pressures tend to place emphasis on this. In many cases, it can embody a variety of political motivations, especially when the carrier is state-owned or receives subsidies.

---

[8]   A number of studies list the types of difficulties resulting in airline alliances either failing to function effectively or breaking up. Many would embrace many of the following items (Flanagan and Marcus, 1993; Lindquist, 1996):
*   Objectives too broadly set
*   Objectives not congruent
*   Asymmetry between partners
*   Unrealistic expectations
*   Differing product services standards
*   Conflicting or competitive priorities
*   Contrasting corporate styles

While this approach pinpoints some important issues, it does not provide a coherent framework or argument for addressing the subject of why so many alliances are short lived or the difficulty of making them operational in the first place.

[9]   As a generalization about alliances, Porter (1990) argues;
"Alliances are not a panacea; most alliances are unstable, difficult to manage (and anyway risk creating a rival). Only alliances that are highly selective will support true competitive advantage".

Equally, international aviation is carried out within a bilateral or multilateral, legal framework of international agreements. Issues of security, national sovereignty and trade are often given dominance over strict economic efficiency in the supply of services. Linked are the background interests of those providing industry hardware and those who work within the system. Then there are the users who exercise preferences through their willingness to pay.

Such diverse priorities inevitably lead to compromise and power brokering between various parties. In some cases, they act to directly influence the way an alliance is devised and operates, but also individual groups can act behind the scenes to influence managerial decisions; organized labor's role is an example of this.

Any coalition is liable to change its attitude to a given situation or, conversely, to break up and end the alliance for a variety of possible reasons.

Other, more powerful or focused coalitions may emerge in aviation. This could involve new carriers or competitors entering the market and attracting partners from the existing coalition. External factors can make the existing alliance less attractive for some partners; changes in bilateral air service agreements or technical changes could affect the costs of individual carriers providing services. Equally, new markets would emerge that bring new players to the game.

Further, attitudes of those in the coalition may change, favoring other structures or adjustments to the way an alliance operates. Patterns of industrial and commercial needs may, for instance, affect the attitudes of business travelers. National policies on subsidies may make airlines or suppliers of infrastructure modify their views.

Attitude may change of the coalitions' functions as their experience grows. This endogenous effect may lead to the internal structure realignment and new internal rules being applied.

Given these and other possible reasons for waxing and waning and new coalitions emerging, it is perhaps surprising so many alliances have survived rather than disintegrated. Within this framework, too, it is possible to consider various factors affecting the marriages (or perhaps more appropriately, liaisons) international airlines make.

6.4.1 New bedfellows

Circumstances change with time as more information about the current situation emerges. This can lead an airline to assess that even while an alliance may be working satisfactorily, new options lead it to seek preferable alternative partners. If an alliance fails to live up to expectations, then the incentive to seek out new opportunities is inevitably greater.

The franchising arrangement between Virgin Atlantic and CityJet, for instance, ended when Virgin decided to move into the short-haul market and acquired the Belgian independent carrier EBA. Equally, British Airways ended two major alliances to form up with new partners. The first, with United Airlines, involved no equity holdings and lasted from 1987 to 1991. More recently, British Airways' alliance with USAir ended when the prospects of linking with American Airlines emerged. More common, however, is the case where individual, point-specific route alliances are terminated as airlines adjust their overall marketing strategy and find more attractive bedfellows for their specific individual routes.

6.4.2 Lack of focus

Some commentators have been concerned about the objectives alliances set for themselves and questioned whether they always have sufficient focus (Coltman, 1995). The underlying objective of any alliance is not always easy to define, given their multiple-membership and multifaceted nature.

General analysis of industry by business school academics such as Porter (1980) indicate that companies have several strategies to deal with the competitive forces found in modern market structures. Particularly, companies can seek out least cost solutions, emphasize differentiation or focus on particular markets or sub-markets. In some cases, a combination may provide the focus, but success normally comes from isolating a single avenue.

Almost by definition, point specific alliances tend to be concerned with targeted geographical markets. Through a lack of adequate information, failure generally comes about because of miscalculations regarding the benefits of such alliances. Actual sunk costs to the partners are relatively small, and rational behavior suggests trial and error may be more cost-effective than seeking out more reliable forecasts.

Strategic alliances are more complicated to disentangle, especially if there are equity holding considerations. Developing focus here involves recognizing that trade-offs may be important across a network of activities. Much the same can be said of public policy response of such alliances; world-wide antitrust legislation is often based on ideas developed for clearly defined markets served by the manufacturing industry that embrace few network implications. Various forms of competition have to be met. Putting together large carriers offers the opportunity to meet competition, but conflicting views may occur in how to handle other markets unique to each partnership carrier. Finding partners with similar overall long-term goals and objectives is not easy in this type of situation. More flexible arrangements are likely to prove more durable.

151

6.4.3 Airline incompatibilities

Airlines are far from homogeneous. This may not automatically pose a problem since diversity can lead to complementary, successful alliances. Nevertheless, if major variations exist in their philosophies or structures, problems inevitably arise in the maintenance of anything but a very loose alliance.

One particular problem is that airlines vary in terms of economic efficiency, particularly internal cost structures. As we have seen, a distinction is needed here between the full costs of operating and those within the control of individual carriers; part of the reason European carriers have higher costs than most US counterparts are higher fixed costs of operating in predominantly in European markets. Caves *et al* (1987) also found that different European route structures adversely affect costs. It is not easy making valid comparisons because of the types of markets served and services provided. But, generally in trans-Atlantic markets, US carriers are more efficient than European scheduled airlines, although conventional charter carriers in Europe offer low cost services. As liberalization occurs, however, the gap is closing.

Referring to the Porter model of managerial strategy, various airlines' cost situations differ, even in competitive markets. This can be a reflection of internal management philosophies rather than external institutional factors or matters of strict efficiency. Alliances which bring together airlines with radically different philosophies do not appear so robust, even if potential synergies exist in terms of complementary networks.

Airline alliances are also run by individuals, and like any business, their attitudes and approaches play an important part in determining how well it functions. As well, differing national approaches to management can pose problems, even if a degree of consensus exists among senior management how an alliance should develop. These types of problems are illustrated between strategic alliance partners such as Northwest and KLM, see Jennings (1996a).

6.4.4 Outside interference

All forms of airline alliances have to be government sanctioned, with most international ones by several countries. In many countries, or groupings such as the European Union, alliance elements run counter to traditional generic anti-trust or merger policies. Problems of conforming to regulatory regimes is why some airline alliances take time to initially arrange or do not operate, despite considerable energies expended in negotiations and discussions.

The problem is particularly acute, as indicated earlier, in the context of larger, multifaceted alliances involving major international airlines. But problems also exist when the scale is much less ambitious but entails such things as equity holdings which affect the position of a national flag carrier.

In these circumstances, the issue of strategic alliances gets enmeshed in broader questions of trade and protectionist policies. This can be seen in the awarding of US anti-trust immunity for the Lufthansa/United Airlines. New bilateral agreements were obtained and horse trading over the US/UK service became part of the decision-making framework for the American/British Airways alliance.

The structure and evolution of any airline alliance is often shaped as much by political factors as commercial considerations, and this puts a strain on its commercial success.

6.4.5 New initiatives

An important feature of the aviation sector in recent years has been its flexibility and inventiveness. The development of CRSs, frequent flyer programs, code-sharing, yield management techniques and hub-and-spoke operations, together with technical advances in aircraft design and air traffic systems, bears witness to the changes that have taken place over the past twenty-five years.

A general agreement exists that aviation is also becoming more internationalized, and this trend will continue. Although there have been major advances in aviation technology but also institutional arrangement governing operations, there will be the need for further changes in the way the sector functions if it is to retain its vitality and contribute fully to the global economic development.

Generally, however, it is more difficult developing coordinated strategies among actors in such a dynamic sector than those operating in a more static environment. It is no accident smaller carriers are often very active in developing 'ticketless' travel and instrumental in introducing no-frill flights. A temptation in any market is for a major player lagging behind to align itself with a more dynamic actor. While this may prove successful, management ethos and structure of more active undertakings differs from those of established counterparts.

6.5   OUR LIMITED KNOWLEDGE

In examining the importance of international airline alliances, we have not attempted any new econometric or statistical analysis in this chapter.

Completed academic and official studies have extensively squeezed a limited database. Rather, the chapter has attempted to bring together in a systematic way what knowledge exists. It looks at the main issues from a managerial standpoint rather than a narrower public policy perspective that has characterized other analysis in this area.

From a point specific basis involving strategic groupings, international airline alliances are an important element in the way aviation markets are evolving. They have offered a mechanism for airlines to enhance the efficiency with which transport services are provided. Particularly, they permit certain types of scale economies to be exploited without the necessity for full mergers to be carried out.

Additionally, alliances allow carriers to circumvent more restrictive institutional barriers common in many international markets. Since they are collusive agreements affecting the way markets function, alliances have implications for anti-trust policy.

Recent surges of alliances between major carriers have gradually increased public awareness of the need to more carefully review their role in the aviation sector and appropriate public policy response to it. In practice, completed empirical studies, academic or governmental, that explore the impact of international airline alliances has been limited. Little is known about economic implications of routes, since where they have taken place tends to focus on the major alliances instead. Researchers have also been handicapped by a scarcity of relevant statistical information and conceptual models of how network industries function.

What information that is available reveals that the main strategic international airline alliances have not, in the short term, resulted in any social welfare net loss. This evidence, small in quantity, is somewhat dated and relies on relatively basic analysis. Even less is known about impacts of the very large and expanding number of point specific and regional airline alliances. Little is known about those involving intra-EU services or services between the EU and non-US destinations. While important individual features exist relating to these numerous alliances, there may also be important common effects for general policy making purposes.

Many alliances involving European carriers have simply fallen apart, while others function only in an environment of friction between participants. If they are to be a serious threat to future competition in the sector, this will come about only if they find ways of holding together. Continual fluctuations in their composition and nature also poses informational problems for potential air travelers.

An important issue is airlines' ability to learn from their experiences in partnerships and other alliances, both within aviation and other sectors. These lessons relate to both the success of airline alliances to function and evolve, but equally to emanate from the marked failure of others. Retrospectively, the industry has been slow to learn; over-extended during good times and lacking viable contingency plans for leaner times had much to do with the problems occurring in the late 1980s. More recently, evidence exists that lessons were learned on the financial front, and this may lead to more stable alliance structures.

One of the major problems analyzing international alliance implications is the lack of relevant data. International air transport data is difficult to obtain, and what is available can be distorted or misinforming. For example, airlines record ticket flight information, but because of code sharing arrangements, passengers may have been carried by another partner airline. The increased use of 'ticketless travel' is likely to compound such problems in the future.

The several studies done on the 1978 US Airline Deregulation Act were only possible because of extensive data bases, especially the ten per cent ticket sample. Comparable studies in Europe and elsewhere reflect, in part, the inadequacy or incompatibility of information sources in other countries. The problem is compounded by the growth of complex, global strategic alliances comprising carriers from a number of countries. The network nature of the sector makes it particularly difficult to define clear markets in this situation.

Linked to this is a need for a more comprehensive understanding of the implications of airline network alliances. Studies conducted in the US have varied in technical sophistication, but they do not incorporate the full richness of airline activities' network features. In some cases where an alliance affects a limited market segment, this may pose few problems. But with a global movement, interactions between sub-markets will inevitably grow, and the lack of full analysis could generate misleading policy conclusions. This is going to become an issue of increasing significance as anti-trust issues begin to arise more frequently.

Understanding how these alliances function and what make them viable is important for the sector and public policy formulation. To date, little detailed work has been done. One reason is that the very notion of alliances is a difficult one, taking many different forms and embracing a diversity of different features. It appears, however, the subject can be examined by treating it as a coalition and applying coalition theory to the topic. And as with any coalition, its success depends on its members sharing a common objective and the ability to control the environment in which it operates.

To date, many alliances have floundered because of a lack of internal focus; forming one is seen as necessary without exploring long-term implications. This may have been expected in the early days when lessons had to be learned, but this infant methodology cannot work today. Also important is understanding that aviation is a dynamic sector operating in an active economic and political climate. Certainly, this accounts for some realignments that have taken place within and between alliances.

7. Stability in European Air Transport Markets

7.1 STABILITY IN AIR TRANSPORT MARKETS

As we have seen over the past twenty years, market liberalization and state withdrawals have been features of virtually all air transport markets and not just aviation (Button and Keeler, 1993). The different effects have been studied to various degrees. The aim of this chapter is to explore one possible implication of the on-going liberalization occurring in the EU area of the aviation market. The focus is on the issue of the stability of free markets in transport industries and the appropriate policy response when instability is potentially severe[1].

We have seen that services in western Europe have been gradually liberalized in line with general global trends. Actual understanding of what motivates airlines in their actions in deregulated aviation conditions is, though, still remarkably limited, despite the considerable experience of US deregulation since 1978 (see also Chapter 2).

Some US commentators talk, for instance, in terms of competition and contestability, albeit in imperfect forms (e.g. Morrison and Winston, 1987), while others analyse workably competitive (Keeler, 1990) or oligopolistic structures (Kahn, 1988). Nor is the intellectual position stable; some leading figures initially suggesting that aviation may be contestable have subsequently changed their minds (Baumol and Willig, 1986).

An important policy issue is whether a deregulated scheduled aviation market is viable long term or if inherent characteristics mean that competition will ultimately prove destructive. This topic attracted considerable media interest in the early 1990s when most of the world's

---

[1]   Button and Nijkamp (1997) offer a more general assessment of these issues. Stability here is used in its economic sense. An unstable market, because of the uncertainty engendered, will lead to suboptimally low or zero supply.

leading airlines, especially US carriers, had significant financial losses. Discussions centered around whether this was a short term phenomenon or if it represented an inherent market problem associated with providing scheduled air transport services[2]. Such topics tend to attract less attention during periods of economic up-turn but are likely to return to the forefront of debate during the next recession.

The stability debate is neither new nor is it unique to recent experiences in air transport regulatory reform[3]. In the early days of commercial aviation, many questioned the viability of offering scheduled services at all (Heppenheimer, 1995). In non-aviation markets, past legislative measures were based around ideas of excessive and destructive competition. These laws ranged from banning jitney, para-transit services in the US in the 1920s to the introduction of bus service licensing in the UK in the 1930s (Foster and Golay, 1986). The intellectual arguments surrounding the creation of a European Common Transport Policy in the 1960s were initially based on the implicit assumption that low supply and demand elasticities naturally resulted in market instability (EEC Commission, 1961).

Much of the recent economic debate around the question of market stability centers on the existence or otherwise of a so-called core[4]. In simplest terms, a core implies that competition will lead to the optimal level of supply. If there are situations where, say, there are indivisibilities in supply (a route would ideally be served by 1.5 planes but obviously only 1 or 2 could be used) then the service may prove unstable, and in the extreme not provided at all. In the indivisibility case one airline may offer the service, obtain high profits on its single daily flight to optimize profits but in doing so attract a second carrier. Two carriers can not generate sufficient revenue to be viable and so one or both leave the service. At the extreme, where there are rational expectations, no risk-adverse carrier will even start to offer a service knowing the probable outcome would be destructive competitive market entry. The core is then said to be empty.

This issue is one implicitly present in recent EU air transport debates. Concerns were expressed that without appropriate institutional safeguards, the aviation market's technical features might prove to be unstable. If competitive conditions do not automatically generate an equilibrium in this case, then what should the policy response be? The rapid expansion of carriers in the US after 1978 and the subsequent concentration of their

[2]   A journalistic assessment of the US domestic market, much along the academic lines of the analysis presented below, can be found in Smith (1995).

[3]   Edgeworth (1881) pioneered work in this area.

[4]   More details of the conditions that form part of the notion of core theory are discussed below in a Technical Appendix.

number (Morrison and Winston, 1995) and the continuing problems of the domestic aviation industries of Canada (Button, 1989) and Australia (Nyathi *et al*, 1993) are used as examples of situations to avoid in Europe[5].

Charged with looking into EU aviation policy, the recent recommendations of the Comité des Sages for Air Transport (1994) implicitly recognized the possibility of instability when accepting mergers and co-operation agreements have 'potential advantages...for users and operators'. The block exemptions under the 1988 EU Package discussed in Section 2.4.4 can also be interpreted this way as well.

7.2 TESTING FOR A CORE

Core theory suggests that competition can frequently be unstable and inefficient by not achieving Pareto optimal results, even under common cost and demand conditions[6].

The problem has long been recognized as a possibility outcome where an industry's unit cost is not a non-increasing function of the industry's output (there is an empty core). Perhaps the clearest exposition of empty core problems is provided by Sjostrom (1993)[7]:

> An empty core arises whenever capacity, defined here as the output associated with minimum short-run average avoidable cost, in the industry exceeds the quantity demanded at the price equal to that minimum average cost. Competitive equilibrium in such an industry requires that at least one firm shut down in the short run, with the resultant price above minimum average cost. However, a group of buyers can join together with that idle seller to upset the competitive equilibrium. The implication is simple: whenever there is short-run excess capacity, there is unlikely to be a competitive equilibrium.

Problems of these types may be particularly acute when indivisible costs exist and demand is finely divisible. Implications of an empty core is a

---

[5]   There are a number of ways of measuring concentration, of which the Herfindahl index is now the most widely used. The Herfindahl index is defined as $C = \Sigma S^2$ where S is the share of each supplier in the market.

[6]   For a technical discussion of the modern theory of the core see Telser, (1978; 1987; 1990; 1991; 1994).

[7]   Similarly, Telser (1991) offers a succinct explanation of the policy implications, 'If the core is empty... (t)his raises important policy problems because then competition needs appropriate rules to make it serve consumers so an efficient equilibrium that maximises real income can emerge'.

lack of a competitive equilibrium and inefficient allocation of resources. The natural reaction of involved actors is to co-operate their activities, such as through the creation of a 'super-firm' of a cartel or by long term agreements between buyers and sellers. Such situations may cover the rates charged, the plants operated and their output or revenue levels.

The empirical work that has been completed seeking out core conditions is, however, relatively limited and generally fairly technical[8]. What should also be emphasized is that the work is purely indicative; it seeks to find whether market and institutional conditions are those where an empty core could exist but cannot offer insights as to whether it does exist.

Bittlingmayer initially focused his research on the US cast-pipe industry in the early 20th century (the Addyston Pipe case) and subsequently produced a link between mergers and changes in antitrust policy. He concluded that the standard Viner case (see Appendix) holds where no competitive equilibrium is composed entirely of forms with identical U-shaped cost curves producing a homogeneous product, unless demand is such that optimum production plans require suppliers to produce where marginal cost equals average cost. But Bittlingmayer also explored the implications of demand shifts. By preventing co-operative action in industries where the core was empty, US antitrust legislation unavoidably forced merger strategies on all those involved.

Sjostrom's work centers on demand conditions in the context of current maritime markets. He focuses on inefficient entry and the need for price-setting agreements to impose an equilibrium on the market. Particularly, Sjostrom explores instances where the core may be empty and isolates a number of possible conditions where this may be so or where market suppliers may seek to make agreements to avoid emerging empty cores[9]. The conclusions reached are:

[8]　　Details of underlying arguments of core theory tend to be abstract, but articles by Bittlingmayer (1982; 1985); Sjostrom (1989; 1993) and Pirrong (1992) provide a practical basis for exploring the likely existence of an empty core. The potential existence of an empty core has also been explored by examining cost function in the context of experimental economics as well as more conventional procedures (Van Boening and Wilcox, 1992).

[9]　　Because the quantity shipped by a conference depends partly on the effectiveness of the cartel, Sjostrom used a two stage estimation of the general form:

$$CON = f[Q, SD, P, REST]$$
$$Q = f[CON, LDC, EXP, IMP]$$

where:

- the greater the variation in suppliers' minimum average costs, the more likely a competitive equilibrium;
- an empty core is more likely when demand is less elastic. (Demand conditions are not considered in detail in later analyses, as low demand elasticities are consistent with an empty core and rent seeking collusion. In aviation, they are extremely variable across markets and customer groups. A recent survey of international studies conducted by Oum *et al* (1992) indicates findings in the range −0.4 to −4.51.);
- the larger a supplier's capacity relative to the market, the more probable the core will be empty;
- agreements to create a core are more likely during an economic recession;
- wide variability in demand or costs increases the probability of agreements; and
- agreements are less likely when legal restrictions exist on entry.

A practical difficulty in apply these is that, albeit with a different direction of correlation, several of these conditions are consistent with collusion for rent seeking purposes. Table 7.1 provides a summary of such situations where this holds. Sjostrom's empirical analysis of structure, conduct, and performance approach looks at conditions in the shipping conference markets to explore the extent they conform, consistent with a rent seeking or empty core scenario. Given the data available, Sjostrom explores for legal restrictions on entry (making core theory for collusion

CON = Conference's share of liner shipments on its route
Q = Quantity shipped on liners
SD = Standard deviation of liner shipments on the route
P = Average value of goods shipped on the route by liner ships
RES = Dummy variable isolating Latin American, Indonesian and Philippine routes
LDC = Dummy variable isolating routes to and from less developed countries
EXP = Total exports of the country in which the liner cargo originated
IMP = Total imports of the region of the cargo's destination
The equations estimated using two-stage least squares yielded:

$$CON = 3.37 - Ln0.22Q + 1.53E\text{-}6SD + 0.03P - 0.54REST$$
$$LnQ = -0.24 + 2.98CON - 0.73LDC + 0.49EXP + 0.48\ IMP \qquad n = 24$$

The signs of the coefficients of the SD and REST variables are consistent with the existence of an empty core. They are significant at the 95% level.

less likely) or severe temporal variations in demand and costs (making it more likely).

Pirrong's approach again in relation to conference shipping, is complementary to Sjostrom's by placing emphasis on exploring costs. In particular, Pirrong explores relations between cost, demand and market organization. He isolates conditions where the demand structure is finely divisible and cost curves are non-homogeneous when describing the circumstances under which competition is not feasible. His conclusions are consistent with Sjostrom's findings and suggest that collusion and coalitions in the shipping market serve to ensure stability and avoid competitive chaos. Whether the exact nature of the particular form of collusion is efficient could not be judged.

Table 7.1 *Differing conditions for rent seeking and stability collusion*

| | Chance of Collusion | |
	Cartel	Empty core
Heterogeneous supply	Low	Low
Less elastic demand	Low	High
Small numbers case	High	High
Industry in slump	Unclear	High
Variable supply/demand	Low	High
Legal restrictions	High	Low

Developments in these empirics regarding shipping provide a basis for assessing the aviation markets. While the analogy cannot be taken too far, we have already argued that important parallels exist between the two sectors. Shipping lines provide regular services that increasingly involve, through electronic data interchange systems, crude yield management procedures like scheduled aviation (Brooks and Button, 1994). Tramp shipping may be seen as akin to aviation charter services. Shipping operations are increasingly moving towards hub-and-spoke structures. Deferred rebates and other loyalty payments in conference markets have similar implications to frequent flyer programs. The move towards consortia in liner shipping has parallels to code-sharing in aviation markets. And shipping berth allocation has much in common with airport slot issues and differential handling charges according to airline.

These types of features have not been fully explored with regard to the probable nature of a reformed European aviation. A number of studies have pointed to inherent similarities and differences between the European scene and the obvious point of comparison, the deregulated US domestic market, but none have gone beyond this (e.g. Good *et al*, 1993; Button and Swann, 1992). To reap potential benefits of greater European market flexibility, however, greater understanding is needed of underlying market conditions. This is important to framing mergers and competition policy. But change is taking place without completely comprehending the potential implications.

A move towards cross share-holdings and alliances can in simple, economic terms be seen in one of three possible contexts. First, it may indicate that airlines are trying to improve overall efficiency by maximizing economies of scale and scope. Second, efforts may exist to exploit rent-seeking potential by acquiring monopoly powers in terms of market advantages enjoyed from offering diverse and extensive frequent flyer programs and operating with common codes. And third, cross-sharing and alliances may indicate the core is empty since other forms of collusive activities are excluded by statute; following Bittlingmayer's (1985) line of reasoning, this is a means by which actors can reduce market instability.

Little to date, however, has been attempted to examine the alternative possibilities listed above.

In the context of the empty core argument, it is important to recall that the EU post 1997 situation will not produce a carbon copy of the US 1978 domestic situation. Council Regulation 2408/92, for example, allows freezing capacity when the market is fundamentally unbalanced, and Regulation 2409/92 allows intervention to prevent downward spirals on air fares. Some institutional concern exists in the EU regarding the possibility of emerging market instabilities. As Telser (1994) says,

> ...a general method of resolving an empty core requires imposition of suitable upper bounds on the quantities that may be sold by certain sellers.

Considerable changes in the intra-EU regulatory environment have not rapidly occurred or without debate. Changes in the general framework of mergers and competition policy within the EU are gradually giving the Commission greater powers where issues are seen as Union wide. Not only has concern been raised about transition management and how to treat high cost flag carriers, but also whether the post 1997 situation will provide a stable market outcome. One way to gain insight is to apply methods used in other sectors to the aviation situation.

163

7.2.1 Market structure considerations

While it is difficult providing conclusive evidence of a non-empty core existence (except in exceptional circumstances), work in the shipping sector provides a framework for establishing indicators. European aviation regarding market entry can first be examined in the context of Sjostrom's (1989) approach. A difference between conferences and EU bilateral air transport cartels is that conferences are organized by the liners themselves, while bilateral air transport cartels are inter-governmental arrangements. Bilateral negotiators are inevitably concerned with flag carriers' interests (or at least national carriers) and seen as the negotiating arms of the airlines. In other words, the objectives of principals and agents generally coincide.

This approach involves looking at pertaining market conditions and exploring if implications consistent with the core theory emerge. Many forces favoring rent seeking cartel behavior are identical to those that lead actors to operate, thus avoiding an empty core (see again Table 7.1). Following Sjostrom, this is more likely when costs and demand are highly variable (the opposite is true if it is purely for rent seeking) and less likely when entry is legally restricted. This limit on the number of actors involved in the market, thus reducing the probability that the number of potential carriers will exceed the number of active airlines, makes coordination agreements less likely.

Cross-sectional data for 1990 was chosen covering air service between most capital and major cities of the current EU members. Cities included Amsterdam, Athens, Barcelona, Birmingham, Brussels, Copenhagen, Dublin, Frankfurt, Glasgow, Lisbon, London, Lyon, Madrid, Manchester, Milan, Munich, Paris and Rome[10]. The period was selected on pragmatic grounds to minimize problems associated with wider developments in European aviation policy. The time immediately follows initiated liberal bilateral arrangements but before implications of gradual EU liberalization processes became effective. The period also pre-dates airlines' movements on a large scale into other national markets by means of mergers and share holdings and before continental European based airlines' major privatization measures[11].

Empirical analysis focuses on relating the share of carried airline passengers from either end of a European route to a set of explanatory

[10]   The routes excluded domestic services, totaled 106, and related to two-way traffic.
[11]   Additionally, a significant increase in fifth freedom operations since 1991 – rising from 16 routes offered per week in July 1991 to 33 routes per week in July 1993 – clouds later data sets.

variables. In Sjostrom's (1989) argument, variation in these can be taken as a reflection of the strength of potential collusive power.

Explanatory variables embrace both allowance for legal restrictions on entry (where a positive sign is consistent with an empty core situation and a negative with cartel rent seeking), and for temporal variation in demand (a positive sign more in line with an empty core of the degree of traffic carried by route end airlines and a negative with conventional rent seeking collusion).

Additionally, a number of normalizing variables included reflect the nature of individual markets but offer little insight into an empty core possibility or likelihood of an empty core existence rather than rent seeking. A high level of market concentration (e.g. number of airlines), is consistent with both situations. As well, other variant sets reflect possible differences in individual market structure incorporated for normalization (e.g. route lengths, time it has been served and competition from charter carriers). Ideally, one would extend this range of variables to embrace such features as heterogeneity in the suppliers (Good *et al*'s, 1993 analysis suggesting European airlines are far from homogeneous) but specifying such a set of features is not tractable. In fact, implications of heterogeneity for the core/cartel debate is unclear (Sjostrum, 1989). But normalization may be relevant in testing other hypotheses.

The general formulation of the model employed is[12]:

$$SE = f(AD, LR, NC, CR, TF, PL, NR, DV) \qquad (7.1)$$

where:
SE = Percentage of traffic on the route carried by airlines from the countries at either end of the route
AD = Distance between airports in kilometers
LR = Acts to reflect the nature of the legal environment and a dummy variable, taking a unitary value if the route is the subject of a liberal bilateral (i.e. no strong legal constraint exists on market entry). The EU routes where liberal bilaterals existed in 1989 were UK–Belgium; UK–France; UK–Eire; UK–Germany; UK–Netherlands; France–Germany; France–Spain and Germany–Spain.
NC = Number of carriers on the route
CR = A dummy variable, taking a value of unity if the route serves north-south traffic to reflect possible competition from charter services

[12] The data was extracted from International Civil Aviation Organisation (various issues).

TF = Total flights
PL = Average load factor
NR = A dummy variable taking the value of unity if there was no service in 1985
DV = Proxies market variability and the annual variability of demand between 1985 and 1990, expressed as the coefficient of variation in annual passengers carried on each route included in the analysis.

A number of alternative linear and logarithmic model specifications were explored but generally made no material difference. For estimation purposes, specification of the dependent variable is in terms of a log-odds transformation to allow for it being bounded in its natural form. This poses problems in deriving elasticities but does not affect the positive/negative nature of the signs of coefficients that are our main interest. The estimation conducted used ordinary least squares. The main results, set out below with standard errors in parentheses, offer tentative support for the possible existence of empty core conditions.

$$Ln[SE/(1-SE)] = 8.855 - 0.001AD + 0.538LR - 2.002NC + 1.512CR +$$
$$(0.002) \quad (1.728) \quad (0.308) \quad (1.820)$$
$$0.001TF + 14.630PL + 5.101NR + 2.200DV \qquad (7.2)$$
$$(0.000) \quad (9.390) \quad (3.813) \quad (3.514)$$
$$n = 106 \quad R^2 = 0.50$$

Variable signs representing legal restrictions (LR) and degree of market stability (DV) are in line with the empty core hypothesis, although low t-statistics indicate limited explanatory power. Given the nature of the variable specification, the positive sign associated with the LR coefficient implies a higher chance of collusion when the market is not legally restricted – hence, a lower probability of co-ordination to prevent instabilities when legal controls are in place. One interpretation is that the institutional framework contains the potential empty core problem through airlines' actions via national governments. Equally, the positive relationship of SE with the market stability variable implies (as the core situation suggests), greater proclivity to co-operative behavior when uncertainties are high. Here, carriers are interpreted limiting the possibility of being caught on a discontinuity in their supply schedules.

Other variables, not considered in Sjostrom's framework, can be seen as weakly consistent. For instance, the load factor variable could be interpreted as conforming with the core theory notion that the industry's discontinuities average total cost curve are more likely as industrial capacity increases. Others take intellectually sensible, if not always significant, signs. The number of carriers is negatively correlated with market share which is in conformity with *a priori* expectation for both empty core and rent seeking hypotheses. The positive sign associated with the number of flights variable can similarly be given either interpretation.

In summary, empirical results based on Sjostrom's market entry approach are indicative but not conclusive that collusion in European aviation markets come about due to an empty core but not beyond that. Statistical associates, although generally in the direction that supports this hypothesis, are extremely weak.

7.2.2 Cost and demand considerations

Detailed analysis of costs conducted along the lines of Pirrong's (1992) work on liner shipping is virtually impossible in the European aviation context because of suitable route level data. What is possible is to highlight general features of the market indicative of the underlying cost structure and to compare these with the demand and costs conditions where an empty core may pertain. Specifically, the types of conditions are summarized by Pirrong (1992) as,

> ...if the cost functions of individual plants contain regions of both increasing and decreasing returns, demand is variable, and if plants serve several customers simultaneously, the core is almost always empty.

As with shipping conferences, it is clear that scheduled aviation services serve customers simultaneously; this factor drives the yield management strategy and discriminate pricing. Further, there is evidence of discontinuity in marginal costs where output is less than average cost. Such conditions could pertain in aviation where the number of passengers a plane carries while still being able to fly is constrained by the aircraft's characteristics.

Even when strict discontinuity does not occur, and the marginal cost curve of carrying more passengers is continuous but rises very steeply, the core with large markets can be empty. This is because the cost penalty of expanding output for a given fleet becomes large as each aircraft's output surpasses the point where marginal costs rise rapidly. The result can mean that it is desirable to pay the financial penalty by activating an additional plane and using the existing fleet below its capacity.

A key issue is whether these types of conditions typify aviation. Tretheway and Oum (1992), whose findings are in line with others (e.g. in Doganis, 1991), provide detailed generalized data that costs begin rising well before an aircraft's capacity is reached. Cost per kilometer falls as the number flown increases, but because of technological constraints after a certain range, the distance can be extended only by reducing aircraft capacity. On a Boeing 747-400, for example, the majority of savings seem to be exhausted after 5,000 kilometers. Yet given the relatively high proportion of quasi-fixed costs associated with any scheduled flight, cost per passenger falls as the number of seats filled increases towards full capacity.

Although some variability exists between carriers, IATA data suggest that indirect costs amount to about 65% of scheduled unit cost services on European routes. Hence, marginal costs rise well before the payload at maximum range is reached. Where hub-and-spoke operations are employed (as is the case of European flag carriers focusing on the national hubs), less flexibility exists to vary capacity for services, given the knock-on costs across the networks they serve. An empty core is more likely when aircraft are intensively used, a situation consistent with the positive and significant coefficient found for the PL variable in regression analysis.

Another way of assessing the situation is in terms of traffic density economies. These, one recalls, exist when the average unit cost of production declines as the amount of traffic increases between any given set of points. Evidence from the US and Canada (Caves *et al*, 1984; Borenstein and Rose, 1994) indicates that unit costs of providing a service fall as the number of passengers on a route increases. There is no reason to anticipate the same is not true for Europe; when discussing airlines, the UK Civil Aviation Authority (1993) observed, '...economies of route density are generally acknowledged'. When they exist on routes with competing services, operators have incentives to cut prices to short run marginal cost in the face of excess capacity periodically occurring when variations in demand exist. The result is that prices will be too low to cover the full costs of operating an efficient set of schedules. The core is thus empty.

In this context, the demand side is clearly important, and Pirrong (1992) agrees with Sjostrom in that 'variable demand is a crucial factor contributing to the failure of competition'. In conditions of fluctuating demand, it is often optimal operating some plants below capacity, thus creating excess capacity. Generally, aviation is typified by marked variations in demand over time, with strong cyclical variations linked to the business cycle (Doganis, 1991). Europe is not isolated from this. In addition, short term shocks are brought about by concerns over safety in times of military conflict. Although not very powerful, regression results are consistent with the core hypothesis.

The intrinsic nature of scheduled aviation markets is still poorly understood. Many policy reforms in recent years have been more general ideological shifts regarding the role of government. And as the result of the ineffectiveness of existing regulatory structures to achieve desired social objectives, a positive response occurs to a higher understanding of how aviation markets function. While the shift towards more liberal regulatory structures generally has brought potential Pareto gains[13], longer term stability necessary for an emerging market equilibrium has not been thoroughly explored. Core theory provides a useful and long established theoretical framework to review this issue in regards to European aviation.

7.3   POLICY OPTIONS

Since there is a *prima facie* for suspecting that scheduled air transport services in the EU may, if left to pure market forces, be confronted by empty core and instability problems, what should be the appropriate policy response? There are four broad ways policies can be developed to counteract market instabilities in network industries or, stating in technical terms, to resolve an empty core;

- the situation may be deemed unimportant and no action taken;
- policies may be instigated with the aim of manipulating the role of markets;
- policies may be instigated involving institutional measures that involve direct provision of networks; and
- policies may allow actors in the market to tackle the problem internally through the adoption of coalition or other measures.

Leaving the situation to market forces may prove the most effective approach. Because of lack of precise knowledge of the mechanisms at work or distrust of the suitability of the remedial policies at hand, intervention failures are likely to outweigh the market failure of instability if the latter is not severe[14]. In general it is difficult being precise about the existence of an

[13]   Strict Pareto improvements are when at least one party gains from an action and none lose. A potential Pareto gain is when there are sufficient net benefits from a change that gainers could afford to compensate the losers and still be better off.

[14]   As with any activity, government intervention may result in intervention failures which produce outcomes worse than those associated with market failures. For instance, to protect a supplier against the full rigors of the market by instigating bankruptcy laws along the lines of Chapter 11 in the USA can worsen the empty core problem. Airlines, for example, have fixed costs associated with their aircraft but have avoidable costs associated with their use on scheduled services. If a relatively small number of airlines compete intensively to fill all seats over a specified route, it is possible their fixed costs

empty core and even more difficult is the design of policies to ameliorate the problems associated with the market failure.

One approach is to directly intervene and limit the degree actors can price down to marginal cost or saturate the market. The EU implicitly exhibited concern about the potential for empty core problems in both trucking and aviation. Trucking policies in the 1970s aimed at deriving a system of 'forked tariffs' with upper and lower limits, with the latter to prevent excessive competition. Equally, EU Council Regulations 2408/92 and 2409/92 allow for market interventions to prevent the downward spiraling of air fares. At a local level, it is normal for taxicab markets to operate under a regime of regulated fares and, in some cases, with market entry controls.

The difficulty with direct actions, however, is to determine the appropriate price floor or capacity ceiling, a problem which is particularly pronounced in a network setting. The issue becomes one of weighing the potential costs of market failures, and the implications of the empty core, against the resources costs of intervention failures where parameters are misspecified. The problems are a mirror reflection of the challenges of specifying antitrust and monopoly regulations when dealing with suppliers' efforts to gain an excess of market power.

Since the main problem of an empty core is insufficient or, at the extreme, no supply, government may intervene to directly provide capacity. This approach has been one argument used in the past to justify the state ownership of networks. In general, removing of market incentives leads to reduced efficiency and higher unit costs of provision especially where policies mean that cross subsidies are deployed. In practice it has been difficult isolating circumstances that are a genuine empty core problem from instances where the demand curve for the network services lies entirely within the cost curve and, *ipso facto*, no capacity could be justified on positive economic criteria. Examples involve situations where there may have been grounds for public provision to meet an empty core problem but subsequent shifts in either costs or demand no longer justify such actions.

The final alternative is to allow those in the market to tackle potentially empty cores themselves – that is develop managerial approaches

will not be recovered. If one or more carriers then seeks Chapter 11 bankruptcy protection this will reduce the fixed costs of their services but put financial pressures on their competitors. The others airlines will, in turn, be forced into bankruptcy to adjust their cost structure. After several successive rounds, fixed costs will fall to zero but also will the incentive to invest in these networks. The supply then falls to zero even though net social benefits would result from its provision.

and market strategies that circumvent the instability implications inherent in many network industries. In passenger aviation, for example, one can explain frequent flier programs in terms of retaining customer loyalty while keeping fares above short run marginal costs in a volatile market[15]. Further, airline mergers, particularly those after the introduction of the 1978 deregulation of US domestic markets, strategic alliances and franchising can be seen as controlling aspects of supply and yield management techniques to price discriminate and generate maximum revenue.

In several ways, this type of approach has been implicitly accepted in some policy areas. It was pursued in the domestic US aviation market when mergers policy, in the hands of the US Department of Transportation, was comparatively lax in the twenty years following deregulation and devices such as the frequent flier program were developed. Equally, EU aviation policy has allowed mergers, provided that certain concessions are made (e.g. the relinquishing of designated routes) to limit resultant market power and has provided block exemptions from elements of competition policy. Further, frequent flyer programs have not been attacked under EU competition policy, and these provide a mechanism for retaining customer loyalty across periods of fluctuating demand. At the international level, the IATA has enjoyed the power to influence fare levels and, more recently, antitrust immunity has been afforded by some governments to the strategic airline alliances that have emerged.

The policy challenge is to ensure if such devices are used, their potential costs in terms of the possible monopoly power do not exceed the benefits of avoiding potential empty core situations. This is particularly difficult in network industries where conventional anti-trust policies pose problems of implementation because appropriate markets over which legal judgments can be made are difficult to define. This is exemplified by recent debates over international strategic airline alliances where policy makers must decide if it is a service, a route, a set of routes or a wider network that forms the basis of the market under review. The complexity of cost allocation over airline networks also poses serious potential problems of regulatory capture.

In the key policy conclusion of core theory, there are benefits for both suppliers and users in the presence of an empty core to forming coalitions and cooperative action. The policy maker's difficulty is deciding when such

---

[15]   Telser (1994) argues the general case thus,
'Participants in a market lacking a core do contrive arrangements that will suitably restrict competition.... Long-term contracts between suppliers and their customers such as the take-or-pay contracts in natural gas are arrangements that restrict competition insofar as they eliminate some spot markets.'

actions are important to establish a stable equilibrium and how they serve as a supplier's device to extract economic rents. It is also important to consider public policy's role in terms of collusive behavior types permitted and how to regulate it once allowed.

While it is not presently possible to establish sufficient empirical conditions for an empty core existence, it is feasible to seek indicators of the state's existence. Evidence is far from conclusive regarding the European aviation market and certainly less convincing than put forward in relation to international shipping conferences. It is not, however, inconsequential. If a possibility exists of an emerging empty core, then caution may be justified, as well as an economic rationale behind the way the EU is liberalizing it. The danger rests in too much caution and continued financial aid given to public-owned flag carriers for fear their demise may lead to instability. This means that potential benefits of greater levels of efficiency are lost.

In pragmatic terms, the EU implicitly recognizes these difficulties in the way mergers and subsidies are treated[16]. Current practice effectively allows mergers, provided certain concessions are made, to limit resultant market power (e.g. the relinquishment of designated routes). Equally, frequent flyer programs have not been attacked under EU competition policy, thus providing a mechanism for retaining customer loyalty across periods of fluctuating demand. This ad hoc approach can only be speculated, since it is dependent on wider international aviation development. It is important, however, to ensure that potential gains from market liberalization are not limited by institutional developments that do not adequately account for problems which could ensue from an empty core existence.

THEORETICAL APPENDIX: NOTIONS OF THE CORE[17]

Core theory focuses on cost and demand structures as determinants of market structure. For Adam Smith's 'Invisible Hand' theorem to eliminate dead-weight loss and prices to guide individuals to outcomes that maximize economic welfare,

---

[16]   See Dutheil de la Rochère (1994) for a discussion of the EU's handling of aviation concentration policy.

[17]   This section contains material that is sometimes a little more technical than other parts of the book. The diagrammatic treatment can be skipped without any major loss of understanding although it does provide a theoretical underpinning for the arguments and empirical analysis in the body of the chapter.

- the aggregate industry production function must be superadditive so that the sum of outputs of two separate organizations do not exceed the total output resulting from their merger and
- the aggregate industry production function must have non decreasing returns to scale.

Telser and others have added to these conditions to embrace problems of empty cores, notably,

> One feature ...[of] empty cores is that the firms' total costs resulting from the factor prices generated by unfettered competition among them for the factors of production exceed the total revenue so that none can survive, although there is a net benefit to the public from having these commodities. (Telser, 1994)

Literature on situations when an empty core arises tends to be highly abstract and often avoided because of the difficulty to access it. This discussion provides verbal and graphic descriptions of actual market situation types when an empty core can emerge. It is not comprehensive but rather, it offers a degree of theoretical support for the more general discussion in this report[18].

The Viner case

The core is often empty when demand is finely divisible but production costs are not. The often-cited Viner case (1931) of a non-core outcome in a network industry is illustrated by taking two identical suppliers (such as airlines on a route) with standard U-shaped average cost curves. Fixed costs are thus assumed. Marginal cost on the route is a discontinuous function of total airline output and equal to the minimum average cost of the aircraft at two points in Figure A7.1, namely Q1 and Q2. The demand is continuous and represented by D.

If one airline operates a flight in this scenario, excess profits will be earned. Expansion to two aircraft, as a second carrier is attracted to the market, will result in both having a loss as competitive pressures lead to prices being driven down to marginal cost. A stable outcome will emerge

---

[18]   In particular, it draws on the theoretical writings of Telser but also Sjostrum's work (1989), that clarifies many points regarding inefficient entry, and Pirrong (1992) that provides analyses cost indivisibilities (see also Button and Nijkamp, 1997).

only if by chance the demand curve intersects the average cost curve at a point coincidental with the marginal cost curve.

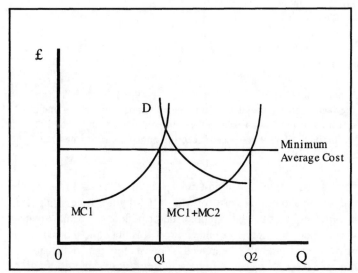

Figure A7.1 *The decreasing cost case*

The problem is created because any increase in the number of firms from n to n+1 affects both the total variable cost and the total fixed cost of the industry. Optimality requires comparing a higher fixed cost of having one more firm, and the reduction in variable cost of each firm producing less where demand is satisfied at a price equal to marginal cost. Efficient industry equilibrium will not generally be where the firm's unit cost is minimized. Increasing their number does not affect the outcome until the number becomes very large, at which point the Pareto-optimal number of undertakings is reached.

Non-identical firms

It is possible for an empty core to emerge if the Viner assumption of firms being identical is relaxed. For example, they may have different minimum average costs associated with the two airlines shown in Figure A7.2. The air transport industry supply curve is depicted as discontinuous and upward sloping. In this case, the core is empty when the continuous market demand curve goes between segments of the industry supply curve. The more homogeneous the supplying airlines and the less their minimum average costs differ, the more likely is the market demand curve to pass through a gap (with perfect homogeneity as in the Viner case). Hence, the higher the probability an empty core outcome will exist. The greater the variation in airline cost curves, the higher the probability of a competitive equilibrium.

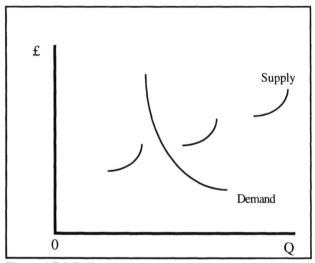

Figure A7.2 *Differing cost curves*

Low elasticity of demand

Figure A7.3 illustrates a situation where supplying airlines on a route are not homogeneous but each has a vertical supply curve. A typical section of the industry supply curve is depicted as VWXY. D1 and D2 represent possible, vertically parallel market demand curves. For the air transport market to have a core, demand must lie between Y and X. From simple observation at any price, the less elastic the demand curve, the more likely it is to fall into a gap in the supply curve (e.g. between X and W). At the extreme when demand is perfectly inelastic, the probability of an empty core is unity. With a perfectly elastic demand curve for air transport services on the route, a core must exist.

The market in a slump

The state of the market can influence supply when fixed costs are involved. If individual suppliers have U-shaped cost curves that imply an element of fixity, they may then remain in the market for a period, even if average total costs are not completely covered, as would costs between C1 and C2 in the left-hand image in Figure A7.4.

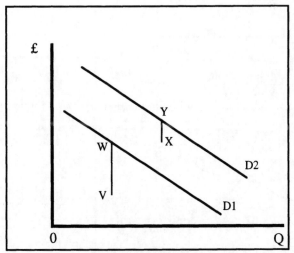

Figure A7.3 *Low demand elasticity*

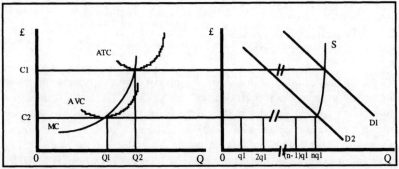

Figure A7.4 *Market recession*

The right hand figure shows the market, with n supplying undertakings. If demand rises slightly above D1, there will be no entry since a newcomer of minimum scale q1 would drive the price down below C1. Equally, a small drop in demand for air travel would not cause an exit of an airline because of the fixed cost factor. In terms of core theory, the core is not empty for a small rise or fall in demand. If demand for air services falls below D2, then an empty core situation does emerge since the market cannot support all the n airlines attempting to operate in it.

From a pragmatic perspective, the core is more likely to be empty when an industry is in a slump. A shift up in the avoidable cost curves confronting airlines has a similar implication.

Fluctuating and uncertain demand

Linked to the above, variability in demand can lead to an empty core. In situations where there is a U-shaped long run cost curve (as in Figure A7.5) but with substantial fluctuations in demand for air travel (between D1 and D2 at the extremes), then establishing a fixed fare at the competitive equilibrium, q, will result in losses at all times except when demand coincidentally cuts the LRAC at the minimum point.

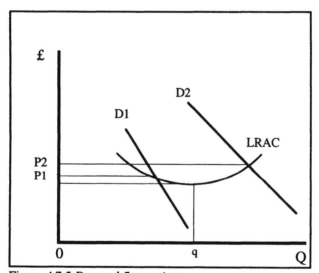

Figure A7.5 *Demand fluctuations*

Perfect market adjustments allowing prices to vary as demand for air transport services fluctuates would remove this problem. But with the provision of scheduled air services where service output and fares or cargo rates are set in advance, there is very limited scope for this. With this information, suppliers will not enter the market unless they can be assured of a price across the range of demand fluctuations ensuring normal profits may be earned.

177

8.   Conclusions

In this book we have examined the way in which the European Union has developed an air transport policy. What we have seen is that the movement forward has been slow, uneven and frequently difficult. Air transport policy embraces a number of different aspects that become even more difficult to handle when brought into the international arena. But it is important that Europe does have a viable approach to air transport.

Air transport is the fastest growing mode of transport. International air transport is the fastest growing segment of the air transport market. It provides an important mode of transport for business travel and is the main transport underpinning of the European tourist industry. Airlines and the associated infrastructure required to allow their efficient operations are major employers. The aviation industry is a leader in both hardware and software technological developments.

Air transport has also traditionally been one of the most regulated modes of transport. This has partly been for reasons such as safety and national defence but interventions of an economic nature have also been extensive. Governments have manipulated prices, market entry, service quality and other aspects of international aviation markets as well as often taking airlines into state ownership in efforts to achieve a variety of non-commercial objectives. Air transport infrastructure is also largely publicly owned.

Recent years have seen changes in virtually all countries with a major aviation interest in the ways that regulation is viewed in general and these changes have permeated the regulatory framework within which air transport is supplied. Indeed, in some ways and in several countries air transport regulatory reform has been pioneering. There has been a move away from detailed governmental regulation of the commercial aspects of supply with a greater focus on wider issues such as the environment.

The institutional changes that began in the US domestic air transport market in the late 1970s and have spread across a number of other national markets such as Australia, Canada and New Zealand have belatedly taken an international dimension. Liberalization of a range of international bilateral agreements have taken place, albeit largely in a piecemeal fashion (Organisation for Economic Cooperation and Development, 1997). The EU has been part of this international process, both as an entity in its own right and also through the actions of individual Member States.

It has taken time for the EU to come to grips with its initial transport priority, the creation of a Common Transport Policy for land transport. The EU has, however, as part of its recent overall transport strategy, since the late 1980s sought to make air transport more efficient and to ensure that imperfections in its supply do not impede the attainment of the wider goals of the Union. The regulatory reforms that have taken place now mean that the market for airline services with the EU differs radically from that of only a decade or so ago. Reforms to the external market have been less dramatic but not insignificant.

The path of regulatory reform in EU has differed markedly from that pursued in the US and also countries such as New Zealand and Australia. It has been one of gradualism, albeit often not entirely planned gradualism. There is an inevitable academic interest in contrasting the trans-Atlantic alternative strategies towards regulatory reform but there is also the public policy interest in that regulatory change is an on-going process and valuable practical lessons are to be learned. This extends beyond the narrow confines of air transport.

Of course, there are variations in the details of individuals markets that reflect different consumer preferences and the local supply conditions. Lessons are seldom immediately transferable but general guidelines may be gleaned. The European Union, for instance, besides having a diverse geography, represents an economic grouping of long standing independent states, each with its own political traditions and social characteristics; it is not legitimate to compare its air transport market with others without recognizing this. The basic infrastructure of the sector as well as institutional structures are legacies of these arrangements.

The developments in the EU can also be assessed on their own merits. For instance, in terms of evaluating the gradualist approach to regulatory changes, there is the question of the usefulness of the EU framework as well as that of gradualism *per se*. The EU path is only one of several that could have been adopted; the pace could have been faster or slower and the details of legislative reform could have been different. Any of these factors could influence the resultant reaction functions of airlines and the extent to which regulatory capture has proved an issue. What does emerge is that the EU has taken a very long time to bring about the same degree of market freedom that has been enjoyed in many domestic markets around the world for a number of years. There is an opportunity cost in retaining a structure that is generally recognized as highly inefficient and Europe has borne this cost by moving less rapidly than, say, the US in bringing about market reforms.

There have been some physical restrictions to the way EU aviation could have developed although these should not be overplayed. The reality of the existing air transport infrastructure in the EU means that there are physical restrictions on the pace and nature of change and on its outcome. Overall capacity problems can result in the full potential of the sector not being realized. Over investment, however, is wasteful of resources that can more effectively be used elsewhere. There exists a set of clear cost-benefit guidelines as to the extent to which capacity should be varied. The practical issue seems more to be one of deriving operational ways of using these policy assessment tools than the underlying theory.

More important, in many cases institutional structures and administrative regimes that distort the way existing infrastructure is used also lead to overall inefficiency within the European air transport market as well as having implications for the distribution of benefits across users and suppliers of services. Airports and air traffic control are not priced in an economic manner and this means user priorities are not reflected in decision making. EU rules on infrastructure pricing are based more on equity criteria than on ensuring the most efficient use is made of facilities. More generally, efforts at transport infrastructure planning in Europe, such as the Trans-European Networks program have generally been modal based and have relied upon trying to bring together national plans rather than seeking a genuine EU intermodal structure.

There have also been changes in the internal structure of air transport as, in particular, airlines have sought to more completely exploit the potential cost economies and, more important, marketing economies associated with various forms of alliance. Code sharing and common frequent flier programs coupled with coordinated schedules are features of these. Public policy makers have in the past tended to stand by while these alliances have been formed and only intervened at the margin. The arguments of enhanced consumer benefits and the creation of greater market stability are influential factors.

This move towards greater coordination amongst suppliers is certainly not unique to aviation but it has involved a number of particularly controversial features. The EU has to date managed to deal with many of the issues internal to the EU market essentially through its framework of competition policy but the trend towards global strategic alliances involving major air carriers poses new problems of accountability and extra-territoriality.

So has the EU's air transport policy been a success? Certainly it has been slow to evolve and problems still remain. Unlike countries such as the US where the focus is almost entirely on letting the user have a very large say in the types of services that are offered, there remains both a high degree of paternalism and a strong element of support for particular suppliers in the EU. This is not something peculiar to aviation but is important in the way that it is treated.

What also emerges is that EU aviation policy is still far from being complete. For example, the matter of responsibility for external relations is still to be settled, the air traffic control system still needs to be harmonized and up-graded, and the application of competition policy still needs to be clarified. The inadequate economic mechanisms for allocating scarce infrastructure capacity remains a serious impediment to more effective interoperability in the EU. Progress has been made on a scale that few would have expected two decades ago, but still the EU does not have the same degree of liberalization of its internal air transport market that is to be found within the US.

References

Airbus Industrie (1993) *Market Perspectives for Civil Jet Aircraft*, Airbus Industrie, Paris.

Alamdari, F. (1997) "Airline labour cost in a liberalised Europe", International Air Transport Conference 1997, Vancouver.

Argyris, N. (1989) "The EEC rules of competition and the air transport sector", *Common Market Law Review*, 26: 5-32.

Ashford, N. and Moore, C.A. (1992) *Airport Finance*, van Nostrand Reinholdt, New York.

Association of European Airlines (1995) *EU External Relations*, AEA, Brussels.

Avmark Aviation Economist (1994) "Is the Anglo-German alliance succeeding?", May: 8-9.

Avmark Aviation Economist (1995) "Moving towards consumer protection", August: 2-5.

Avmark Aviation Economist (1996) "American reality", April/May: 2.

Avmark Aviation Economist (1996) "An alliance too many", June: 2.

Avmark Aviation Economist (1996) "Euro-US hopes and frustrations", January/February: 5-6.

Barrett, S.A. (1987) *Flying High: Airline Prices and European Regulation*, Avebury, Aldershot.

Barrett, S.D. (1990) "Deregulating European aviation – A case study", *Transportation*, 16: 311-27.

Baum, H. and Weingarten, F. (1992) *Kooperation zwischen Schienen- und Luftverkehr in Deutschland* Studie für das Deutsche Verkehrsforume, Köln.

Baumol, W.J. and Willig, R.D. (1986) "Contestability: developments since the book", *Oxford Economic Papers*, 38: 9–36.

Baumol, W.J.; Panzar, J.C. and Willig, R.D. (1982) *Contestable Markets and the Theory of Industrial Structure*, Harcourt Brace, New York.

Bittlingmayer, G. (1982) "Decreasing average cost and competition", *Journal of Law and Economics*, 25: 201-29.

Bittlingmayer, G. (1985) "Did antitrust policy cause the great merger wave?", *Journal of Law and Economics*, 28: 77–118.

Boeing Commercial Airplane Group (1996) *Current Market Outlook, 1996*, Boeing, Seattle.

Borenstein, S. (1992a) "The evolution of US airline competition", *Journal of Economic Perspectives*, April: 45-73.

Borenstein, S. (1992b) "Prospects for competitive air travel in Europe", in Adams, W.J. (ed.) *Singular Europe: Economics and Polity of the European Community after 1992*, University of Michigan Press, Ann Arbor.

Borenstein, S. and Rose, N. (1994) "Competition and price dispersion in the US airline industry", *Journal of Political Economy*, 102: 653–83.

Borenstein, S. and Zimmerman, M.B. (1988) "Market incentives for safe commercial airline operation", *American Economic Review*, 78: 913-35.

Brooks, M. and Button, K.J. (1994) "Yield management: a phenomenon of the 1980s and 1990s?", *International Journal of Transport Economics*, 21: 177–96.

Bruecker, J. and Spiller, P. (1994) "Economies of traffic density in the deregulated airline industry", *Journal of Law and Economics*, 37: 379-415.

Button, K.J. (1989) "Liberalising the Canadian scheduled aviation market: the gradualist approach to deregulation", *Fiscal Studies*, 10: 19-52.

Button, K.J. (ed.) (1990) *Airline Deregulation: An International Perspective*, David Fulton, London.

Button, K.J. (1992) "The liberalisation of transport services", in Swann, D. (ed.), *1992 and Beyond*, Routledge, London.

Button, K.J. (1996a) "Aviation deregulation in European Union: do actors learn in the regulation game?", *Contemporary Economic Policy*, 14: 70–80.

Button, K.J. (1996b) "Liberalising European aviation: is there an empty core problem", *Journal of Transport Economics and Policy*, 30: 275–291.

Button, K.J. (1997) "Interactions of global competition, airline strategic alliances and air traffic safety", in Soekkha (ed.) *Aviation Safety*, VSP, Utrecht.

Button, K.J. and Gillingwater, D. (1986) *Future Transport Policy*, Croom Helm, London.

Button, K.J. and Keeler, T.E. (1993) "The regulation of transport markets", *Economic Journal*, 103: 1017-28.

Button, K.J. and Nijkamp, P. (1997) "Network industries, economic stability and spatial integration", paper to the 36th Annual Meeting of the Western Regional Science Association, Hawaii.

Button, K.J. and Swann, D. (1989) "European Community airlines - deregulation and its problems", *Journal of Common Market Studies*, 27: 259-282.

Button, K.J. and Swann, D. (1992) "Transatlantic lessons in aviation deregulation: EEC and US experiences", *Antitrust Bulletin*, 37: 207-55.

Button, K.J. and Weyman-Jones, T. (1994) "The impacts of privatisation policy in Europe", *Contemporary Economic Policy*, 12: 23–33.

Bylow, L.F. and Savage, I. (1991) "The effect of airline deregulation on automobile fatalities", *Accident Analysis and Prevention*, 23: 443-52.

Carlton, D., Landes, W. and Posner, R. (1980) "Benefits and costs of airline mergers: a case study", *Bell Journal of Economics,* 11: 65-83.

Castles, C. (1997) "Development of airport slot allocation in the European Community", paper to the Privatisation and Deregulation in Transport Seminar, Oxford University.

Caves, D.W., Christensen, L.R. and Tretheway, M.W. (1984) "Economies of density versus economies of scale: why trunk and local services airline costs differ", *RAND Journal of Economics*, 15: 471-89.

Caves, R., Christensen, L., Tretheway, M. and Windle, R.J. (1987) "An assessment of the efficiency of US airline deregulation via an international comparison", in Elizebeth Bailey (ed.), *Public Regulation: New Perspectives on Institutions and Policies*, MIT Press, Cambridge.

Chalk, A. (1986) "Market forces and aircraft safety: the case of the DC-10", *Economic Inquiry*, 24: 43-60.

Chance, D.M. and Ferris, S.P (1987) "The effect of aviation disasters on the air transport industry: a financial market perspective", *Journal of Transport Economics and Policy*, 21: 151-65.

Close, G. (1990) "External relations in the air transport sector: air transport policy or the common commercial policy?" *Common Market Law Review*, 27: 107–127.

Coltman, D. (1995) "The challenge of a successful alliance", paper to the 4th Annual Phoenix International Aviation Symposium.

Comité des Sages for Air Transport (1994) *Expanding Horizons – Civil Aviation in Europe, An Action Programme for the Future,* European Commission, Brussels.

Commission of the European Communities (1979) Contribution of the European Communities to the Development of Air Transport Services, *Bulletin of the European Communities,* Supplement 5, Brussels.

Commission of the European Communities (1979) *Towards the Development of a Community Air Transport Policy, Civil Aviation Memorandum No. 2,* COM(84) 72 Final, Brussels.

Commission of the European Communities (1981) *Scheduled Passenger Air Fares in the EEC,* COM(81) 398 Final, Brussels.

Commission of the European Communities (1985) Completing the Common Market, COM(85)310 Final, Brussels

Commission of the European Communities (1993) *Outline Plan of the Trans-European Airport Network,* Draft Communication VII-C4/Com 2/, Brussels.

Commission of the European Communities (1994) *The Way Forward for Civil Aviation in Europe,* COM(94)218 Final, Brussels.

Commission of the European Communities (1995) *Consultation Paper on Airport Charges,* Commission of the European Communities, Directorate General VII, Brussels.

Commission of the European Communities (1996) *Impact of the Third Package of Air Transport Liberalization Measures,* COM(96) 415 Final.

Demsetz, H. (1968) "Why regulate utilities?" *Journal of Law and Economics,* 11: 55-66

Dewatripont, M. and Roland, G. (1992) "The virtues of gradualism and legitimacy in the transition to a market economy", *Economic Journal,* 102: 291-300.

Dodgson, J.; Katsoulacous, Y. and Pryke, R. (1991) *Predatory Behaviour in Aviation,* EC Official Publications, Luxembourg.

Doganis, R. (1991) *Flying of Course: The Economics of International Aviation* (2nd Ed.), George Allen and Unwin, London.

Doganis, R. (1992) *The Airport Business,* Routledge, London.

Doganis, R. (1994) "The impact of liberalisation on European airline strategies and operations", *Journal of Air Transport Management,* 1: 15-25.

Doganis, R. and Lobbenberg, A. (1994) "The 'true' cost of monopolies", *Airports International,* May:29-31.

186

Dresner, M. and Windle, R. (1995) "Are US air carriers to be feared? Implications of hubbing to North Atlantic competition", *Transport Policy*, 2: 195-202.

Dresner, M. and Windle, R. (1996) "Alliances and code-sharing in the international airline industry", *Built Environment*, 22: 201-11.

Dresner, M., Flipcop, S. and Windle, R. (1995) "Trans-Atlantic airline alliances: a preliminary evaluation", *Journal of the Transportation Research Forum*, 35: 13-25.

Dutheil de la Rochère, J. (1994) "European Community policies on airline concentration", *Journal of Air Transport Management,* 1: 103–107.

Eckel, C.; Eckel, D. and Singal, V. (forthcoming, 1997) "Privatization and efficiency: industry effects of the sale of British Airways", *Journal of Financial Economics.*

Economides, N. (1996) "The economics of networks", *International Journal of Industrial Organisation*, 14: 673-699.

Economist (1995) "Airline alliances: flying in formation", July: 50-60.

Edgeworth, F.Y. (1881) *Mathematical Physics*, Kegan Paul, London.

EEC Commission (1961) *Memorandum on the General Lines of a Common Transport Policy,* EEC, Brussels.

Encaoua, D. (1991) "Liberalizing European airlines: cost and factor productivity evidence", *International Journal of Industrial Organisation*, 9: 109–24.

European Civil Aviation Conference (1981) *Report of the Task Force on Competition in Intra-European Air Services,* ECAC.

European Court of Justice (1973) "Europemballage Corpn. and Continental Can Co. Inc v. EC Commission", *Common Market Law Review*, 12: 199.

European Court of Justice (1974), "The French Merchant Seamen: E.C. Commission v France", *Common Market Law Review*, 14: 216.

European Court of Justice (1986) "Ministere Public v. Lucas Asjes and others", *Common Market Law Review*, 44: 173.

European Court of Justice (1994) "State v. Saachi", *Common Market Law Review*, 14: 177.

Flanagan, A. and Marcus, M. (1993) "Airline alliances: secret of a successful liaison", *Avmark Aviation Economist*, January/February: 20-3.

Forsyth, P. (1991) " The regulation and deregulation of Australia's domestic airline industry", in Button, K.J. (ed.) *Airline Deregulation: An International Perspective,* David Fulton, London.

Forsyth, P. (1996) "Air liberalization, privatization and consolidation in Australia and New Zealand", *Built Environment*, 22: 192-200.

Foster, C.D. and Golay, J. (1986) "Some curious old practices and their relevance to equilibrium in bus competition", *Journal of Transport Economics and Policy*, 20: 191–216.

Friedman, M. (1962) *Capitalism and Freedom*, University of Chicago Press, Chicago.

Gallacher, J. (1996a) "A clearer direction", *Airline Business*, June: 22-52.

Gallacher, J. (1996b) "Bow to no man", *Airline Business*, August: 32-35.

Gellman Research Associates (1994) *A Study of International Airline Code Sharing, Office of Aviation and International Economics*, Office of the Secretary of US Department of Transportation, Washington.

Gillen, D.W.; Oum, T.H. and Tretheway, M.W. (1988) "Entry barriers and anti-competitive behavior in a deregulated airline market: the case of Canada", *International Journal of Transport Economics*, 15: 29-41.

Gillen, D.W.; Oum, T.H. and Tretheway, M.W. (1989) "Privatization of Air Canada: Why is it necessary in a deregulated environment", *Canadian Public Policy*, 15: 285-99.

Golbe, D.L. (1986) "Safety and profits in the airline industry", *Journal of Industrial Economics*, 34: 305-18.

Good, D.H., Röller, L-H. and Sickles, R.C. (1993) "US airline deregulation: implications for European transport", *Economic Journal*, 103: 1028–1041.

Hanlon, P. (1994) "Discriminatory fares: identifying predatory behaviour", *Journal of Air Transport Management*, 1: 89-102.

Hanlon, P. (1996) *Global Airline Competition in a Transnational Industry*, Butterworth, London.

Hayes, M.T. (1992) *Incrementalism and Public Policy*, Longman, London.

Heppenheimer, T.A. (1995) *Turbulent Skies: The History of Commercial Aviation*, Wiley, New York.

Hill, L. (1996) "Such a bad experience", *Air Transport World*, 33: 398-40.

Hoen, H.W. (1996) "'Shock versus gradualism' in Central Europe reconsidered", *Comparative Economic Studies*, 38: 1-20.

Humphreys, B. (1994a) *New Developments in CRSs*, ITA Documents and Reports 32, Paris.

Humphreys, B. (1994b) "The implications of international code sharing", *Journal of Air Transport Management*, 1: 195-207.

International Civil Aviation Organisation (various issues) *On Flight Origin and Destination*, Montreal, ICAO.

International Civil Aviation Organisation (1994) *North Atlantic Air Traffic Forecasts for the Years 1994-1999, 2000, 2005, 2010*, ICAO, Paris.

Jennings, M. (1996a) "Poisoned pals?" *Airline Business*, 12: 22-4.

Jennings, M. (1996b) "Alliances still not immune from risk", *Airline Business*, July: 74.

Jones, L. (1996) "Keeping up appearances", *Airline Business*, 12: 38-42.

Kahn. A.E. (1988) "Surprises of airline deregulation", *American Economic Review, Papers and Proceedings*, 78: 316-22.

Karels, G.V. (1989) "Market forces and aircraft safety: an extension:, *Economic Inquiry*, 27: 345-54.

Kasper, D. (1988) *Deregulation and Globalisation: Liberalizing International Trade in Air Services,* American Enterprise Institute, Washington, DC.

Katz, R. (1995) "The great GATS", *Airline Business*, September: 81-2.

Keeler, T.E. (1984) "Theories of regulation and the deregulation movement", *Public Choice*, 3: 399-424.

Keeler, T.E. (1990) "Airline deregulation and market performance: the economic basis for regulatory reform and lessons from the US experience", in Banister, D. and Button, K.J. (eds.), *Transport in a Free Market Economy*, Macmillan, London.

Kraft, J.H.; Oum, T.H. and Tretheway, M.W. (1986) "Airline seat management", *Logistics and Transportation Review*, 22: 115-30.

Kuijper, P.J. (1983) "Airline fare-fixing and competition: an English lord, Commission proposals and US parallels", *Common Market Law Review*, 20: 203.

Lakshmanan, T.R. (1989) "Infrastructure and economic transformation", in Andersson, A.E., Batten, D.F., Johansson, B. and Nijkamp, P. (eds), *Advances in Spatial Theory and Dynamics* North Holland, Amsterdam.

Lederer, J.F. and Enders, J.H. (1989) "Aviation Safety: the Global Conditions and Prospects", in Moses, L. and Savage, I., *Transportation Safety in an Age of Deregulation*, Oxford University Press: Oxford.

Lindquist, J. (1996) "Marriages made in heaven", *Avmark Aviation Economist*, January/ February: 12-13.

McGowan, F. and Seabright, P. (1989) "Deregulating European airlines", *Economic Policy*, October: 283-344.

Meersman, H. and van de Voorde, E. (1996) "The privatisation of air transport in Europe: interaction between policy, economic power and market performamce", *Built Environment*, 22: 177-191.

Mencik von Zebinsky, A.A. (1996) *European Union External Competence and External Relations in Air Transport*, Kluwer, The Hague.

Midttun, A. (1992) "The European market for aviation: a sociological inquiry into the political economy of a complexly organized market", *Journal of Economic Issues*, December: 1063-1094.

Mitchell, M.L. and Maloney, M.T. (1989) "Crisis in the cockpit? The role of market forces in promoting air travel safety", *Journal of Law and Economics*, 32: 329-55.

Morrison, S.A. and Winston, C. (1987) "Empirical implications and tests of the contestability hypothesis", *Journal of Law and Economics*, 30: 53–66.

Morrison, S.A. and Winston, C. (1988) "Air safety, deregulation and public policy", *The Brookings Review*, 6: 10-15.

Morrison, S.A. and Winston, C. (1995) *The Evolution of the Airline Industry*, Brookings Institution, Washington, DC.

Moses, L.N. and Savage, I. (1990) "Aviation deregulation and safety", *Journal of Transport Economics and Policy*, 24: 171-88.

Müller, J. (1997) "Integration and competition in the European Airline Industry", in *Europe: The Single Market Review, Subseries V, Vol. 3, Competition Issues*, Kogen Page, London.

Ng, C. and Seabright, P. (1995) "Regulation, competition and cost efficiency of European flag carriers", paper to the New England Conference on Efficiency and Productivity, Armidale.

Nyathi, M.; Hooper, P. and Hensher, D. (1993) "Compass Airlines: 1 December 1990 to 20 December 1991, what went wrong?", *Transport Reviews*, Part 1, 13: 112–149; Part 2, 13: 185–206.

Organisation for Economic Cooperation and Development (1993) *International Air Transport: The Challenges Ahead*, OECD, Paris.

Organisation for Economic Cooperation and Development (1997) *The Future of International Air Transport Policy: responding to Global Change*, OECD, Paris.

Oster, C. and Pickrell D. (1986) "Marketing alliances and competitive strategy in the aviation industry", *Logistics and Transportation Review*, 22: 371-87.

Oster, C.V. and Zorn, C.K. (1989) "Airline deregulation: is it still safe to fly?", in Moses, L. and Savage, I., *Transportation Safety in an Age of Deregulation*, Oxford University Press: Oxford.

Oum, T.H. (1995) (ed.) *Airline Economics and Policy: Selected Papers of Tae Hoon Oum*, Korean Research Foundation for the 21st Century, Seoul.

Oum, T.H. and Yu, C. (1996) "A comparative study of total factor productivity of the world's major airlines", in Hensher, D., King, J.

and Oum, T.H. (eds.) World *Transport Research Vol. 4, Transport Management*, Pergamon, Oxford.

Oum, T.H.; Chen, H-M. and Fok, A.K. (1994) "Productivity and Cost Competitiveness of the World's Major Airlines", paper to the 29th Annual Meeting of the Canadian Transportation Research Forum, Victoria.

Oum, T.H.; Gillen, D.W. and Noble, S.E. (1986) "Demands for fare classes and pricing in airline markets" *Logistics and Transportation Review*, 22: 195-222.

Oum, T.H.; Waters, W.G. and Yong, J-S. (1992) "Concepts of price elasticities of transport demand and recent empirical estimates", *Journal of Transport Economics and Policy*, 27: 139-154.

Pelksman, J. (1986) "Deregulation of European air transport", in de Jong, H.W. and Shepherd, W.G. (eds.) *Mainstreams in Industrial Organisation,* Martinus Nijhoff, Dordrecht.

Perl, A., Patterson, J. and Perez, M. (1997) "Putting a price on aircraft emissions at Lyon-Satolas Airport", *Transportation Research D: Transport and Environment,* 2: 89-106.

Pirrong, S.C. (1992) "An application of core theory to the analysis of ocean shipping markets", *Journal of Law and Economics*, 35: 89–131.

Porter, M. (1980) *Competitive Strategy: Techniques for Analysing Industries and Competitors*, Free Press, New York.

Porter, M. (1990) *The Competitive Advantage of Nations*, Macmillan, New York.

Prodromidis, K.P and Frangos, T. (1995) "Public or private enterprises in the airline industry", *International Journal of Transport Economics*, 22: 85-95.

Pryke, R.W.S. (1991) "American deregulation and European liberalisation", in Banister, D. and Button, K.J. (eds.), *Transport in a Free Market Economy*, Macmillan, Basingstoke.

Pustay, M. (1992) "Towards a global airline industry: prospects and impediments", *Logistics and Transportation Review*, 28: 103-28.

Reynolds-Feighan, A. (1997) "Airport services and airport charging systems: a critical review of the EU common framework", paper to the International Air Transport Conference 1997, Vancouver.

Roland, G. (1993) "The political economy of restructuring and privatization in Eastern Europe", *European Economic Review*, 37: 533-40.

Rose, N.L. (1989) "Financial influences on airline safety", in Moses, L. and Savage, I., *Transportation Safety in an Age of Deregulation*, Oxford University Press: Oxford.

Rose, N. L. (1990) "Profitability and product quality: economic determinants of airline safety performance", *Journal of Political Economy*, 98: 944-64.

Sharkey, W. (1986) *The Theory of Natural Monopoly*, Cambridge University Press, Cambridge.

Shenton, H. (1994) "Code-sharing is airlines' gain consumers' loss", *Avmark Aviation Economist*, October: 13-20.

Sjostrom, W. (1989) "Collusion in ocean shipping: a test of monopoly and empty core models", *Journal of Political Economy*, 97: 1160-79.

Sjostrom, W. (1993) "Antitrust immunity for shipping conferences: an empty core approach", *Antitrust Bulletin*, 38: 419-23.

Smith, T.K. (1995) "Why air travel doesn't work", *Fortune*, April 3: 26-36.

Soames, T. (1997) "Ground handling liberalisation", *Journal of Air Traffic Management*, 3: 83-94.

Spraggins, H.B. (1989) "The impact of airline size upon efficiency and profitability", *Journal of Transportation Management*, 23: 73-104.

Starkie, D. (1997) "Re-appraising airport regulations", paper to the Privatisation and Deregulation in Transport Seminar, Oxford University.

Stasinopoulos, D. (1992) "The second aviation package of the European community", *Journal of Transport Economics and Policy*, 26: 83-87.

Stasinopoulos, D. (1993) "The third phase of liberalisation in community aviation and the need for supplementary measures", *Journal of Transport Economics and Policy*, 27: 323-328.

Stevens, H. (1997) *Liberalisation of Air Transport in Europe*, The European Institute, London School of Economics, London.

Stigler, G. (1971) "The theory of economic regulation", *Bell Journal of Economics and Management*, 2: 3-21.

Telser, L.G. (1978) *Economic Theory and the Core*, University of Chicago Press, Chicago.

Telser, L.G. (1987) *A Theory of Efficient Cooperation and Competition*, Cambridge University Press, Cambridge.

Telser, L.G. (1990) "Theory of corporations: an application of the theory of the core", *Journal of Accounting, Auditing and Finance*, 5: 159-201.

Telser, L.G. (1991) "Industry total cost functions and the status of the core", *Journal of Industrial Economics*, 39: 225-40.

Telser, L.G. (1994) "The usefulness of core theory in economics", *Journal of Economic Perspectives*, 8: 151-64.

Thurow, L. (1996) *The Future of Capitalism: How Today's Economic Forces will Shape Tomorrow's Future*, W. Morrow, New York.

Toms, M.R. (1994) "Charging for airports: the new BAA approach", *Journal of Air Transport Management*, 1: 77-82.

Treitel, D. and Smick, E. (1996) "All change", *Airline Business*, 12: 34-36.

Tretheway, M. (1990) "Globalisation of the airline industry and implications for Canada", *Logistics and Transportation Review*, 26: 357-67.

Tretheway, M. and Oum, T. (1992) *Airline Economics: Foundations for Strategy and Policy*, Vancouver, Centre for Transportation Studies, University of British Columbia,

UK Civil Aviation Authority (1988) *Statement of Policies on Air Transport Licensing – June 1988*, CAP 539, London, CAA.

UK Civil Aviation Authority (1993) *Airline Competition in the Single European Market*, CAP 623, CAA, London.

UK Civil Aviation Authority (1994) *Airline Competition on European Long Haul Routes*, CAP 639, CAA, London.

UK House of Commons Transport Committee (1996) *Sixth Report: The Proposed Alliance between Britsih Airways and American Airlines*, HC598, HMSO, London.

UK House of Lords European Communities Committee (1980) *Forty-ninth Report from the European Communities Committe – European Air Fares*, HL235, HMSO, London.

US Federal Aviation Administration (various years) *Airport Activity Statistics of the Certificated Route Air Carriers*, US Department of Transportation, Washington.

US General Accounting Office (1995) *International Aviation: Airline Alliances Produce Benefits but Effect on Competition is Uncertain*, GAO/RCED-95-99, Washington, DC.

US General Accounting Office (1997) *International Aviation: Competition Issues in the US-UK Market*, Testimony of J.H. Anderson before the Subcommitte on Aviation, Committee on Commerce, Science, and Transportation US Senate, GAO/T-97-103.

US National Commission to Ensure a Strong Competitive Airline Industry (1993) *Change, Challenge and Competition*, US Government Printing Office, Washington, DC.

Van Boening, M. and Wilcox, N. (1992) "Avoidable cost: ride a double-auction roller coaster", paper to the Economic Science Association, Tucson.

Vincent, D. and Stasinopoulos, D. (1990) "The aviation policy of the European community", *Journal of Transport Economics and Policy*, 24: 95–100.

Viner, J. (1931) "Cost curves and supply curves", *Zeitschrift für Nationalokonomie*, 3: 23–46.

Youssef, W. (1992) *Causes and Effects of International Airline Equity Alliances*, Ph.D. Dissertation Series UCB-ITS-DS-92-1, Institute of Transportation Studies, University of California at Berkeley.

Youssef, W. and Hansen, M. (1994) "Consequences of strategic alliances between international airlines: the case of Swissair and SAS", *Transportation Research*, 28A: 415-31.

Index

Printed and bound by CPI Group (UK) Ltd, Croydon, CR0 4YY

24/04/2025

14661322-0001